ERIC NEWBY was born in London in 1919 and was educated at St Paul's School. In 1938 he joined the four-masted Finnish barque *Moshulu* as an apprentice and sailed in the last Grain Race from Australia to Europe by way of Cape Horn. During the Second World War he served in the Black Watch and Special Boat Section, and was a prisoner-of-war from 1942 to 1945. After the war, his world expanded still further – into the fashion business and book publishing. Whatever else he was doing, he always travelled on a grand scale, either under his own steam or as Travel Editor of the *Observer*.

BY THE SAME AUTHOR

A Short Walk in the Hindu Kush
Slowly down the Ganges
Love and War in the Apennines
On the Shores of the Mediterranean
Round Ireland in Low Gear
A Small Place in Italy

ERIC NEWBY

The Last
Grain Race

LONELY PLANET PUBLICATIONS

Melbourne • Oakland • London

The Last Grain Race

Published by Lonely Planet Publications
    Head Office: 90 Maribyrnong Street, Footscray, Vic 3011, Australia
                    Locked Bag 1, Footscray, Vic 3011, Australia
    Branches: 150 Linden Street, Oakland, CA 94607, USA
                    2nd floor, 186 City Road, London, EC1V 2NT, UK

First published 1956 by Martin Secker & Warburg Ltd
First US edition published 1999 by Lonely Planet Publications
This US edition published 2008 by Lonely Planet Publications

Printed by The Bookmaker International Ltd
Printed in China

Author photograph by Wanda Newby

National Library of Australia Cataloguing in Publication Data

Newby, Eric, 1919-2006 .

The last grain race.

ISBN 978 1 74179 526 4.

1. Newby, Eric, 1919-2006. 2. Moshulu (Ship).
3. Voyages around the world. 4. Ocean travel.
5. Sailing ships. I. Title

910.45

Text © Eric Newby 1956

Contents

Acknowledgements

I wish to express my gratitude to Mr F. A. Hawkes, Shipping Editor at Lloyd's, for allowing me to search the archives of *Lloyd's Shipping Index* for information concerning *Moshulu*; to Mr George Dickinson, Editor of the magazine *Sea Breezes*, and Mr Richard Sayer for much valuable assistance; to Mr John Daviel for the drawing of *Moshulu*; and finally to Mr Kiril Gray for all the help he so unselfishly gave me with the typing and revision of the book.

On April 18th there was launched at Port Glasgow by Messrs William Hamilton and Co. a four-masted barque of about 3,200 tons gross, the last of the two sister vessels built for Messrs G. H. J. Siemers and Co. of Hamburg, for their nitrate trade: the vessel has a length of 320 feet (b.p.), a beam of 47 feet and a depth of 28 feet to main deck, and is classed at Germanischer Lloyd's under special survey. With the view of minimizing labour numerous winches are fitted on board for working of sails and the equipment also includes one 6-h.p. and one 10-h.p. petrol winch. During construction the vessel has been supervised by Mr Alexander Craig on behalf of Germanischer Lloyd's, and by Captains Opitz and Gerdau on behalf of the owners. The barque was named *Kurt* (by Mrs T. W. Hamilton).

MOSHULU (ex 'Kurt') – Steel four-masted barque; 5,300 tons d.w., 3,116 gross, 2,911 net. Built Port Glasgow, 1904. Sold by the Charles Nelson Company, Inc., San Francisco, to Captain Gustaf Erikson, Mariehamn. It is understood that the sale is 'subject to survey'.

SAILS (*Mizzen staysails omitted for clarity*)

1 Gaff topsail
2 Upper spanker
3 Spanker
4 Jigger topgallant staysail
5 Jigger topmast staysail
6 Jigger staysail
7 Mizzen royal
8 Mizzen upper topgallant
9 Mizzen lower topgallant
10 Mizzen upper topsail
11 Mizzen lower topsail
12 Crojack (or crossjack)
13 Main royal
14 Main upper topgallant
15 Main lower topgallant
16 Main upper topsail
17 Main lower topsail
18 Mainsail (or main course)
19 Main royal staysail
20 Main topgallant staysail
21 Main topmast staysail
22 Fore royal
23 Fore upper topgallant
24 Fore lower topgallant
25 Fore upper topsail
26 Fore lower topsail
27 Foresail (or fore course)
28 Flying jib
29 Outer jib
30 Inner jib
31 Fore topmast staysail

RUNNING RIGGING (*Buntlines, clewlines, lifts, downhauls, and some sheets omitted for clarity. Some halliards also omitted.*)

32 Upper spanker outhaul
33 Spanker outhaul
34 Spanker sheet
35 Mizzen royal braces
36 Mizzen upper topgallant braces
37 Mizzen lower topgallant braces
38 Jigger topgallant staysail halliard
39 Mizzen upper topsail brace (port)
40 Jigger topmast staysail halliard
41 Mizzen lower topsail brace (port)
42 Jigger staysail halliard
43 Jigger topgallant staysail sheets
44 Crojack brace (port)
45 Jigger topmast staysail sheets
46 Jigger staysail sheets
47 Mizzen upper topsail brace (starboard)
48 Main upper topsail brace (port)
49 Mizzen lower topsail brace (starboard)
50 Main lower topsail brace (port)
51 Crojack brace (starboard)
52 Main brace
53 Main royal braces
54 Main upper topgallant braces
55 Main lower topgallant braces
56 Main upper topsail brace (starboard)
57 Fore upper topsail brace (port)
58 Main lower topsail brace (starboard)
59 Fore lower topsail brace (port)
60 Main brace (starboard)
61 Fore brace (port)
62 Fore royal braces
63 Fore upper topgallant braces
64 Fore lower topgallant braces
65 Fore upper topsail brace (starboard)
66 Fore lower topsail brace (starboard)
67 Fore brace (starboard)
68 Flying jib halliard
69 Flying jib sheets
70 Crojack tacks
71 Crojack sheets
72 Crojack sheets
73 Crojack tacks
74 Mainsail sheets (port sheets not shown)
75 Foresail sheets
76 Mainsail tacks (port tacks not shown)
77 Foresail tacks
78 Foresail sheets
79 Foresail tacks

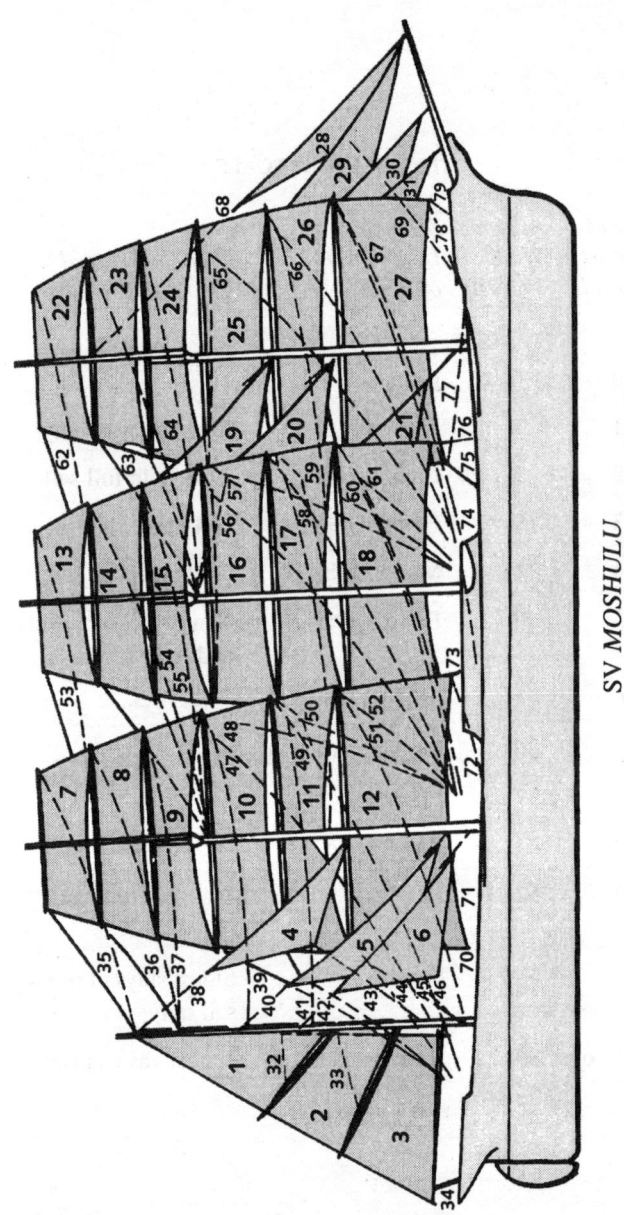

SV MOSHULU
SAIL PLAN AND DIAGRAM OF RUNNING RIGGING
(adapted from the drawing by Mr John Daviel)

THE BEAUFORT SCALE

Admiral Beaufort's Numerals	Average Wind Velocity	Seaman's Description of Wind	Steel full-rigged ship – deeploaded
0	0	Calm	—
1	2	Light air	Steerage way only
2	5	Light breeze	2 knots in full sail
3	9	Gentle breeze	3–4 knots full sail
4	14	Moderate breeze	5–6 knots full sail
5	19	Fresh breeze	Can just carry royals and light staysails
6	24	Strong breeze	—
7	30	Moderate (half) gale	—
8	37	Fresh gale	—
9	44	Strong gale	—
10	52	Heavy (whole gale)	Main lower topsail only
11	60	Storm	Storm staysail or try-sail only
12	over 80	Hurricane	No canvas can stand

Introduction to
the Grafton Edition

ALTHOUGH I did not know it when I joined the four-masted barque *Moshulu* in Belfast in the autumn of 1938, this was to be her last voyage in the Australian grain trade, as it was to be for the rest of Gustav Erikson's fleet of sailing ships, as well as for most of the German and Swedish ships which took part in the 1939 sailings from South Australia to Europe. In that year thirteen three and four-masted barques sailed for Europe, eleven of them by way of Cape Horn, and by the autumn all of them were back in European waters; but although one or two of them continued to sail during the first year or so of the war, carrying various cargoes, and some even survived into the post-war years, the big Finnish fleet of Gustav Erikson was dispersed and the ships never came together again to form the great concourse of vessels which lay in Spencer Gulf, South Australia, in the early months of 1939.

Today them are no more steel, square-rigged sailing ships left trading on the oceans of the world. If any more are built for commercial purposes it seems certain that they will be as different from the barques that I knew as the crews which will be employed to man them will be different.

Gustav Erikson of Mariehamn in the Baltic was the last man to own a great fleet of sailing ships. He employed no P.R.O.s to improve his image. I never met any foremast hand who liked him – it would be as reasonable to expect a present day citizen of Britain to 'like' the Prime Minister or an Inspector of Taxes. In our ship he was known as 'Ploddy Gustav', although most of us had never set eyes on him The thing that warmed one to him was the certainty that he was completely indifferent as to whether anyone liked him or not. He was only interested in his crews in so far as they were necessary to sail his ships efficiently, and for that reason he ensured that they were adequately fed by sailing ship standards, and that the ships they manned were supplied with enough rope, canvas, paint and other necessary gear to enable them to be thoroughly seaworthy. He certainly knew about ships. Originally, as a boy of nine, he had gone to sea in a sailing vessel engaged in the North Sea timber trade. At the age of nineteen he got his first command in the North Sea, and after that spent six years in deep-water sail as a mate. From 1902 to 1913 he was master of a number of square-rigged vessels before becoming an owner. By the thirties the grain trade from South Australia to Europe was the last enterprise in which square-riggers could engage with any real hope of profit, and then only if the owner had an obsessional interest in reducing running costs. Erikson had to pay his crews (which had to be as small as was commensurate with safety) as little as possible. He could not afford to insure his ships, most of which he had obtained at shipbreaker's prices; but at the same time he had to maintain them at such a standard that they were all rated 100 A1 at Lloyd's, or an equivalent classification elsewhere. He was respected and feared as a man over whose eyes no wool could be pulled by the masters whom he employed to sail his ships, and the tremors they felt were passed on down to the newest joined apprentice. Of such stuff discipline is made. A now out-moded word, but sailing ships do not stay afloat and make fast passages at the pleasure of committees of seamen.

The work of handling the great acreages of sail was very heavy, even for men and boys with strong constitutions. Thirty-four days out from Port Victoria, two days after we had passed the Falkland Islands on the homeward run, with a crew of twenty-eight, which included officers, cook, steward, etc., we started bending a complete suit of old, patched fair-weather canvas for the tropics in order to save wear and tear on the strong stuff, sending the storm canvas down on gant-lines. Sail changing was done always when entering and leaving the Trade Winds, four times on a round voyage. While we were engaged in this work it started to blow hard from the south-east; then it went to the south, blowing force 9 and then 10 and then 11 from the south-south-west, when the mizzen lower topsail blew out. This was followed by a flat calm and torrential rain. In the middle of the night a Pampero, a wind that comes off the cast coast of South America, hit the ship when it was practically in full sail. Because the Captain knew his job we only lost one sail, the fore upper topgallant.

In those twenty-four hours the port and starboard watches, eight men to a watch, took in, re-set, took and re-set again twenty-eight sails – the heaviest of which weighed 1ĕ tons – a total of 112 operations; bent two new sails and wore the ship on to a new tack twice, an operation which required all hands, including the cook, and which took an hour each time it was done. The starboard watch were unlucky, having to spend eleven consecutive hours on deck. This was by no means uncommon. Yet strangely enough, I look back on the time I spent in *Moshulu* with great pleasure.

CHAPTER ONE

Wurzel's

ON the day we lost the Cereal Account I finally decided to go to sea.

'You've 'ad it,' said the Porter with gloomy relish as I clocked in a little after the appointed hour at the advertising agency where I was learning the business.

I was not surprised. I was eighteen years old and had been at The Wurzel Agency for two years after leaving school on the crest of one of my parents' more violent financial crises. They had known George Wurzel in his earlier, uncomplicated days and had placed me with him in the fond belief that the sooner I got down to learning business methods the better. By now they were beginning to feel that they might have been wrong. Wurzel's had long held a similar opinion. Since I had ridden a bicycle into Miss Phrygian's office they had been more than cool. Julian Pringle, the most rebellious copywriter Wurzel's ever had, bet me that I could not ride it round the entire building without dismounting. The coast had been clear, the numerous swing doors held open, and the bicycle, which was being sketched for the front page of the *Daily Mail*, borrowed from the Art Department.

It was a pity that Julian did not tell me that the brake blocks were missing; perhaps he removed them. Whatever the reason, I failed to take the dangerous corner at the bottom of the main corridor and ended on Miss Phrygian's desk. She was the Secretary to the Managing Director and carried Wurzel's on her capable shoulders. Though it was by no means obvious at the time, she apparently never bore me any ill-feeling, and during the war Miss Phrygian's enormous parcels of cigarettes were the only ones that consistently got through to the various P.O.W. camps I inhabited. But this kind of antic was only condoned in Layout and Ideas men of the calibre of Julian Pringle, who kept their sanity and independence by behaving atrociously whenever a Director appeared. It was nothing for a client being hurried past the Layout Department to less controversial regions to be treated to a display of paper dart flying. (Once a potential customer was hit on the nose by an ink pellet.) The Prep-School Heart still beat strongly in Layout and Ideas.

I had started my uneasy career in the Checking Department at the age of sixteen. Miss Phrygian had escorted me there. On the way we passed the Porter's cubby hole; inside, half a dozen evil-looking messenger boys were waiting to take blocks to Fleet Street. There were more seats than messenger boys and I found Miss Phrygian casting a speculative look at the empty places. For a moment I thought she was going to enlist me in their ranks, but she must have remembered my father's insistence on the value of the business methods I was going to learn, and we passed on.

In the narrow, airless transepts of the Checking Department, where the electric lights burned permanently, I thumbed my way through the newspapers and periodicals of the world to make sure that our advertisements were appearing on schedule and the right way up, which they failed to do quite frequently in some of the more unsophisticated newspapers from rugged and distant parts of the globe. Some of the advertisements had to be cut out and pasted in a book. We always cut out Carter's Little Liver Pills, but I never discovered the reason. Turning the pages of thousands of newspapers day after day, I accumulated knowledge of the most recondite subjects – croquet matches between missionaries in Basutoland, reports of conventions of undertakers at South Bend, Indiana, great exhibitions for tram ticket collectors in the Midlands – the world spread out before me.

When I was not speculating about what I read, I would fight with Stan, a great dark brute of a boy, one of the two assistants in the Department, to whom I had become quite attached. Both Stan and Les, the second assistant, called me 'Noob'.

''Ere, Noob, what abaht a pummel?' Stan would croak invitingly, and we would pummel one another until Miss Phrygian banged furiously on the frosted glass of her office door to stop the din.

Les, the other checker, had a less rugged exterior than Stan and a passion for Italian opera on which he spent all his money. He would often appear in the morning, dark-eyed and lifeless after long hours in the Gallery at Covent Garden, drop a leaden hand on my shoulder and greet me: ''Lo, Noob. Jer 'ear Gilli lars ni'? . . . Bleedin' marvellous.'

The Department was presided over by a gnome-like little man who knew everything there was to know about his job and had such a retentive memory that he could tell you without hesitation on which page of some old Regimental magazine a sherry advertisement had appeared. Quite naturally our behaviour often exasperated him and he would turn to Stan and me, who were locked in an orgy of 'pummelling', and say: ''Ere, for Christ sake! turn it in!'

From time to time we would be visited by the Contact Men who dealt personally with Wurzel's clients and handled the advertising accounts. They would stand gingerly in our den and turn the pages of the glossy magazines with beautifully manicured fingers. They were all youngish, perfectly dressed in Hawes and Curtis suits, and they smelled of bay rum. The amorous complications of their private lives were hair-raising. One of them owned a Bentley. They all wore clove carnations every day except Saturdays when they were in tweeds and went to the 'country' around Sunningdale. I always felt a clod in their presence and for some time after their visits disinclined to pummel. More popular were the visits of the typists. Wurzel's was run on pseudo-American lines and had a splendid collection. Two of the most popular were Lettice Rundle and Lilly Reidenfelt. Lilly was the more provocative of the two. It was generally conceded that Lettice was the sort of girl you married and had children by after trying Miss Reidenfelt, who was expected to run to fat.

When Miss Reidenfelt entered the Checking Department, Stan,

the Man of Action, would be stricken dumb and with eyes cast down would trace bashful circles amongst the waste paper with his toe. Les, Socialite and Dreamer, knew better how to please, and, more forthcoming, usually succeeded in pinching her. At such times what little air there was would be so heavy with lust that I would develop an enormous headache of the kind usually brought on by thundery weather. When Miss Reidenfelt had finally minced away inviolate, Stan would fling himself at the piles of newspaper in the steel fixtures and punch them in torment, crying: 'Oh, you lovely bit of gravy.'

After what seemed an eternity in this very unhealthy place, I graduated to the Filing Department where the proofs of the advertisements were kept. Here I had Miss Reidenfelt all to myself when she visited me in search of proofs; but I was much too much in awe of her to take advantage of my hard-won advancement. I found that the white-collar boys in the outer office, where twenty telephones rang incessantly, felt just the same about Miss Reidenfelt as Les, Stan and I had in our more private labyrinth. In a more primitive society Miss Reidenfelt would have been the central figure in a fertility rite and would by now have rated a six-figure entry in the index to *The Golden Bough*.

Next I went to 'Art', of which I remember little except wearing a smock, being covered with bicycle tyre solution (which 'Art' used in gallons), and my surprise, when, after standing for hours being sketched for an advertisement for mass-produced clothes, I found that I had emerged on paper as a sunburned, moustached figure wearing a Brigade Tie and a bowler hat. Long afterwards I cherished the hope that this picture might lure some unwary Adjutant of the Grenadiers into our clients' emporium, where he would certainly be provided with a very remarkable suit. Julian had had one of them by his desk for some time. He said it inspired him. The canvas used in its construction was so stiff that with a little effort it could be made to stand up alone like a suit of armour.

From Art I moved to the outer office and bought myself some white collars and a more grown-up suit. Here I was in full view of Mr McBean, the Scots Manager, who, with his bald head, horn rims and slightly indignant expression, seemed to swim in his glass-bound office like some gigantic turbot; only the absence of bubbles when he dictated to Miss Rundle showed that Mr McBean breathed the same air as the rest of us. He had a facility shared by fish and London taxis for turning very rapidly in his tracks, and sometimes, thinking myself undetected, I would find him glowering at me from his aquarium. He disapproved of frivolity and my reputation had preceded me when I joined his department.

✠

With such experiences behind me it was easy to believe the Porter when he said I was going to be sacked, and when I went into the main office through the swing doors in the reception counter I was filled with strangely pleasant forebodings. By this time the place would normally have been a babel, but this morning the atmosphere was chilly, tragic, and unnaturally quiet. Lettice Rundle was having a good cry over her Remington and the group of young men who handled the Cereal Account were shovelling piles of proofs and stereos into a dustbin and removing their personal belongings from drawers. Years later I was to witness similar scenes in Cairo when Middle East headquarters became a great funeral pyre of burning documents as the Germans moved towards the Delta. But this was my first experience of an evacuation.

It was easy to see that besides myself quite a number of people were about to leave. Those remaining pored over their tasks with unnatural solicitude and averted their eyes from their unfortunate fellows. I had no personal possessions to put together. My hat was in the cloakroom where it had remained for two years. I had never taken it out but sometimes I dusted it, as Mr McBean from time to time checked up on the whereabouts of the more junior and unstable members of the staff by identifying the hats in the cloakroom. This was my alibi; with my hat in its place I was permanently somewhere in the building.

This morning Mr McBean was not in his office He was not an unkindly man and the decimation of his staff had probably upset him. I went up to Leopold, the bright and intelligent Jew who looked and sounded so much like Groucho Marx that I had once seen him signing the autograph albums of eager fans in the street. He was smoking an enormous Trichinopoly cheroot – the product of one of the smaller accounts which he helped to handle in addition to breakfast food. I asked him what went on.

'We've lost Brekkabitz, dear boy.'

'I suppose it was your fault, Leo. I must say I thought some of the stuff you put out was positively filthy.'

He removed the cheroot from his mouth and blew a great cloud of smoke in my face. I began to understand why the sales of this particular brand needed all the impetus Wurzel's could give them. His voice came through the smoke: '. . . And when dear Wurzel went to America he got a very chilly reception. The client didn't like our handling of the Digestive Tract. Neither did anybody else. Nobody wants to be reminded at breakfast how many feet of gut he's got. Wurzel stuck out for the last foot.'

'Statistics show that the average is thirty-nine feet,' I said.

'Boy,' said Leopold eagerly, 'I am glad to meet you. So you really read the series?'

'The whole hundred-and-twenty-six of them. I had to in the Checking Department. They made me stick them in a book. They were terrible. They made my flesh creep.'

'So you're the only living creature who ever read them . . . I disliked them so much I used to look at them with my eyes shut. At any rate, they were a flop and this is the pay-off. We're all going, even Robbie and Johnny.'

'What about me?'

'Unless you received a registered letter with your oven-crisp Brekkabitz this morning you're still here.'

I looked at Robbie and Johnny. They were calm, a little icy and slightly green about the gills, but this may have been due to the Annual Staff Party which had been held the night before. They too were preparing to leave.

'Why Robbie and Johnny?' I asked. 'Why are they packing up? They handle the Bicycle Account. That's nothing to do with Brekkabitz.'

'My boy,' said Leopold, biting a great soggy chunk off his cheroot, 'when the heads finish rolling in this place it will look like a field full of swedes.'

'What about Lettice?'

'Joke,' said Leopold. 'Lettice is just a nice girl with a good heart and she types like a dream. They'll never sack Lettice. I don't know what she'll do without me. It's a pity that this should happen after such a heavenly party,' he added.

The Annual Staff Party had been held at a rather raffish roadhouse on a by-pass. With its peeling stucco, bulbous thatched minarets, and empty liquid soap jars over the basins in the washroom, it still holds for me, in retrospect, the essential uneasy spirit of the thirties. We arrived at the road-house after a treasure hunt in motor cars to find that the whole place had been reserved for Wurzel's. People who had driven out for dinner were being turned away.

It had not been a lively evening. Sporadic outbursts of drunkenness were extinguished early. Only Leopold had really enjoyed himself. He had appeared dressed as a waiter in a loathsome greasy suit of tails; the service was so dilatory and the food so bad that he managed to serve the Managing Director with a leg of chicken made of plaster of paris without being detected. Mr McBean had been grateful to find a large helping of smoked salmon on his plate, but this proved to be skilfully fashioned from a rubber bathmat with 'Welcome' in white letters on the reverse side.

When the tables were cleared the Managing Director had risen to his feet. He was shiny and palm-beach-suited. In office hours he was disagreeable; now, filled with wary bonhomie, he was unspeakable. He began his speech by referring to us as 'Boys and Girls', at which a premonitory and quite audible shudder ran through the assembly. He went on to regret the absence of Mr Wurzel, our Chairman, who had unexpectedly been called away.

Although, he said, we had made progress in the last year, we might have to draw in our horns and retrench in the very near future.

After what seemed a lifetime, the Managing Director reached the final peroration: 'What I always feel,' he said, 'is that we're just one big happy family.' He then sat down to a round of rather limited applause.

Now, in the grey morning, the party was over and the happy family was breaking up fast. In Layout and Ideas packing was going on with end-of-term abandon. The illusion was heightened by Julian Pringle, an enormous creature dressed in a green jacket of primitive homespun and a flaming tomato tie. He was sitting on his desk chanting 'No more Latin, no more French' whilst he tied up a great parcel of Left Book Club editions. This was nothing to him. Ideas men lived the uneasy life of King's favourites, and if not discharged would very often take themselves off to another agency, sometimes with a client in tow. At nine-thirty this morning Julian had already been in touch with a well-known rival to Wurzel's, who was glad to have him.

Before Robbie left I asked him why I had not been sacked with the rest of them. Robbie only called you 'old boy' in moments of stress. He was reluctant to answer my question. He called me 'old boy' now.

'Well, old boy, they did think about it but they decided that it cost them so little that it didn't make any difference whether you stayed or not.'

I was furious. The Porter had been wrong and I hadn't ''ad it'. I was perhaps the only member of the staff who would have actively welcomed the sack. Wurzel's was a prison to me. All the way home in the Underground I seethed . . . too unimportant to be sacked . . . At Piccadilly the train was full but the guards packed in more and more people. At Knightsbridge two of them tried to force an inoffensive little man into the train by putting their shoulders to the back of his head and shoving. Someone began to Baa loudly and hysterically. There was an embarrassed silence and nobody laughed. We were all too much like real sheep to find it funny.

At Hammersmith where I emerged sticky and wretched from the train, I found that we had been so closely packed that somebody had taken my handkerchief out of my pocket, used it, and put it back under the impression that it was his own.

I bought an evening paper. It had some very depressing headlines about the breakdown of Runciman's negotiations at Prague.

The next day I went to Salcombe for my holiday. During that fortnight while swimming in Starehole Bay I dived down and saw beneath me the remains of the four-masted barque *Herzogin Cecilie* lying broken-backed, half buried in the sand.

On my way back to London there was an hour to wait for the connexion at Newton Abbot, and wandering up the hot and empty street in the afternoon sunshine I went into a café and wrote to Gustav Erikson of Mariehamn for a place on one of his grain ships.

I never went back to Wurzel's.

CHAPTER TWO

Mountstewart

THE sea had always attracted me. I had inherited my enthusiasm, from my father, who had once tried to run away to sea and had been brought bark from Milwall in a hackney cab. He had not repeated the attempt but ever since, the sound of a ship's siren or the proximity of a great harbour would unsettle him He was, and still is, the sort of man who would crush other people's toes underfoot to look out of a crowded compartment as the train passed Southampton Water, simply to gain a fleeting glimpse of the liners berthed there. Seagulls wheeling over a ploughed field would bring the comment: 'There must be dirty weather at sea to drive them so far inland.'

My interest in sailing ships was being constantly renewed by my visits to the house of a certain Mr Mountstewart whose daughter had been a great friend of mine ever since I could remember. Although Mr Mountstewart was not old-looking when I first met him at the age of six or seven, he could not have been particularly young even then. He had taken part in the Matabele War, the Jameson Raid, and various other skirmishes. Buchan would have loved him. In fact if he had known Mr Mountstewart he would probably have incorporated him in *The Thirty-Nine Steps* instead of Hannay, who always seemed to me to be a creature unduly favoured by fortune.

You could not imagine Mr Mountstewart needing luck or coincidence to help him, although he was by no means well off and would probably have welcomed the chance that Buchan gave his heroes to make their piles before returning to 'The Old Country'. Later, when he lent me Erskine Childers' *Riddle of the Sands*, I immediately identified him with Davies, that splendid sailor and enthusiastic patriot. It did not surprise me when I learnt that he had known Erskine Childers. To this day I am convinced that Mr Mountstewart was a member of the British Secret Service.

At some time towards the end of the eighties he had made a voyage from Calcutta to London in a clipper ship which carried skysails above the royals. His description of sitting astride the skysail yard, which was as thin as a broomstick and shook violently, filled me with apprehension. He had shipped as a passenger, lived aft and had had leisure for reading and speculation. His reminiscences were to prove highly misleading.

The study where he worked was extraordinary, and nothing like it can conceivably have existed outside the British Museum and those sections of the Royal College of Surgeons not accessible to the general public. On the wall facing the door was the longest muzzle-loading punt gun I had ever seen. Below it was a smaller model. Mr Mountstewart was a Fen man and still occasionally discharged this piece from a specially strengthened canoe. Both punt guns hung close up to the ceiling, I suspect, because they were loaded. Beneath them a shark's head, its jaws agape, protruded from the wall. Next door was the bathroom; sometimes when I called, Mr Mountstewart would be having a bath, and the sounds coming from it made me think that it was the invisible hind parts of the shark happily threshing the water.

On the back of the door hung a spiked pickelhaube from a volunteer regiment that Mr Mountstewart had joined in some sudden emergency. On one side it was flanked by a narwhal's tusk and on the other by the sword of a swordfish.

To the left of the door over the fireplace was an oil-painting of the skysail yarder outside Foochow. She was shown with her ports painted black and white, which according to him was supposed to discourage piracy in the China Sea. The picture was by a Chinese artist whose imagination had overburdened the vessel with canvas.

For the rest the room contained a fantastic medley; faded photographs of early submarines at Spithead and the first turbine vessel *Turbina*, filled with apprehensive-looking men in bowler hats roaring through a crowded anchorage; assegais and knobkerries; devil masks and kris; Martini-Henry rifles and bandoliers of soft-nosed bullets.

In a recess stood a large bookcase, the top shelf filled with bottles containing nasty things in pickle, including a foetus, of what species I never dared to ask, only hoping it wasn't human. The second shelf contained a quantity of Nobel explosive and, within dangerous proximity, an electric exploder. The shelves below were filled with books of travel, charts, maps, and text-books which instructed you how to behave in the most difficult circumstances. One of these, a work on first aid *in extremis*, contained the account of a North American trapper successfully amputating his leg with a bowie knife after an affray with Red Indians. It also contained instructions for setting a broken collar bone by hurling yourself backwards off a rock.

Near the window, in a polished brass shell-case of a Gatling gun, stood a sheaf of large rockets with metal sticks which served the same decorative purposes as the Pampas grass in the front window of the next house. One Fifth of November Mr Mountstewart had appeared in our garden by Hammersmith Bridge with a number of these rockets which he fired off in series in the direction of the poorer and more inflammable parts of Fulham. They had disappeared into the night with a satisfying scream, and I am quite certain did a large amount of damage. Mr Mountstewart always maintained they were life-saving rockets but it is more probable that they had been constructed for offensive purposes at the time of the Napoleonic Wars.

The following year he appeared with a spherical object called a Gerb which he insisted was a firework. The bomb, for that is what it proved to be, was lowered into a thick iron mortar which was supposed to be deeply embedded in the earth. Unfortunately, this was not carried out properly, as the gardens were the common property of the flats in which we lived and it was felt that the grass would be damaged. It would have been cheaper to damage the grass. The initial explosion jerked the mouth of the mortar into an upright position, and instead of going over the river the Gerb, like its modern counterpart the V-2, shot vertically into the air with increasing velocity. At eighty feet it should have exploded, but it failed to do so and began to descend on us with a tremendous whining sound. In spite of his age, Mr Mountstewart was farthest from the Gerb when it finally exploded, breaking a number of windows.

I do not think my parents approved of Mr Mountstewart. In any event they never mentioned his name and my visits to his house became more or less clandestine. There I first read Slocum's *Sailing Alone Round the World* and Shackleton's *South*, with its description of the journey in a small open boat in the Antarctic winter from Elephant Island to South Georgia and the subsequent crossing of that island on foot which resulted in the rescue of the rest of the members of the expedition.

I always felt that Mr Mountstewart resembled the Seafaring Rat in *The Wind in the Willows* who persuades the Water Rat to renounce everything and go to sea. By the time I had been at Wurzel's a year his plans for me were nearly coming to fruition. Not only had he succeeded in making me think of nothing but sailing ships; he had also made me feel that discomfort and worse were preferable to my present situation. We would be discussing some proposed voyage and the victuals required and he would bring out the *South American Pilot* (Part 2), which was full of passages like this:

Off Cape St John, the eastern point of Staten Island, a heavy tide rip extends for a distance of five or six miles or even more, to seaward. When the wind is strong and opposed to the tidal stream the overfalls are overwhelming and very dangerous even to a large and well found vessel. Seamen must use every precaution to avoid this dangerous area.

A horrid picture of the Fuegian scene was conjured up by the following extract under 'Refuge Station – Lifeboat':

A refuge station has been established by the Argentine Government in this harbour (St John), provided with a lifeboat for the assistance of shipwrecked mariners. A report made in 1911 states that there was only one inhabitant of Staten Island who had been left alone at Port Cook, in charge of some machinery for extracting fat from seals, for six years.

Mr Mountstewart's strongest card in this game of getting me to sea was the one about time running out. For me time running out meant an outbreak of war, for him it meant waking one morning to find the seas stripped of four-masted barques. There were still in 1938 thirteen vessels entirely propelled by sail, engaged in carrying grain from South Australia to Europe by way of Cape Horn. There were other cargoes for these ships; timber from Finland to East Africa, guano (a sinister kind of bird dung) from Mauritius and the Seychelles to New Zealand, and very rarely, for the two remaining German barques, cargoes of nitrate from Tocopilla, Mejillones and other ports on the Chilean Coast to be carried round the Horn to Hamburg. But for the most part the outward voyages from Europe to South Australia round the Cape of Good Hope and across the Southern Indian Ocean were ballast passages. Grain was the staple cargo. If that failed most of these thirteen ships would soon be rusting at forgotten anchorages.

The survival of the big sailing ships in this trade was due to several favourable circumstances. Grain was not dependent on season, neither was it perishable. In the primitive ports of the Spencer Gulf, where the grain was brought down from the back blocks in sacks, steamers found it difficult to load a cargo in an economical time. Although at some ports there were mile-long jetties, at most places the grain had to be brought alongside the ships in lightering ketches and slung into the hold with the vessel's own gear, which might, and frequently did, take weeks. But a sailing ship run with utmost economy and a low-paid crew could still in 1938 take six weeks to load her cargo of 4,000 tons of grain, reach Falmouth or Queenstown for orders after 120 days on passage and still make a profit on a round voyage of about 30,000 miles, the outward 15,000 having been made in ballast.

CHAPTER THREE
Fitting Out

W HEN I returned from my holiday, events started to happen with increasing momentum so that I began to feel like the central figure in one of those films of the twenties, in which the actors flash in and out of buildings in the twinkling of an eye. With suspicious promptness a letter arrived from Gustav Erikson in Mariehamn, in which that man of iron told me to get in touch with his London Agents, Messrs H Clarkson of Bishopsgate.

Captain Gustav Erikson of Mariehamn, 'Ploddy Gustav' as he was known more or less affectionately by the men and boys who sailed his ships, was in 1938 the owner of the largest fleet of square-rigged deep-water sailing vessels in the world. The great French sailing fleet of Dom Borde Fils of Bordeaux had melted away upon the withdrawal of government subsidies in the twenties; only two barques, *Padua* and *Priwall*, still belonged to the once great house of Laeisz of Hamburg; Erikson remained. He was not only the proprietor of twelve four- and three-masted barques, he also owned a number of wooden barquentines and schooners, the majority of which were engaged in the 'onker' (timber trade) in the Baltic and across the North Sea.

At the time I went to sea he was sixty-five years old. Unlike most twentieth-century shipowners he had been a sailor with wide practical experience before he had become a shipowner. At the age of nine he had shipped as a boy aboard a vessel engaged in the North Sea trade. Ten years later he had his first command in the same traffic and then, for six years, he had shipped as mate in ocean-going ships. Between 1902 and 1913, when he finally left the sea to concentrate on being an owner, he was master of a number of square-rigged vessels.

If I had imagined that Clarkson's would be impressed when I approached them, I should have been disappointed. I was one of a number of Englishmen who applied to join the Grain Fleet every year, and Clarkson's could not know that I was to be one of the last. From this small mahogany-bound office, saved from being prosaic by the numerous pictures of sailing ships on the walls, they looked after the destinies of practically every grain sailer in the world. Even the Germans came to Clarkson. In 1937 they fixed the high freight of 42s 6d a ton for the *Kommodore Johnsen*. Most cargoes were for British ports and Clarkson fixed the freights. Erikson was well served by them.

I learned some of these things from a little white-haired man, who said that to make the voyage at all I must be bound apprentice and pay a premium of fifty pounds. He made no suggestions except that I would probably be better advised not to go at all. I left Bishopsgate with a form of indenture which among other provisions stipulated that my parents were to bind me to the owner for eighteen months or a round voyage; that if I deserted the ship in any foreign port my premium would be forfeited; that if I died or became incapacitated, a pro-rata repayment of premium could be claimed; that I should receive 120 Fin-marks (10s) a month, and that I should be subject to Finnish law and custom.

This document my father reluctantly signed after hopelessly trying to discover something about Finnish law and custom. I remember that he was particularly concerned to find out whether the death penalty was still enforced and in what manner it was carried out. Even more reluctantly he paid out £50 and sent off the Indentures with two doctors' certificates attesting that I was robust enough for the voyage, and one from a clergyman which stated that I was of good moral character. By this time I began to feel that I was destined for Roedean rather than the fo'c'sle of a barque.

During this time Mr Mountstewart had not been inactive. For him the balloon had gone up, this was what he had been waiting for. In the language of his generation it was 'Der Tag'. With memories of long periods of inactivity in the skysail yarder, he had got into touch with an acquaintance of his, a fashionable ship's chandler, whose interest lay principally in the fitting out of yachts in the Solent and the Hamble River. Between them they had drawn up a formidable list of books on navigation and seamanship which I would peruse under the direction of the Master. This was a heaven-sent opportunity for Mr Mountstewart's friend, and he was not backward in loading me with his wares, which included a particularly repellent kind of sea-water soap. I staggered from his showrooms to a taxi with a great pile of logarithm tables, nautical almanacks and seaman's manuals, all slightly shop-soiled. He had tried to persuade me that I needed a sextant but a premonitory and for once accurate voice told me that where I was going I might find difficulty in living it down.

His conscience had not allowed him to recommend his 'yacht-ing' brand of oilskins and clothing, and he had sent me off to the East India Dock Road where I might obtain more suitable garments than his own, which were no doubt excellent for the purpose for which they were designed. Perhaps he knew more than I imagined about sailing ships and feared that I might return after the voyage to accuse him of selling oilskins that split.

When the manager of the store in the East India Dock Road heard who had sent me and what I was proposing to do, he decided to give me his personal attention. He was far grander and more sure of himself than the neighbourhood in which the outfit-ters was situated would have led me to expect. The complete out-fitting of a hundred shipwrecked lascars would have been nothing to him. I was a smallish order and he proposed to deal with me accordingly. He swept me down the staircase to the basement past rails of hideous shore-going suits. 'Now, sir,' he said, taking a deep and well-practised breath, 'you will be wanting pilot coat heavy trousers two suits working clothes heavy underwear heavy seaboots long oilskin coat oilskin trousers seaboot stockings stormcap knife and spike, mattress straw.'

It was a hot September day. I put on the long thick vest and underpants; like all their counterparts in England they were supported mysteriously by a number of tapes which once tied in a knot could never be undone but had to be severed. Over these foundation garments I put layers of unseasonable clothing: thick navy working shirts and trousers, of itchy cloth, a seaman's jersey, stockings and seaboots. Over these went the oilskin coat and trousers, the latter insecurely supported by a single cord. On my head was the storm cap. Even this was disappointing: it was made of patent leather trimmed with imitation Astrakhan. There were flaps that let down over the ears or could be tied up on top of the hat like a deerstalker. Everything was unnecessarily ugly.

The manager was delighted at my transformation. 'Now, sir,' he said briskly, 'if you would like to move about a little . . . I walked a few feet to get what he called 'the feel' of the things and the waterproof trousers fell down.

'You will also require a trunk,' said the manager. At this moment one of his assistants wheeled one in. It was the sort of trunk that stingy murderers use for the disposal of their victims; covered with bright yellow fabric and fitted with imitation brass locks, it gave off a gluey smell and was sticky to the touch.

I was sweating profusely, unhappy to be looking so ridiculous, and miserable about the trunk.

'I want a wooden sea-chest, not a trunk. That thing will fall to pieces if it gets wet.'

The manager smirked. He was accustomed to this kind of complaint. 'The sea-chest is a thing of the past,' he said, 'are you expecting the fo'c'sle to be filled with water?'

'As a matter of fact, I am.'

'In that case,' he replied rather stiffly, 'you will no doubt want to take your own precautions. We will wrap these in brown paper.'

On the way back to Hammersmith, from the top of a bus I saw a magnificent trunk in the window of a shop that disposed of railway lost property. The trunk in the East India Dock Road had been an octavo trunk; this was a folio and the next day when I went to see it, I found that it even opened like a book. One side contained numbers of drawers intended for shoes and the other a big space for hanging clothes. It was blacker and grander than I had imagined. A small ticket said: 'This trunk by Louis Vuitton for sale', and underneath, more despairingly, 'Must be disposed of'. I bought it for four pounds, and put my shore-going clothes and my pilot jacket, of which at the time I was inordinately proud, in the space once filled with Paquin dresses. Its small white label, *Louis Vuitton. Paris. Nice. Vichy*, with its false promise of more gracious living supported me through periods of homesickness and depression.

At about this time occurred the Business with the Caribou Skin Sleeping-bag. It took up a great deal of time that I could have spent more profitably in eating. One of my chief sources of information about life in sailing ships was Basil Lubbock's *Round the Horn Before the Mast*. Lubbock, a tall, tough Etonian, had taken part in the gold rush to the Yukon; returning from the Gold Fields in 1899, he had shipped out of 'Frisco in an iron barque and worked his passage home before the mast. Among his possessions was a Caribou sleeping-bag for which he had given a pair of 12 lb blankets 'to a man who was camped alongside me at Lake Bennett, on the way into the Klondyke'. He described it as having been made in Newfoundland by the Indians from two caribou skins sewn together with the sinews of the animals. The following passage convinced me that I too must have a caribou skin sleeping-bag.

'How delightful and cosy I felt turning into my sleeping-bag in the first watch, better far than a dozen blankets. Off the Horn the air is so moist that once one's blankets are damp they never get dry again; besides which the iron side of the half-deck sweats awfully, and drops on to everything. But when everybody and everything else was wet off the Horn I would crawl into my bag, my underclothes wet, my socks dripping, I did not take them off as the only chance to get them dry was by the heat of my body, and in turning out again I would find my clothes dry, and my feet smoking hot notwithstanding the wet socks.'

The demand for caribou bags had slumped since the Gold Rush of 98. I learned this after visiting the showrooms of half a dozen manufacturers of camping equipment. In most of them I was met with blank stares of incomprehension. True to type, the assistants in those of the better sort, being asked for something outside their experience, refused to admit the existence of such a bag. In the most elegant of Piccadilly outfitters I was told by a man in a tail coat who looked like an aloof penguin that he had not been made aware of the caribou, and I returned home feeling like a character in an undiscovered sequel to *Alice Through the Looking-glass*. Mr Mountstewart suggested the Army and Navy Stores. I was naturally a little wary of him by this time, but he produced that most remarkable work, the Stores Catalogue, which was as thick as a telephone directory, and this, although it did not list caribou skin bags, hinted that even more extraordinary articles could be obtained to order. I therefore decided to pay a visit to Victoria Street.

The man in the department which dealt with camping equipment received my request very well. He had heard of the caribou and could see no reason why its skin should not be turned into a sleeping-bag.

'I suppose we could get one,' he remarked rather gloomily. 'It'll have to come from one of the Hudson's Bay posts. We'll have to barter for it but I'll take your name and address and let you know.'

'When will it be here?' I asked anxiously; time was getting short.

'It should be here in two years. They're nasty things. The last one gave the man who slept in it anthrax.'

I thanked him and after looking up 'Anthrax' in an encyclopedia in the book department, I gave up the struggle. I was content. I knew now that if I really wanted a caribou skin bag I could have one. Instead I bought from him a real camel-hair sleeping-bag of four thicknesses made by Jaeger. In 1956 the hair of the camel is as rare as the skin of the caribou and much more expensive. I used it until 1942, when an athletic Egyptian leapt into the back of the truck in which we were driving down from the Desert, and removed three large bedding rolls belonging to myself and two brother officers; mine contained, in addition to all my other possessions, the sleeping-bag.

When I returned home I found a letter from the owner's agents telling me to join the sailing vessel *Moshulu* in Belfast. She was the one ship I had never heard of, and none of the more popular works on sailing ships gave any information about her. Even Mr Mountstewart knew nothing. However, just before I left for Euston he telephoned me. 'I understand,' he boomed, 'that she is extremely large.'

CHAPTER FOUR

Op the Rigging

I crossed on the night steamer from Heysham and as we came into Belfast in the cold early morning I saw for the first time the mast and spars of *Moshulu*. By comparison the scaffolding of the shipyards, where riveting hammers reverberated about the dark bulk of a new Union Castle liner, seemed solid and rooted in the earth. The barque was invisible, but the four enormously tall masts, fore, main and mizzen, and the less lofty jigger mast, towered into the sky above the sheds of the dockside, not white as I had imagined them, but yellow in the October sunshine.

'Anyone's welcome to that,' said the smooth young steward as he plonked a pot of Oxford marmalade on my table. 'Nasty great thing.'

I did not have the strength to argue with him. All through breakfast I had felt like someone in a condemned cell and my knees had been knocking together under the influence of a nervous impulse which I had been unable to control.

On the quay when I landed there had been some competition among the waiting taximen for my Vuitton trunk. 'You'll be wanting the Grand Central Hotel, most likely?' said the shaggy owner of the most dilapidated taxi who had finally secured me as a fare. I told him I wanted to go to the *Moshulu* and as this did not seem to mean anything to him, I pointed to the towering masts, upon which he mumbled something about 'that big sailer full of Chinks' and we set off at a crazy speed, lurching into the puddles where the cobbles had subsided and slewing dangerously across the tracks of tank engines that bore down upon us at full steam. I barely noticed these things as I was in terror at the thought of climbing those masts which had a beautiful cold remoteness about them like the North Col on Everest. For the first time in my life I wished that a taxi ride would never end, but it was only three or four hundred yards to where the ship was discharging her cargo in York Dock and, too soon for me, we drew up alongside her. There was no sign of life aboard except on the well deck forward, where some stevedores were still unloading her cargo of grain.

I left the taximan extracting my trunk from the fore part of his vehicle where it had become jammed between the floor and the roof, and went forward to explore, waiting for a lull in the unloading operations to go up a slippery plank which led over the bulwarks and so on to the deck. When I reached it I began to feel that the taximan might be right about the ship being full of Chinese, for I found myself face to face with a rather squat, flat-nosed boy of about seventeen who would have looked more at home outside a nomad tent in Central Asia. From beneath a great shock of disordered hair his eyes stared unwaveringly at me. Only the filthy dungarees in which he was dressed and the oilcan he carried proclaimed him to be a child of the West.

It was his face that finally reassured me. Surely, I thought to myself, such an ugly face has something better behind it. I held out my hand and said: 'I am Newby, a new apprentice.'

The slant eyes looked at me suspiciously but I thought I could detect a glimmer of interest in them. He did not take my hand but a deep voice finally said, in a way that made me jump, 'Doonkey.' Believing this to be an epithet directed at me, I began to prepare myself for a fight. None of the books I had read said anything about a situation like this. Their heroes fought only after months of insult. Fortunately I was mistaken and he put me at ease by pointing at himself and saying: 'Jansson, "Doonkey", orl-right,' and at the same time grasping my hand which completely disappeared in his.

This was one of the two Donkeymen responsible for the proper functioning of the donkey engine, the diesel, brace and halliard winches and all things mechanical on board. In spite of his villainous appearance he was really the most tolerant and long-suffering of people, and we went through the entire voyage without trouble.

I indicated the trunk on the dock, and Jansson said: 'Orlright' again, and we went down the gangplank to the taxi. The driver was waving a piece of the roof of his vehicle which had broken off in his efforts to dislodge the trunk and was telling a little knot of stevedores everything he knew about me. As our acquaintance had been short he was drawing effortlessly on his own ample imagination. I was anxious to be rid of him and overpaid him considerably, but this encouraged him to ask for a large sum for the damage to his taxi, for which he said I was responsible. The stevedores closed in to support their countryman, but Jansson made such a threatening gesture with his tattooed forearm that they dispersed and the driver, finding himself outnumbered, gave up the struggle and drove away.

We now lifted the trunk and tried to make our way up the plank, but it was steep and my leather-soled shoes slipped backwards. 'Orlright,' said Jansson. He spat on his hands, slung the trunk on his back and shot up the incline like a mountain goat, depositing it with a great crash on the deck. I followed him. My luggage and I were aboard.

We were now on the starboard side of the foredeck by the square opening of No. 2 hatch. A travelling crane was dipping over it like a long-legged bird, pecking up great beakfuls of sacks. Underfoot was a slush of oil and grain; the oil came from a diesel winch which lay about the deck completely dismembered.

'Kom,' said Jansson and kicked open a door. I followed him through it and found myself in the starboard fo'c'sle. I had imagined the ship to be deserted but once I was accustomed to the half light and the thick pall of cigarette smoke that hung between the dock and the low ceiling, I was able to make out the figures of half a dozen men in overalls who were silently regarding me whilst sitting at a long table which ran the whole length of the fo'c'sle. Most of them seemed to be between seventeen and twenty years of age; all were muscular and pallid.

'Good morning,' I said, and their silent impassive staring went on until, like a long-awaited echo, they rumbled some kind of reply. Fortunately Jansson handed me a mug of coffee which he poured from a big white enamel jug. Someone else on the other side of the table shoved over a can of milk, a loaf of bread, and a ten-pound tin of margarine. I helped myself to my second breakfast; there were some perfunctory introductions, and munching steadily, I listened to them discussing (without visible enthusiasm) my English nationality. At the same time I was able to take note of my surroundings. They were not inviting.

The fo'c'sle was about twenty feet long and thirteen feet wide; its steel bulkheads were painted light grey; round the four sides were bunks which looked like double-banked coffins in an Italian cemetery. The lower ones mostly had home-made curtains which could be drawn when the owner was inside. Only one of the bunks was now occupied, but the curtains were half open, revealing an inert figure with its face to the wall, from which groans escaped at intervals. Down the centre of the fo'c'sle was the long narrow table, its feet screwed to the deck, the top pitted by the scrubbing and scouring of several generations of sailors. Around the edge was a raised beading, or fiddle, intended to stop the crockery sliding off in heavy weather. On either side of the table were heavy wooden benches cleated down to the deck.

Some natural illumination came from the portholes in the ship's side, one or two of which looked out on to the well-deck; but the light was more or less obscured by a chaos of wooden sea-chests, oilskins and mysterious roped bundles which completely filled the upper bunks. Above my head was a teak skylight with a number of thick glasses set in it through which daylight seeped reluctantly. Artificial light was provided by a heavy lantern swinging perilously low above the centre of the table. Behind me was a cupboard with a shelf for crockery, and another for bread, margarine and condensed milk. Below the cupboard was a white drinking-water tank with a brass tap. The crew had just finished breakfast; on the table were the remains of this ghastly repast:

some sort of thick brown stew with macaroni, now rapidly congealing, and what seemed to me, judging by the mounds of skins, an unhealthy quantity of potatoes. Standing among the ruins was an archaic gramophone with a fluted horn. This was now wound up and amidst sighs of anticipation a record was put on. There followed a preparatory churning as the needle engaged itself in the grooves and then the most appalling dissonance of sounds burst upon my ears. After I had become used to the din, I distinguished the words:

> There's a little Dutch mill on a little Dutch hill
> Where the little Dutch stars shine bright.
> Now a little Dutch boy and his little Dutch girl
> Fell in love by the light of the moon one night . . .*

This was *Moshulu*'s only record and though I may probably never hear it again, it will always remind me of Belfast and the time after Munich.

The playing of the record released any inhibitions my arrival had imposed on the company. Conversation became animated and deafening, and as the song ground itself to a standstill the boy sitting next to me, a Lithuanian whose name I later discovered was Vytautas Bagdanavicius, turned to me, flashed a brilliant smile and said happily 'No good' as he wound the motor and started the record again.

Jansson, wishing to show off every item of interest, pointed at the body in the bunk and winked significantly.

'Is he sick?' I asked.

'Bloddy sick, drank too much Akvavit last night,' said Jansson. To confirm this he began prodding the blankets and when this had no effect started to roll whoever it was backwards and forwards like a piece of dough on a pastry-board, roaring, 'Rise op, rise op.' Upon this there was a violent heaving among the blankets.

* Copyright Campbell Connelly, 1936.

'*Perkele, perkele, perkele*; devils, devils, devils,' screamed a furious voice from the bed, mounting to a crescendo like an engine on a bench being tested to destruction. Even the hardened audience jibbed at the rich descriptive obscenity which followed and begged Jansson to leave him alone. He did so, and just like an engine, the voice died away.

Somewhere on the deck, a whistle blew. One by one the occupants of the starboard fo'c'sle went out to continue their work and soon the sounds of hammering proceeded from the port side of the ship where most of them were over the side chipping rust and painting.

Because Vytautas, the Lithuanian, had been watchman all night, he did not go with them. He advised me to get into my working clothes and report my arrival to the Mate. First he helped me stow my trunk in a convenient space behind the fo'c'sle door. Gingerly I put on my navy blue dungarees which seemed stiff and unprofessional compared with the faded blue overalls worn by most of the boys.

'Do not leave anything in the fo'c'sle,' said Vytautas in his rather oriental sing-song. 'These stevedores are thieves. At sea we are all right. Here . . . nobody is good.'

I asked him whether he had just joined the ship, but he replied that this would be his second voyage. *Moshulu* had been on the timber run from Finland to Lourenço Marques in Portuguese East Africa in 1937 before going to Australia for her grain cargo. I was glad; at least he was not leaving, as many of the others were. I had already begun to cling to any acquaintance as a drowning man clutches a straw.

It so happened that I met not the First Mate but the Second, as everything was in a state of flux: some members of the crew were signing off and returning to Mariehamn, others arriving to take their place. The old Captain, Boman, who had commanded her since she joined the Erikson fleet, was going home and being replaced by Captain Sjögren who was coming from the *Archibald Russell*.

The Second Mate was thin, watery-eyed and bad-tempered. At

sea he was to prove much better than he looked to me this morning. He did not like ports and he did not like to see the ship in her present state. My arrival did not seem propitious and after dressing me down for not reporting aft directly I had come on board, he suddenly shot at me: 'Ever been aloft before?'

'No, sir.'

We were standing amidships by the mainmast. He pointed to the lower main shrouds which supported the mast and said simply: 'Op you go then.' I could scarcely believe my ears. I had imagined that I should be allowed at least a day or two to become used to the ship and the feel of things, but this was my introduction to discipline. I looked at the Mate. He had a nasty glint in his eye and I decided I was more afraid of him than of the rigging. If I was killed it would be his fault, not mine, I said to myself with little satisfaction. Nevertheless I asked him if I could change my shoes which had slippery soles.

'Change your shoes? Op the rigging.' He was becoming impatient.

At this time *Moshulu* was the greatest sailing ship in commission, and probably the tallest. Her main mast cap was 198 feet above the keel. I started towards the main rigging on the starboard side nearest the quay but was brought back by a cry from the Mate.

'Babord, port side. If you fall you may fall in the dock. When we're at sea you will always use the weather rigging, that's the side from which the wind blows. Never the lee rigging. And when I give you an order you repeat it.'

'Op the rigging,' I said.

The first part of the climb seemed easy enough. The lower main shrouds supporting the mast were of heavy wire made from plough steel and the first five ratlines were iron bars seized across four shrouds to make a kind of ladder which several men could climb at once. Above them the ratlines were wooden bars seized to the two centre shrouds only, the space for the feet becoming narrower as they converged at the 'top', eighty feet up, where it was difficult to insert a foot as large as mine in the ratlines at all.

Before reaching this point, however, I came abreast of the main yard. It was of tapered steel, ninety-five and a half feet from arm to arm, two and a half feet in diameter at the centre, and weighed over five tons. It was trussed to the mainmast by an iron axle and preventer chain which allowed it to be swung horizontally from side to side by means of tackle to the yardarms; an operation known as 'bracing'.

Above me was the 'top', a roughly semi-circular platform with gratings in it. This was braced to the mast by steel struts called futtock shrouds. To get to the 'top' I had to climb outwards on the rope ratlines seized to the futtock shrouds. There was a hole in the 'top' which it was considered unsporting to use. I only did so once for the experience and cut my ear badly on a sharp projection which was probably put there as a deterrent. I found difficulty in reaching the top this first time and remained transfixed, my back nearly parallel with the deck below, whilst I felt for a rope ratline with one foot. I found it at last and heaved myself, nearly sick with apprehension, on to the platform, where I stood for a moment, my heart thumping. There was only a moment's respite, in which I noticed that the mainmast and the topmast were in one piece – not doubled as in most ships – before the dreadful voice of the Mate came rasping up at me:

'Get on op.'

The next part was nearly fifty feet of rope ratlines seized to the topmast shrouds. Almost vertical, they swayed violently as I went aloft; many of them were rotten and one broke underfoot when I was at the level of the topsail yards. Again the voice from the deck:

'If you want to live, hold on to those shrouds and leave the bloody ratlines alone.'

The lower topsail yard was slung from an iron crane but the upper topsail yard above it was attached to a track on the foreside of the topmast allowing the yard to be raised by means of a halliard more than twenty-five feet almost to the level of the crosstrees. The crosstrees formed an open frame of steel girdering about 130 feet up, at the heel of the topgallant mast. Originally the topsail had been a single sail, but to make it easier for the reduced crews to take in sail, it had been divided into two. At the moment the upper topsail yard was in its lowered position, immediately on top of the lower topsail yard. The crosstrees seemed flimsy when I reached them; two long arms extended aft from the triangle, spreading the backstays of the royal mast, the highest mast of all. I stood gingerly on this slippery construction; the soles of my shoes were like glass; all Belfast spread out below. I looked between my knees down to a deck as thin as a ruler and nearly fell from sheer funk.

'Op to the royal yard,' came the imperious voice, fainter now. Another forty feet or so of trembling topgallant shroud, past the lower and upper topgallant yards, the upper one, like the upper topsail yard, movable on its greased track. The ratlines were very narrow now and ceased altogether just below the level of the royal yard.

I was pretty well all in emotionally and physically but the by now expected cry of 'Out on the yard' helped me to heave myself on to it. In doing so I covered myself with grease from the mast track on which the royal yard moved up and down. It was fifty feet long and thinner than those below it. As on all the other yards, an iron rail ran along the top. This was the jackstay, to which the sail was bent. (In cadet training ships this rail would have had another parallel to hold on to, as, with the sail bent to the forward jackstay, there was little or no handhold. *Moshulu* had not been built for cadets and this refinement was lacking. With no sails bent what I had to do was easy, but I did not appreciate my good fortune at the time.) Underneath the yard was a wire rope which extended the length of it and was supported halfway between the mast and either yard-arm by vertical stirrups. This footrope was called the 'horse' and when I ventured out on it I found it slippery as well as slack so that both feet skidded in opposite directions, leaving me like a dancer about to do the splits, hanging on grimly to the jackstay.

'Out. Right out to the yardarm,' came the Mate's voice, fainter still. I hated him at this moment. There were none of the 'joosts' and 'ploddys' of the stylized Scandinavian to make me feel superior to this grim officer. He spoke excellent English.

Somehow I reached the yardarm. I tried to rest my stomach on it, and stick my legs out behind me but I was too tall; the footrope came very close up to the yard at this point, where it was shackled to the brace pendant, and my knees reached to the place on the yard where the riggers had intended my stomach to be, so that I had the sensation of pitching headlong over it. Fortunately there was a lift shackled to the yardarm band, a wire tackle which supported the yard in its lowered position, and to this I clung while I looked about me.

What I saw was very impressive and disagreeable. By now I had forgotten what the Mate had said about falling into the dock and I was right out at the starboard yardarm, 160 feet above the sheds into which *Moshulu*'s 62,000 sacks of grain were being unloaded. The rooftops of these sheds were glass and I remember wondering what would happen if I fell. Would I avoid being cut to pieces by the maze of wires below, or miss them and make either a large expensive crater in the roof or a smaller one shaped like me? I also wondered what kind of technique the ambulance men employed to scoop up what was left of people who fell from such heights. I tried to dismiss these melancholy thoughts but the beetle-like figures on the dock below that were stevedores only accentuated my remoteness. The distant prospect was more supportable: a tremendous panorama beyond the city to the Antrim Hills and far up the Lough to the sea.

'Orlright,' called the Mate. 'Come in to the mast.' I did so with alacrity, but was not pleased when he told me to go to the truck on the very top of the mast. I knew that with these blasted shoes I could never climb the bare pole, so I took them off, and my socks too, and wedged them under the jackstay.

There were two or three very rotten ratlines seized across the royal backstays. The lowest broke under my weight so I used the backstays alone to climb up to the level of the royal halliard sheave to which the yard was raised when sail was set. Above this was nothing. Only six feet of bare pole to the truck. I was past caring whether I fell or not.

I embraced the royal mast and shinned up. The wind blew my hair over my nose and made me want to sneeze. I stretched out my arm and grasped the round hardwood cap 198 feet above the keel and was surprised to find it was not loose or full of chocolate creams as a prize. Now the bloody man below me was telling me to sit on it, but I ignored him. I could think of no emergency that would make it necessary. So I slid down to the royal halliard and to the yard again.

'You can come down now,' shouted the Mate. I did. It was worse than going up and more agonizing as I was barefoot, with my shoes stuffed inside my shirt.

'You were a fool to take your shoes off,' said the Mate when I reached the deck. 'Now can you learn to clean the lavatories.'

Since that day I have been aloft in high rigging many hundreds of times and in every kind of weather but I still get that cold feeling in the pit of the stomach when I think of the first morning out on the royal yard with the sheds of the York Dock below.

TECHNICAL INTERLUDE
(Surface at page 56)

In the afternoon I went with a number of other newly arrived crew to sign some papers at the office of the Finnish Consul. Afterwards Vytautas took me over the ship. The strength and size of her steel top hamper was matched by that of her immense steel hull – into which more than 4,800 tons of grain would be packed. *Moshulu*'s gross tonnage (that is to say, the entire internal volume expressed in units of 100 cubic feet to a ton) was 3,116. She drew twenty-six feet of water when loaded and measured 335 feet on the waterline.

She had a very handsome, fine bow entrance somehow disproportionate to her rather heavy overall appearance; a tiny poop only twenty feet long also contrived to spoil her looks when seen from the beam, but the general effect was undeniably impressive. Like *Archibald Russell*, *Moshulu* was fitted ·with bilge keels to make her more stable. Above the loadline the hull was painted black except for the upper works of the amidships, which were white. Her masts and spars were light yellow. Under the bowsprit there was no splendid figurehead like those of the *Killoran* and *Pommern*, only on the beak beneath the bowsprit a carved boss with a coat-of-arms picked out in yellow and blue, the house mark of Siemers, the Hamburg owners who had had her originally in the nitrate trade.

The masts, fore, main, mizzen and jigger, were each supported by a system of heavy fore-and-aft stays, six on the foremast, four on the main and mizzen, three on the jigger. On the foremast the forestay that supported it was a double stay set up taut with rigging screws shackled into the deck on the fo'c'sle head. The fore topmast stay, the next above the forestay, was also a double stay led through blocks on either side of the bowsprit and passed round rigging screws. The bowsprit itself was held rigid by two stays underneath it, the outer and inner bobstays, and on each side by three bowsprit guys shackled into the bows.

The three square-rigged masts were supported by shrouds of heavy wire; three pairs of lower shrouds extending from the bulwarks to the 'top', round the mast and back to the bulwarks; three topmast shrouds extending from the 'top' to the crosstrees; and two topgallant shrouds above. From aft came great stresses and there were nine backstays on each mast to meet them. Both lower shrouds and backstays were set up to the hull plating and tautened by heavy rigging screws. All the doublings were wormed, parcelled, served and painted black; the seizings were white, one of the few concessions to the picturesque in the whole ship.

In the days when a ship's masts and yards were wooden, the rigging was of hemp, set up with lanyards and deadeyes. In a dismasting it was sometimes possible to cut away the wreckage and allow it to go by the board; but the shrouds and backstays of *Moshulu*'s standing rigging were of steel wire so thick and strong that if the masts went over the side and one set of rigging screws was torn bodily out of the ship, it would be a tremendous job to cut away the slack rigging on the lee side without special equipment if the rigging screws stripped their threads.

Each square-rigged mast crossed six yards to which six sails were bent, a total of eighteen: the royal, upper and lower topgallants, upper and lower topsails and below these the big course-sails, fore, main and mizzen. There was a total of thirteen fore-and-aft sails: four head sails set on the forestays to the bowsprit – the flying jib outermost, set on the fore topgallant stay, the outer and inner jibs and the fore topmost staysail all set on their respective stays. In addition there were two staysails set on the topmost and topgallant forestays between each mast, six in all. There could have been royal staysails too, but they were never set in *Moshulu* while I was in her. With a small crew topgallant staysails were more than enough. Once we set a fore royal staysail beyond the flying jib, but it blew out in a squall and the experiment was not repeated. All the fore-and-aft sails had downhauls for taking them in and halliards for setting them. On the jigger mast there were three fore-and-aft sails, a triangular gaff topsail, an upper spanker between the upper gaff and the gaff boom, and, biggest of all, the lower spanker. The two lower sails were controlled by brails and were difficult to furl. The arrangement of three sails on the after mast was peculiar to the ex-German nitrate traders. Most barques only had two. With all these sails set, *Moshulu*'s sail area was in the region of 45,000 square feet.

Vytautas took me right out on the bowsprit. Into the tip of it several nails had been driven, to which some dried horny fragments adhered.

'Shark's fin's,' said Vytautas. 'Good luck, not much of it left now.' We were facing one another on the footrope. 'Very dangerous here,' he said happily. 'No netting under the bowsprit. If she runs heavily she may dip and wash you off. If you are sent to furl the "Jagare", that's the flying jib, look out for the sheet block, it can easily knock you into the water. Remember, please,' he added a little more wistfully, 'if you fall from here the ship will go over you and by the time she can heave-to it will be too late to find you.'

I was suitably impressed by these observations and had reason to remember them on many occasions during the voyage.

We worked our way down the bowsprit to the white-railed fo'c'sle head deck, the raised part of the ship at the bows. To port and starboard were *Moshulu*'s bower anchors, the old-fashioned kind with stocks, lashed down to the deck. Their stocks prevented them being hauled close up to the hawse pipes, and there was a mall crane to lift them on board. Beneath the crane was a teak pin rail with iron pins in it to which the downhauls of the headsails were belayed. The sheets led to pin rails on either side of the fo'c'sle head just above the well deck. In addition there was a capstan with square holes in it to take the heads of the wooden capstan bars. At sea this capstan was used for hauling down the tack of the foresail when the vessel was beating into the wind, but it could also be geared to the anchor windlass beneath the fo'c'sle head. On both sides of the capstan there were massive bitts to which the tack of the foresail could be made fast.

At the break of the raised deck were the two lighthouses which protected the port and starboard navigation lights; each could be entered through a hole in the roof of the lamp rooms under the fo'c'sle head. In port, the copper domes of these lighthouses were neglected and bright green from exposure, but at sea, unless the weather was very bad, they were kept brightly burnished. Two companion ladders led to the well-deck below, and between them hung in a sort of gallows the big bronze bell with *Kurt, Hamburg* (the name given her by her German owners) engraved on it.

Lashed up next to the bell, with its heel on the deck, was the spare sheet-anchor. Immediately below the lighthouses on the well-deck were the pigsties, built solidly of steel but for the present untenanted.

Underneath the fo'c'sle head-deck were the lavatories, ablution rooms, blacksmith's stores, the boatswain's store, and the port and starboard lamp-rooms. It was a draughty, smelly part of the ship. The lavatories were very gruesome, with no locks on the doors and no flushing arrangements. I had spent a memorable half-hour on the first morning cleaning them with a long iron rod and innumerable buckets of dirty dock-water. This was the most disgusting task I have ever been called upon to perform in peace or war. In war not even the pits beside the railway tracks so thoughtfully provided by the Germans for our convenience when we were being moved westwards in chains from Czechoslovakia equalled the lavatories in *Moshulu*.

Between the two washrooms stood the anchor windlass with its massive cables, and the salt-water pump, a very rickety affair with a pipeline aft to the main deck.

Immediately aft of the pump was No. 1 hatch, a tiny thing eight feet square, leading down into the 'tween-deck space and also to the forepeak where the bulk of the coal for the galley was kept. Forward of the coal store were the chain lockers, two vertical shafts in which the anchor cables were faked down link by link as they came in over the windlass pawls above. In the forepeak were great coils of wire strop, mooring springs and towing hawser, and for some distance aft in the 'tween-deck the space was filled with a pell-mell of bundled sail. The 'tween-deck was really an upper hold eight feet high, extending the length and breadth of the ship as far as the after peak, or lazarette, beneath the poop. This deck was pierced through by tonnage openings of the same size as the hatches above them. At sea both the hatches above and the tonnage openings below were battened down, cutting off the upper and lower holds. There was no artificial light below and because of this there was to be a nasty accident quite soon.

Next to No. 1 hatch the great trunk of the foremast rose up through the deck from its roots on the keelson of the ship. By the mast was a teak fife rail with iron belaying pins to which the headsail halliards and the sheets of four square sails above the lower topsail were belayed; the lower topsail and foresail sheets were belayed to cleats on the fore part of the mast itself. Not far distant from the foremast were the halliard winches for raising the upper topsail yards and topgallant yards when setting sail. The royal halliards rove through blocks and were belayed to the pin rails. It took ten men to raise a royal yard. The square sail halliards were so placed that with the yards raised they became in effect additional backstays.

Abaft the foremast was the donkey boiler room with a hinged funnel on top where Jansson and his even more savage-looking superior tended their charge, which was intended to raise the anchors. On very rare occasions it provided power for sending aloft the heavier sails. Here the Donkeymen kept the tools of their trade, which included a blacksmith's forge, spares for the winches and, an important item, a blow-lamp with which they were always brewing cocoa, happily independent of the irascible cook. On either side of the donkey house was a capstan to which the sheets of the great foresail were brought through fairleads in the bulwarks. They were also used to send sail aloft by manpower.

Between the donkey house and the raised bridge deck amidships was No. 2 hatch with Jansson's dismantled winch beside it. Here the Belfast stevedores, using shore cranes, were unloading with an almost ritualistic deliberation, like figures in a slow-motion film of a coronation ceremony. To port and starboard were the pin rails for the forebraces which controlled the final angle or trim of the foresail and upper and lower topsail yards after they had been roughly braced round with a Jarvis brace winch. Only the course and topsail yards on each mast were operated by winches. The hand braces for the topgallant and royal yards came down to the deck still farther aft on the midships section, and were belayed to the fife rail at the mainmast.

Next to the mainmast was the Jarvis brace winch for the foremast yards with which four men could brace round the course and upper and lower topsail yards according to the direction of the wind, the wire braces paying out on cone-shaped drums on one side of the winch, whilst the slack was taken up by a similar set on the other side. There were three Jarvis brace winches in *Moshulu*, which eased what would otherwise have been an almost impossible task in so large a vessel for a crew as small as ours. The remaining yards, the two topgallants and the royals, were braced round with long rope braces. In the same way those operated by the winch had also to be trimmed properly by hand.

The forepart of the raised bridge-deck was painted white and had brass scuttles set in it. These portholes shed some light into the port and starboard fo'c'sles and into the galley where the Cook, that most wretched of men, lived in a stifling atmosphere filled with escaping steam, looking very much like 'the Spirit of the Industrial Revolution' in a Nursery History of England. The bridge deck, sixty-five feet long, forty-seven feet on the beam, was connected with the fo'c'sle head and poop decks by flying bridges over the fore and main decks which enabled the Mates to move about more quickly when issuing orders. On the bridge-deck was the charthouse, a massive construction where the charts, sailing directions, log-book, barometer and navigational instruments were housed. A companion-way led below to the Officers' quarters.

Right amidships were the two massive teak wheels connected with the steering-gear aft by well-greased wire cables running through sheaves in the deck. These cables would sometimes break when a heavy sea was running. In a big gale three men would stand on the raised platforms to assist the helmsman who checked the more violent movements of the wheel with a foot-brake set in the floor. In front of the wheel was the big brass binnacle and behind the helmsman was the ship's bell on which he echoed the striking of the clock inside the charthouse. On a brass plaque below the bell was engraved: *Wm. Hamilton, Shipbuilders, Port Glasgow*.

Beneath the bridge-deck, in the forepart, were the port and starboard fo'c'sles with the galley in between them; the Petty Officers' cabin, which housed Carpenter, Donkeymen, and the Sailmaker's assistant who normally worked by day; and the Sailmaker's loft. In the after part were the six rooms of the Master's accommodation – saloon, bathroom, cabin, etc – spare room for guests – and the Officers' quarters, also the accommodation for the Steward and Cook. The Steward, Steward's boy and Cook lived aft but helped to work the ship, and even went aloft when the necessity arose.

Short ladders to port and starboard led down to the 130-foot long main deck, where the ports of the Captain's saloon amidships faced on to No. 3 hatch. By the mizzen mast was another

Jarvis winch for the mainbraces, the mizzen halliard winches and the main pumps. On either side of it were skids supporting the ship's motor-boat and a gig. Farther aft, to port and starboard, were two sets of davits each supporting a lifeboat. Between them was the standard compass on a raised platform, level with the flying bridge and connected with it, a henhouse on skids above the deck, No. 4 hatch, a freshwater tank, just before the break of the short poop and the jigger mast with the mizzen brace winch. On the poop was the patent sounding machine, a capstan, and the spare kedge-anchor.

Beneath the poop was the entrance to the after peak where the stores were kept. It was covered with a grating, heavily padlocked. Also under the poop was a pair of auxiliary wheels which could be connected to the steering-gear if the cables parted; there was also a binnacle with a compass card that displayed the most extraordinary aberrations. The helmsman's head projected right through the deck, but he was so walled-in by a curved steel coaming above and on either side that only a very imperfect view aloft could be had through the glass window in the front of it. There were six compartments under the poop. Two were originally intended for the apprentices, one was appropriated by the Sailmaker as a cabin in cold weather, another served the Carpenter as a workshop.

The bulwarks on the fore-well and main decks were shoulder-high and fitted with steel doors at intervals, hinging outwards from the top. These freeing ports enabled the water to drain off when the ship took a heavy sea. They made an abominable din and ropes were often washed off belaying pins and jammed in them.

All the slack of running rigging was coiled down on these belaying pins. There were a couple of hundred pins with some 300 lines belayed to them, some miles of hemp, wire and chain. As no sails were bent aloft, they seemed mystifying and without purpose.

All this I learned from Vytautas.

'The higher the gear, the farther aft, is the rule,' he said. 'You see, it's quite easy.'

'I don't.'

'You know the names of all the yards?' asked Vytautas.

'Yes,' I said. I thought I did.

'But do you know buntlines from leechlines and clewlines and the difference between a sheet and a tack? You will have to know these things, you will have to know them in Swedish, and you will have to find them at night.'

'How?'

'We must see Sömmarström. He's the Sailmaker and the only one who can help you.'

✦

That night I went ashore with Jansson and Vytautas Bagdanavicius to have a 'liddle trink'. It was the farewell to the boys who were going back to Mariehamn. A steady Ulster drizzle was falling as we came on to the dockside and the cobblestones shone greasily in the glare of the arc lights.

It was a long way to the main gate. We passed a steamer moored astern of us, brilliantly lit, throbbing with the movement of hidden machinery; there was no one about her, no one on the dockside, only a mangy cat scrabbling at a rubbish pile, whilst the rain swished down into the filthy water of the dock. After what seemed an interminable walk, for my feet still ached after the business in the rigging, we arrived at the dock gates, where in addition to the watchman there were two vast Belfast policemen, hard as nails, armed with pistols and long sticks, who eyed us unlovingly. Outside the gate we were on the Donegal Quay where, what now seemed a whole life ago, I had put my trunk in a taxi. Facing us, across the quay, was a wild and woolly-looking pub with its name 'Rotterdam Bar' over the door in letters of blood.

Inside, most of the crew had already gathered. Many of them I had never seen. Those I had were unrecognizable in the shore-going uniform, single-breasted blue serge suits of very Teutonic cut and light-coloured caps. In their company the evening passed in a haze. I remember meeting an Englishman called Sowerby who had just completed a round voyage in *Moshulu* as a passenger. As the evening wore on and people became drunker and spoke more freely I got the impression that the ship had not been very happy or the Captain very popular.

I was unused to beer in large quantities and, downing pint after pint, I quite soon found myself drunk. Leaning my forehead on the brickwork in the lavatory, I remember being sick and groaning to myself : 'Oh, God, I'm drunk, oh, Christ, I'm drunk, what am I here for?'

There was a lot of singing of a dark, Nordic kind. Then, after a long while, I heard a voice calling 'Time'. Lights were dimmed and we reeled out into the wet unfriendly night.

Someone suggested that we should dance and we set off down a street of heart-breaking squalor in the direction of a dance hall on the first floor of a building in Corporation Street. We went up a flight of narrow stairs and paid a shilling each to a man who, in any Police Court, would have been described by the Magistrate as a 'Corrupter of Youth'. The pleasures which we were made free of appeared innocuous enough. The room was large and to the music of a modernist radiogram two or three couples were circling rather gingerly. At intervals the music was drowned by the noise of passing tramcars which swayed past the uncurtained windows like 'Flying Dutchmen'. The seats round the walls were filled with a lot of girls heavily powdered but well below the age of consent. Some were drinking fizzy lemonade. Most of them looked like schoolgirls who ought to have been in bed asleep by this time after finishing their homework. Soon I was prancing round the room with a big, niffy red-headed girl who was liberally covered with the wrong shade of powder. I tried to talk to her but was relieved to find that she spoke no known tongue. I was very tired.

I was almost glad when a quarrel broke out between one of our crew and one of the natives; chairs were raised and began to fly through the air, the lights went out, there was the crash of glass and a bottle landed in Corporation Street. My partner vanished to join the opposition and soon we were fighting a rear-guard action on the stairs. By the time we reached the street police whistles were trilling merrily.

The march back to the ship was like the 'Retreat from Moscow', painted by an elderly spinster. The injured and the incapable were being supported by their companions. Jansson, who was very far gone, was being held up by Vytautas and myself, one on either side.

'The police will not like this,' said Vytautas, who was almost sober. 'I also do not like this place.'

At his suggestion we disengaged ourselves from the main body and made for a different entrance to the dock. Just then Jansson passed out completely and we dragged him forward along the street with his feet scuffling the granite cobbles.

'We must lift him now,' said Vytautas, as we came up to the gate. There were the inevitable two policemen, suspicious and broken-nosed. They bore down on us as we hoisted the wretched Jansson into a vertical, more lifelike position.

'Where are you going?' one of them demanded accusingly.

'*Moshulu*,' said Vytautas, in a disarming way.

'What's the matter with him?' asked the other, flourishing his great bludgeon in the direction of Jansson whose head unfortunately chose this moment to fall forward with an audible click.

'He is suffering from overwork,' I said with drunken insolence, and hiccuped. Nothing seemed to matter any more. Fortunately the policeman failed to understand my English accent. At the same time the drizzle of rain increased to a downpour and they both retired to their hut. Otherwise we should probably have been arrested.

We proceeded on our miserable and interminable way. To reach the *Moshulu* we had to pass round three sides of the York Dock. On the way we tripped over a hawser in a patch of shadow and nearly dropped Jansson in the water.

At the gangplank we were met by a bedraggled watchman armed with a pick helve who scrutinized us minutely before allowing us on board. Exhausted and wet we reeled into the fo'c'sle and after removing Jansson's boots, pushed him into his bunk and sought our own. As soon as I lay down on my straw mattress the fo'c'sle began to revolve like a gramophone record. I crawled on deck, barking my shins on all sorts of projections, and sticking my head over the rail, was fearfully sick for the second time. It had been a long, long day.

CHAPTER FIVE
Over the Side

WE were awakened at 5.30 in the morning after our 'liddle trink' by a dreadful voice crying, 'Resa upp, Resa upp.' This summons, with its medieval implications of Hell and Judgement, made me feel like a corpse in a Dürer engraving, and the illusion was sustained when I sat up in the coffin-like bunk and hit my head a great crack on the bedboards of the bunk above.

'Shot op,' came an angry voice from the occupant of the upper bunk. I lay still in the stifling blackness until the fo'c'sle door was kicked open and the night-watchman, in oilskins, appeared with a lantern, which he hooked to the ceiling, and a pot of coffee which he banged down on the table. One by one groaning figures began to roll out of their coffins and grovel for boots. From outside came the hiss of rain in the darkness of the too-early morning.

This was to be such an invariable routine, the watchman impatient and bad-tempered after a night on deck, surrounded by the terrors of Belfast that I no longer remember individual days but only that awful first morning.

With two others I was given the job of carrying coal to the galley from the small hatch near the fo'c'sle head. In the coal store by the forepeak we filled great oil-drums with coal, manhandled them in the darkness below decks to the hatch opening, hauled them on deck, and carried them to the galley, slung on a capstan bar – hard work for my unpractised arms. We made ten journeys like this before the Cook was satisfied. Afterwards I again cleaned the lavatories.

At eight o'clock came breakfast, which was a mess of pungent beans and very pickled bacon. I was then told to collect a hammer, a pot of red lead, and a brush and go over the side forward to chip the rust off the topsides – a job the more experienced and favoured members of the crew had been engaged in since 6 a.m. Rain was still falling steadily. There were already two or three precarious platforms over the side when I got there. They were simply planks with ropes made fast to either end and belayed on deck.

I do not think it was by design that the platform I inherited was in the most difficult position right over the bows, about two feet above the water. Grimly I lowered myself twenty feet to the platform, to find that it was immediately below the lavatory which I had just cleaned. I began to wish that I had used two or three more buckets of water, and this was a good lesson to me in doing a job thoroughly. At sea one was very likely to find oneself let down by one's own mistakes. I had not the strength to climb the rope again and shift to a more wholesome area, so I settled down to work where I was.

Set perilously above the dirty waters I first chipped and then red-leaded a large irregular piece of the ship's side, using red lead from the pot which hung in front of me on a cord. Horizontal movement of the platform was controlled by a system of ropes. In trying to move my platform so that I could work in a fresh and more agreeable situation, and being unable to regain the deck to shift the head-ropes, I inadvertently let slip a clove-hitch which was keeping my platform about four feet to the left of its proper position. The whole construction, thus released, swooped sideways and hit the platform of the man who early that same morning had told me to 'shot op' when I hit my head on his bedboards. He was an able seaman called Sedelquist, made more bad-tempered than usual by the events of the previous evening. The shock of the collision made me drop my hammer in the dock, upset the red lead on Sedelquist's overalls, and knocked the brush out of his hand. It gave him a bad fright. I had not imagined that he could speak English, as up to now we had not spoken, but he immediately called me a 'focking* bastard' and disappeared on deck. Soon he returned with the same Mate who had sent me aloft the day before.

'What d'you bloody well think you're doing?' he shrieked down at me.

'I'm terribly sorry,' I replied. This piece of English courtesy was wasted on the Mate. In fact it made him more angry.

'I'm sorry you're in this ship. Where's your hammer?'

'I'm afraid it's gone,' I replied, almost bashfully.

'Jesus,' said the Mate. 'Because you're English you think you can lose my hammers. I'll take it off your pay.'

When, months later, I got to Australia and collected part of my pay, amongst the deductions for cigarettes and so on made by the Captain was my little hammer.

'You are zorry, I am zorry,' said Sedelquist, when the Mate had gone, looking at his beautiful dungarees covered with red lead.

My morale, which had been dropping since I arrived in Belfast, fell to new depths. But I was learning. I vowed that I would never again, whilst in the ship, be sorry for anything, and apart from some lapses I managed to keep this resolve. I had been outraged by Sedelquist's action in rushing on deck to tell the Mate what had happened. Years of school life, happily behind me, told me that by schoolboy standards, Sedelquist had 'sneaked'. At my prep school he would have been sent to Coventry. Here I seemed to be in danger of suffering the fate which should have been his.

After some hours on the freezing platform, during which I brooded on these questions and hit viciously at the ship's side, a whistle blew. It was the dinner hour. Sedelquist swarmed up his rope with agility. Pride prevented me from asking his help. I had never been very good at climbing at school and I had always loathed the glib, bouncy, P.T. instructor who used to disport himself on the comfortably thick ropes in the gym. This rope was

* Fock – Swedish word meaning foresail.

different. It was two-inch manilla and very greasy. With great efforts I rose seven or eight feet and then slipped miserably down again. My second try took me higher but I could not see how I could climb out over the flared bow.

I managed to get within an inch or two of the lower rung of the rail and then I was back on my platform, almost in tears. I considered jumping in the dock and swimming or shouting to attract attention. Neither of these courses really appealed to me. Eventually I managed to traverse the side of the ship and reach the platform beyond Sedelquist's. Here I got my foot in a hawse-pipe and reached the deck easily.

Dinner was over and the 'Little Dutch Mill' was being played when I arrived. I was greeted with derisive cheers. I had learned another lesson, not to be late for meals.

'You are zorry,' said Sedelquist, 'and you are noh strong.'

There was no reply to this and I got on with the cold remains of the dinner which I had begged from the Cook and which seemed unaccountably good.

Although my popularity was at a low ebb, it received a tremendous fillip the next day, my third on board, a short period which already seemed to me like an eternity. The coal supplies were low and we were replenishing them from the shore. I was therefore rather dirtier than usual and was looking forward to a bath at the Salvation Army Refuge, of which I thought very highly, having had a hot one for next to nothing the night before. I was standing at the rail when I saw a very fast and luxurious sports car nose its way along the dock and come to a halt by the ship. There was a flurry of skirts as the occupant emerged, and a distant vision of legs of timeless elegance as a woman, clutching a splendidly unpractical hat, came up the gang-plank.

Naturally all work on board ceased, and the crew gave themselves up to an orgy of speculation. There was a short interval before she appeared by the mainmast, escorted by two Mates (the First having just joined); both wore social expressions and braid caps which they had put on with miraculous speed. According to Sedelquist, they kept their hats handy in the officers' lavatory for just such an emergency. I was not used to the Second Mate in this new social role, but by now I had recognized the visitor and was not as surprised as the rest of the crew when I was called aft.

The visitor was a great friend of my parents, called Lucy, whom I had always worshipped from afar. Whenever possible I would refer to her as 'my aunt in Ireland', but it was only practicable to do so when she was not present and to people who did not know her. I had been debarred from any other pretence by my extreme youth. Now, here she was, dressed in black, the most elegant woman in Ireland. I must have looked pretty bad, because her first words were. 'Och, Eric, come away home now, your mother's crying her eyes out.'

'I'm afraid I can't, Lucy,' I said, lying bravely. 'It's tremendous fun really, and I'm not always as dirty as this.'

'Can he come home with me?' she asked the Mate, who was goggling.

'We stop work at twelve o'clock on Saturday. He must be on board by six o'clock on Monday morning.' I really thought that he was going to choke as the words came dragging out of his boots.

'How sweet of you,' said Lucy, going over him with a lovely smile. 'I'll pick him up here. Now, can he please show me the ship?'

I didn't think that even Lucy could pull this one off but she did, inserting a parenthetic: 'Perhaps you could come too. I am sure Eric knows very little about it.'

Both Mates escorted her to the car when she drove away. It may have been autumn in the York Dock, but over the deck of the *Moshulu* hung the expensive scent of springtime.

The boys crowded round. Just like school again.

It was Sedelquist who led the interrogation.

'Who is hee?'

'She's called Lucy.'

'Hee is very good. Hee is your friend?'

'She's all right,' I parried.

Sedelquist persisted: 'Hee is your girl friend.' I pondered

this, wondering why he had not said boy friend. I thought too of my diminished status, all the mistakes I had made in three short days. If we did not sail soon I should be a laughing-stock.

Sedelquist was about to ask the same question again.

'Hee . . .'

'Well, sort of,' I said. 'She's a sort of aunt.'

Whatever the Scandinavian interpretation of 'aunt', it satisfied everybody. I was 'noh strong', but Lucy was my aunt and in the dark days to come, before I became 'you strongbody' and could take it out of other people, it was the respect that the crew had for her that kept the mass of them on my side whatever violent battles I might have to fight individually.

CHAPTER SIX
Sömmarström and His Sails

O N Monday morning I was delighted to find that two more 'foreigners' had arrived on board and had been allotted to the starboard fo'c'sle. One of them, George White, was a tall thin young man from Massachusetts; the other was a young Dutchman called Jack Kroner who spoke fluent English. Both had signed on as apprentices, but Jack, who had been to sea before, had very sensibly evaded the premium which my father had been required to pay on my behalf, by arriving unheralded at the ship and striking a bargain on the spot.

Belfast after dark, into which we used to sally with Vytautas on modest porter-drinking expeditions, was a strange city, like a studio set for a Hitchcock thriller and equally deserted. The rain shone on the cobblestones and the wind howled down the dismal thoroughfares, rattling the glasses of the gas-lamps above our heads.

The only people we ever encountered off the main streets were numbers of apparently able-bodied men who would emerge from the shadows outside public houses and demand money. If not satisfied they would become abusive. One of the Finns who was being repatriated became so enraged by their attentions that he picked one of them up and threw him bodily into a glass shopfront. His departure was delayed for some days by this act, but he was saved from serious consequences by his ignorance of English and the ingenious plea put forward on his behalf that he had misunderstood the nature of the importunity. The four of us never had any compunction about refusing these requests for money as we had so little ourselves.

During these innocuous evenings spent in the snug of one of the less wild pubs we gradually drew up, to use the idiom of the times, a multi-lateral pact to resist those Finns and Swedes who already showed signs of becoming aggressive. Vytautas was not included in these arrangements. He had already made a round voyage in *Moshulu* and his position was established; besides, he had the happy temperament that did not attract trouble. Like other pacts in the world outside, to which we gave so little heed, it was to be rendered invalid by the loss of one of the contracting parties and the isolation of the remaining two, which made it impossible for one to help the other.

For the most part our thoughts were dominated by The Voyage. Sometimes, tired of the squalor in which we found ourselves, it seemed that we would never sail. It was Vytautas, by far the most resilient, who made us feel, by some reminiscence of life in the Trade Winds or in the high latitudes, that our present discomforts were bearable.

The last of the cargo was unloaded and the ship was warped down the dock to a deserted quay where we were to take on board our ballast stiffening for the voyage to Australia. There we cleared hundreds of blind baby mice from the frames in the hold; cleaned out the bilges which were filled with rotting grain and very smelly bilge-water, and set to work sweeping out the 'tween-decks. It was here that the accident occurred. The weather had been abominable and the open hatches were covered loosely with tarpaulins. In the 'tween-decks it was pitch black. We had two lanterns, and by the light of one of these George was sweeping with a will, working his way aft. Soon he was outside the circle of light thrown by his lamp; unused to the 'tween-decks, he stepped backwards over the tonnage opening below No. 3 hatch and fell into the empty hold, hitting the keelson twenty feet below. When we reached him he was rigid, but still breathing. By the time we had got him out of the hold on a stretcher he was conscious and in pain. In the ambulance on the way to hospital he said, 'I guess you're going to have to do without me.'

One of his legs was broken and quite a lot of other things as well. He remained in hospital until December, two months after we sailed. It was a bitter disappointment for George; unlike the American of European imagination, he was not a rich young man. He had worked his passage to England and spent most of his savings to realize his ambition. I was downcast too. I had been long enough in the ship to realize that the confined space in which we lived would become very irksome once we were at sea. I was now deprived of my principal ally.

The following day Vytautas fell off the donkey house and broke an arm. *Moshulu* was dangerous for the unwary.

At the quay we took in our ballast, fifteen hundred tons of coarse dark sand used in the manufacture of pig-iron, huge lumps of paving-stone, granite blocks and the best part of a small house. At the same time the stevedores added two dead dogs, but we did not discover this until we reached Australia in January, the hottest month of the year.

✢

John Sömmarström, Sailmaker and Bosun of *Moshulu*, was a famous figure in the Erikson ships. If ever a man deserved the title of 'shellback' it was he.

When I first met him he was fifty-eight years old and had been forty-three years at sea, all of them in sail, most of them in square rig. He had served in Scottish ships like *Loch Vennachar* in the 1900s and he had been for a time in the china-clay trade between Par in Cornwall and other West of England ports. In later years he had been Sailmaker in the barquentine *Mozart* which he described as 'a cow', the four-masted barque *L'Avenir* (he had served four years in *L'Avenir* when Erikson still had her), and a year in the *Archibald Russell*.

As I entered the sail loft I had an impression of a solid chunky man with spectacles set on a rather snub nose and a face covered with grey stubble. He was sitting in his shirt sleeves reading *The Seven Pillars of Wisdom*. In his mouth was a pipe that had gone out and on his head a unique hat. It was an ordinary grey felt hat, tweeked up in the middle like a scoutmaster's, punctured with a number of holes that might have been made by bullets, intended, he said, to allow the air to circulate. I noticed that his fingers were rather stubby but the nails were very finely formed. He had a wonderful smell about him compounded of hemp and Stockholm tar.

When he began to speak I was surprised that he spoke really fluent English, or rather Scots, with the accent of the Clyde. Perhaps he had picked it up in the *Loch Vennachar*. I told him what I wanted.

'It's a funny thing that most of the people who get killed in these ships are Englishmen,' he grunted. 'Limeys we used to call them. There were Limeys, Squareheads and Dagoes. You're a Limey. You hang on tight.'

(Readers who are discouraged by technical details about sails and sailmaking should skip the rest of this chapter.)

'If you like,' he went on, 'I'll tell you something about square sails. First, they're not square at all, they're four-sided and square at the head but the foot's cut on an arc, called the roach, to allow the sails to clear the fore-and-aft stays when they're set.

'Most people seem to think that a sail's cut in one piece. A sail's cut cloth by cloth. I already know how wide the sail has to be because all square sails extend to within eighteen inches of the yardarm cleats on the head, and the depth depends on the height of the mast and the distance between the yards.

'That's the material over there.' He pointed his pipe at a heavy bolt of canvas. 'Webster's 24-in. Standard Flax Canvas from Arbroath. The finest stuff in the world and expensive.'

'How much would it cost to make a complete new set for the ship?'

He glared at me. 'About £2,500. But you listen to me. It doesn't matter to you, does it, how much it costs? I'm telling you something more important.' His pipe had gone out so I offered him some tobacco, rather diffidently, afraid that Fribourg and Treyers's mixture would not be strong enough for him. It made him splutter a bit at first but he appeared mollified. 'Where was I?' he said. Fortunately this was a purely rhetorical question and did not require an answer from me.

'I said that a sail is cut cloth by cloth and before I start the actual cutting I have to calculate the number of cloths the width requires, allowing for seams, tabling on the leeches, and slack. The leeches are the perpendicular edges, and you have to allow some slack when sewing on the bolt ropes, otherwise when the bolt rope stretches in wear, the sail might split.'

'What is tabling?'

'Tabling is a broad hem made on the skirt of the sail by turning the edge and sewing it down. It strengthens the sail for sewing on the bolt rope. You needn't be afraid to ask if you don't understand. I only get wild if you ask me questions like a bloody fool reporter.'

He continued: 'In the depth I've got to allow for tabling at the head and the foot. There are gores in a sail too, they're the angles cut at the ends of the cloth to increase the width or the depth. The canvas for the gores is cut on the cross, the longest gored side of one cloth makes the shortest side of the next. After the first gore is cut the rest are cut by it.'

'Christ,' I muttered, overcome by the Sailmaker's command of technical and outmoded English with which he seemed equally at home as with his native Swedish. He began to explain how he found the number of yards of canvas needed. 'It comes in bolts twenty-four inches wide. I add the number of cloths in the head and the foot together and halve them to make them square. Then I multiply the number of squared cloths by the depth of the sail and add to that the additional canvas contained in the foot gores and linings, and the four buntline cloths. The linings are sewn to the leeches and middle to strengthen it. The buntline cloths are to stop chafing on the sail. That's why the sails are heavy. A course, that's the big sail on the fore, main and mizzen – weighs more than a ton, and much more when it's wet.

'If you're interested,' went on the Sailmaker, 'I'll tell you something about sailmaking. This is my sail-loft.' He waved his hand to indicate the austere and cramped quarters in which he worked. 'And these are my tools: palm and needles; a sail-hook.' He held up a small iron hook with a cord spliced to an eye in the shank. 'Used for holding still the work. Marline-spikes for opening rope strands when I splice. A wooden fid for the same purpose. A pinker, like a marline-spike but straight, and a heaving-mallet.' This was a hammer with a small cylindrical head used as a lever to haul tight the cross-stitches when sewing the bolt-ropes on the sail.

'What are the bolt ropes?' I asked, having wanted to know all this time.

'The bolt rope is sewn to the edge of a sail to stop it splitting. It's either wire or hemp, mostly wire now. If it's hemp it's sewn with three-thread twine. The rope has to be well twisted while this is being done and it has to be cross-stitched on the leeches every twelve inches on every seam and at the middle of every cloth in the foot. In the head of the sail are the cringles through which the rope-yarns are passed securing the sail to the jackstay on the yard. In the foot are the cringles to which the buntlines are fastened and by which the sail is drawn up to the yard for furling.'

'And what's this?' I asked him, holding up another hammer with a grooved head. 'Another sort of heaving-mallet?'

'It's a serving-mallet,' he replied. 'And this is the way I serve a clew – which, by the way, is the lower corner of a sail to which the sheet is fastened.'

On the leech of the sail was a cringle, a ring made by working a strand of rope round an iron thimble. This cringle he hooked on to a bulkhead, hung off a block and tackle on the bolt rope where the clew was to be, and set it up taut between a vertical iron post and the bulkhead. He took a ball of spun yarn, made two or three turns round the bolt rope, confining the end under the turns; he placed the serving mallet on the rope, passing the yarn round the rope, the head of the mallet and the handle. 'Take hold of this,' he ordered, handing me the ball of yarn to pass round the rope as he turned the hammer which wound the yarn tightly on to the rope.

'This is serving,' said the Sailmaker, after he had made a few turns to show me the idea, 'but first you must worm the rope by winding spun yarn along the contour of it to get a level surface and after that you parcel it with tarred canvas wrapped on before you serve it.

'Now that you know how to make a sail,' the Sailmaker went on optimistically, 'you must know how to sail the ship. Do you know anything at all about square rig?'

I said that I knew very little.

'Huh,' he sniffed contemptuously. 'Well, you'd better bloody well wake up and learn.'

He immediately launched into a long and clear exposition of the theory of square sails and the action of the water on the ship's rudder. How, when *Moshulu*'s wheel was put to starboard, the rudder would go to starboard and the vessel turn to starboard; that the greater the angle of the rudder the more the ship's way would be impeded. It was therefore important so to balance the ship with sails that only a slight touch on the helm was necessary.

'Now suppose,' said the Sailmaker, 'that *Moshulu* has the wind on her starboard beam, that is to say at right angles to the direction in which she is heading. Sails are set on the foremast only and the yards are braced so that the sails are full. What happens? I'll tell you,' he said before I could open my mouth. 'Her bows will fall off and her stern will come into the wind. That's because she rotates on her pivotal turning point, which is forward of the mainmast when she's trimmed properly. With sail set on the mizzen, her head will come into the wind. With sail on the main only she will go ahead, and if the yards are braced so that the wind blows on the forepart of the square sails, she'll go astern.'

He went on for an hour and I only understood half of what he told me. Finally he lumbered to his feet, saying: 'I'm off to see the Consul. Leave that list of English words, I'll write down the Swedish later.'

Now he was getting restive, rummaging in a box. 'Aw hell, I've got to see the Consul.'

'Which Consul?' I asked, wondering why he suddenly wanted one at five o'clock on a wet October night.

'The one under the fo'c'sle head, on the port side,' he grunted triumphantly, for he had just found a copy of the *New Statesman and Nation* to serve his need, and departed on this urgent mission.

The next morning, in spite of consultations between the Mates and the Sailmaker, the utmost confusion prevailed. For winter in the North Atlantic we needed a complete suit of thirty-one storm-sails. Some of them were in the sail-loft but the rest were in the 'tween-decks mixed up with tropical sails we would need later and old blown-out rags too rotten to mend. None of the crew seemed to know which sails were wanted or where they were to be found. The sails were three and four deep in the darkness and as heavy and intractable as lead. The Mates flashed electric torches and groped for the lower leeches of the square sails on which were stencilled the name of the sail, together with the initials of the maker. There were some very old sails amongst the newer ones. One or two, of American cotton, must have been made for her before she was laid up in Seattle after the 1927 voyage to Melbourne; others were out of a well-known ship, the *Star of England*. There was also a mainsail with reef-points in it from *Herzogin Cecilie*, which must have been made before 1921 when she passed to the Finns, and was probably made long before 1914, at the time when she was a training-ship and cargo-carrier for the Norddeutscher Lloyd Company.

Some sails were marked in Swedish, some in English, others in German and, as each sailmaker had his own system of marking, the Mates tied themselves in tri-lingual knots.

After about half an hour of sweating and swearing, they sent for the Sailmaker. He lumbered about in the darkness saying 'Aw, shit,' when he tripped over some obstacle. Occasionally he borrowed a torch to consult a grubby and almost illegible piece of paper. Very soon we were heaving the chosen sails on deck: long, sausage-shaped bundles which cut into our shoulders as we tottered along the flying bridge with them.

The first sail I helped to send aloft and bend was a main lower topsail. It was stretched out across the deck and the head earrings (the ropes with which the head of the sail was stretched out along the yards) made fast to their cringles. Then the robands, the rope yarns with which the sail was bent to the jackstay, were put through each eyelet hole in the head. Next the sail was made up with its head and foot together and a gantline was rove through a block on the mast-head. One end of it was made fast to the centre of the sail, which was then hauled aloft with the help of the donkey-engine, a refinement we were not to enjoy at sea because the donkey-engine guzzled too much coal and water. Once at sea every sail was sent aloft on a gantline by hand capstan.

At the yard, clewlines, buntlines and chain sheets were ready to be bent to the lower topsail which now swung on the gantline above the yard. The sheets for the lower topsail had been cast off the cleats on the mainmast and enough chain hauled up from below to enable them to be shackled to the clew of the sail. The clewlines were shackled on and the buntlines were passed through the wooden thimbles on the front of the sail and clinched to the cringles in the bottom of the sail by a buntline knot which would not jam. The sail was now ready to be brought to the yard. Those on deck hauled away at the buntlines and those on the yard hauled on the head of the sail, one man sitting astride each yardarm to reeve the head earring through straps on the yard and haul out the head of the sail to make it quite square. The head of the sail was then made fast to the jackstay with the robands already in the cringles.

The sail was now bent, with the clews of the lower corners of the sail drawn right up to the yardarm by the clewlines and the body or bunt of the sail hauled upwards by the buntlines. Now we had to furl it, as we were making a neat harbour stow. The weather leech had to be taken in first and the heavy weight of sheet and clew earring taken as far in towards the mast as possible. Next, the body of the sail was hauled up and beaten down in a neat package on top of the yard and the rope gaskets passed round both the yard and the sail, and secured.

To set the same sail one hand would be sent aloft to cast off the gaskets and overhaul the bunt and clewlines, leaving them slack. The lee sheet would be hauled down, then the weather sheet, and, on a movable yard such as the upper topsail, the yard would be raised by the hands on deck applying themselves to the topsail halliard winch. The last job for the man aloft was to overhaul the buntlines and make up the gaskets neatly on top of the yard, seizing them to the jackstays.

All this was mystifying to me. I had read of these things and, with the aid of the Sailmaker's list, had tried to memorize the Swedish for buntlines, clewlines, and so on, but it was different up in the rigging. In the fo'c'sle I might know that the upper topsail outer buntline on the port side was 'babords övre märs yttre bukgårding'. In practice my mind became blank. It was difficult enough to hang on and furl sail in a flat calm in dock. I trembled to think of performing these feats in the Atlantic.

CHAPTER SEVEN

Wild Life in the Irish Sea

WE sailed from Belfast on Tuesday, October 18th, 1938, our destination Port Lincoln for orders. On board were a crew of twenty-eight, including the Captain, a man of huge size, who had come to us from Erikson's four-masted barque *Archibald Russell*. His name was Mikael Sjögren.

The crew consisted of three Mates – 'Förste Styrman', 'Andre Styrman', 'Tredje Styrman' as they were called in Swedish, the working language of the ship; the Sailmaker, who was also the Bosun; the two Donkeymen, both called 'Doonkey'; the Carpenter or 'Timmerman'; the Steward and Steward's boy, and the Cook or 'Kock'. I always found this title comic, but nobody else did. They all lived aft except the Sailmaker, the Carpenter and Donkeymen who had their meals in the middle fo'c'sle and normally stood no watches. Jansson, the second Donkeyman, was the only one who did. There were eighteen foremast hands, nine in each watch. Two 'Matros' Able Seamen; seven 'Lättmatros', Ordinary Seamen (Jansson rating as Lättmatros); five 'Jungmän' or boys; and four apprentices. The Jungmän in *Moshulu* were either pure-blooded Finns from the mainland or Åland Islanders with Swedish blood. They were really equal in rank with the Apprentices, who were all foreigners, two Danes, a Dutchman and myself.

These and a number of bedraggled hens in a henhouse on the main deck did not seem an over heavy complement for such a big barque as the *Moshulu*, but it was the normal one.

By half past three in the afternoon everything was ready. On board we had four tons of potatoes, the staple food, and a large number of harness-casks filled with pickled beef and pork, giving promise of an endless succession of nasty meals. Drinking water cost £5 a ton at our destination, so we had on board sixty tons of it, enough for a round voyage of thirty thousand miles. Fortunately we had a good steward who had just forced the none-too-scrupulous ship's chandler to take ashore with him several sacks of potatoes which had been rejected. This gentleman had been one of the last to leave the ship, to be followed shortly afterwards by the wife and son of the Captain. The latter, only five years old, was in miniature bell-bottoms and although red-eyed bore himself bravely. As they left, the Pilot had come aboard, looking every inch a Pilot, and was now pacing the amidships deck with the Captain.

In another quarter of an hour the graving deck, which had seemed to fill with painful slowness, was up to the brim. The caisson was raised and hove out clear and men who would soon be sitting down to supper in their own homes strained at great capstans on the dockside, warping us out into the stream. In this way, without bands, without crowds and without cheering, watched by a score of unemotional labourers standing in the soft rain, we set off on our fifteen-thousand-mile voyage.

I had been watchman on our last night in Belfast. Now, for a little longer, I was still free. The silence of our departure was uncanny. Standing with Vytautas, whose arm was still in plaster of paris, I returned the steady gaze of the dockers. A voice called 'Good luck,' but I could not say from where it came; it might have been a prayer offered by any of us.

I was glad to be leaving the miles of grey streets and the squalor and filth that had beset the ship during her weeks in port. I had said my goodbyes to my mother, who had come over to stay with Lucy, in the latter's house, not wanting my resolve to be sapped by scenes of Victorian emotion on the dockside. Then, as now, I felt that tears should be reserved for the happy return. Everything was too novel and interesting for regrets.

The majority of the crew were going pell-mell along the deck and struggling with festoons of mooring wires, encouraged by the Mates on the flying bridges. The Sailmaker, a tower of strength, had emerged from his quarters wearing his punctured hat and a remarkable pair of trousers with a very large rectangular patch in their massive seat.

An energetic little tug with a red and black funnel took us in tow. Soon we were out in the deep-water channel, marked by black conical beacons to port, and to starboard by red cans. The black cones were numbered in a descending scale, the cans lettered from H to A.

We passed a red can marked 'D'. On it was perched a sea-bird with a long beak, seen for a moment, but I still remember it. All around us was the rushing, hissing tide.

Astern, Belfast was enveloped in a pall of yellow smoke, and beyond the city were the Antrim hills drenched in mist and rain.

'Belfast, the arse of the earth,' grunted the Sailmaker, spitting neatly over the side and clamping his hat firmly over his eyes. Three months later, when we finally made a landfall at Cape Catastrophe, he was to make the same observation about the Eyre Peninsula, and on both occasions I agreed with him wholeheartedly.

Night was falling and I was told to be ready to go aloft. I struggled into my oilskin coat from which I had lopped eighteen inches, to bring it into line with those worn by the rest of the crew, after Sedelquist had asked me if I thought I was 'Keeng of Englant'. The trousers which had fallen down when I first put them on in the East India Dock Road still continued to do so. I had hoped to prevent this by sewing on a lot of buttons to which I attached my braces, but the braces were of the inelastic kind and after the first night in the Irish Sea all the buttons disappeared and the braces went over the side. On my head I stuck a brand new sou'wester which I had been dubious about wearing as I looked such a dolt in it, but everyone else was wearing one and looked equally doltish and it did not seem to matter.

Now I could see the light on Black Head, away on the port quarter, flashing every three seconds and the Mew Island light to starboard flashing four times every half-minute. Somewhere on the starboard shore Lucy and my Mother would be drinking tea. I was roused by a dig in the back and a request to 'Horry op the rigging', and found myself going aloft to loose a lower topsail. All the way up I was pursued by the 'Horry ops' of other more experienced members of the crew close behind me, who were in danger of having their fingers trodden on. Out on the yard we cast off the gaskets which secured the furled sail. It bellied out below and was sheeted home by those on deck. I was left aloft to overhaul the buntlines. This was the apprentice's job. To prevent chafe on the front of the sail he had to haul enough spare line through the bunt blocks to leave some slack at the bunt and stop it running back with seizings of yarn at the blocks.

With topsails set on main and mizzen, *Moshulu* began to gather way and cut the water by her own power and gain on the tug. It was time to part from her. The towing cable was cast off from the bitts forward and vanished through the hawse pipe with a zipping sound; there was a momentary view of the little tug surrounded by churned water, of dark figures hauling frantically aboard her as she turned, then her siren gave long blasts of farewell as she faded into the murk astern.

Aloft sail was billowing out in miraculous fashion. We seemed to be moving through the water quite fast, but when I asked Kroner what speed he thought we were doing he said only about four knots. I was disappointed.

Between six o'clock and midnight we tacked the ship three times; at least I think we did. It was pitch black and I had no idea how we were heading. The order to tack ship was 'Stagvända', which meant putting the vessel about by bringing her head across the wind, a tricky thing to do at night with a new, green crew. For all I knew then we may have done a 'Kovända', that is to say, wearing ship by turning her head away from the wind before putting her on the new course, an operation which required much more sea room. On the first night it made little difference to Kroner or myself whether we were tacking or wearing ship; neither of us could understand the orders. Although he was an experienced sailor our sensations must have been somewhat similar. Ropes were thrust into my hands and I hauled on them; I was propelled not very gently towards brace winches and turned handles almost interminably After winding came more hauling at the rope braces so that I soon lost all the skin from my over-civilized hands. At the head of the rope with five or six of us tailing behind him was Jansson's boss, the Donkeyman, a savage-looking lout in a cloth cap. 'Doonkey' encouraged us with the most extraordinary noise. 'Hor vay . . . ooooh . . . Han or han . . . Eee-or . . . curm up.' We newcomers tried to echo them. At first I felt rather like Christopher Robin bellowing 'Eee-or' at the top of my voice, but soon I began to enjoy it.

'Ooooh . . . Eee-or . . . oooh . . . Eee-or,' roared the Donkeyman like a real donkey in anguish. 'Eee-or,' we echoed lustily. Now the brace had to be belayed. 'Slack oop,' he said in a more conversational voice. Everyone except me let go of the rope as if it were red hot. 'Doonkey' gave a great heave at the slack, sending me flying into the scuppers where I hit my head on a solid oak slide which was used for tipping rubbish into the sea.

'Name of Sarrtan,' said 'Doonkey', 'was slack oop,' taking several turns with the brace round an iron belaying-pin. Each time we tacked ship the operation took an hour, as all the ropes had to be coiled down properly on the pins and the braces left ready. I was in despair at the complexity of the running rigging. Aloft it was simpler; each sail had four buntlines and two clewlines for hauling the foot up to the yard, and sheets to the bottom corners. There were halliards for raising certain yards. In addition there were braces for controlling the angle of the yards and downhauls, halliards and sheets for the fore and aft sails. On deck it was very difficult. Every rope rove through blocks and was belayed to the long banks of pins on the rail below the bulwarks. Some pins had two different ropes belayed to them. For an ignorant person like myself it would be very easy to cast off a royal halliard by mistake in the darkness, releasing the yard which would come crashing down, perhaps tearing the mast out of the ship.

It began to blow harder. 'Bräck bukgårdingarna på fock övre

bram,' said the First Mate, a little man in big boots. With the aid of the Sailmaker's notes, I had passed the long hours of my night watchman's job learning the names of the sails. 'Fock övre bram' was an upper topgallant, but what in heaven's name were 'bukgårdingarna' and why did we 'bräck' them? I thought of this problem as we scurried up the ladder from the main deck, across the midships deck, and down to the fore rigging in the well-deck. Then suddenly I remembered how I had been made to overhaul the buntlines when we set the topsail. 'Bukgårdingarna' must be the buntlines, and we were going to break the spun yarn stoppings at the blocks which kept slack at the bunt.

We hung grimly on these buntlines, vainly trying to break each in turn. Eventually Jansson went aloft and found each buntline neatly stopped at the block with unbreakable twine which some over-zealous 'Jungmän' had used instead of the thin stuff.

'Oh, bräck dem,' said the Mate. 'Bräck dose tings,' just at the moment when Jansson, having discovered the trouble, cut the stopping. Five of us were hanging on the buntline when the slack came roaring down on us and we collapsed on deck in a heap with the Mate on the top.

'Orlright,' said the First Mate when we had got up. 'Tag i gigtåget.'

'Gigtåget' proved to be clewlines and we hauled away at 'gigtåget' and 'bukgårdingarna' until the bunt and clews were close up to the yard.

'Orlright, två block,' said the Mate. 'Mikelsonn, Newby, Taanila, upp och göra fast.'

It was very dark and wet aloft and when we reached the yard I could just see the weather-clew of the sail flailing about in a very alarming fashion.

'A Sarrtan's bloody job for tree,' grunted Mikelsonn, a good-natured Danish apprentice who had been a cadet in the schoolship *Danmark*, where things like this were tackled by numbers as a drill.

'Längre ut på nock,' he shouted, shoving Taanila and me out towards the weather yardarm. 'Ut, ut,' he urged.

We went out on the yard. It was dark and Taanila, a tiny sixteen-year-old Finn who, like me, understood no Swedish, was where he should not have been, at the weather yardarm. Soon he began to be sick over Mikelsonn and myself.

'Sarrtan, Sarrtan,' said Mikelsonn, embracing big armfuls of canvas. ('*Satan*' was the most popular Swedish expletive, equivalent to 'blast' or 'hell' in English.)

'*Perkele, Perkele,*' sobbed Taanila in the Finnish equivalent. I contented myself by repeating a habit-forming monosyllable that I had picked up at school. We had made little progress; we were unused to the footrope which was bucking wildly underfoot, and it was difficult for our three nationalities to work in concert owing to the barriers of language. As a maximum deterrent Taanila seemed to have switched over to a freshly filled stomach. To make matters worse he lost his temper; perhaps he was frightened. I know that I was. I saw Mikelsonn edging towards the mast and soon I heard him screaming for more men. What we really needed was an interpreter. The Mate's reply came crackling up from below and exploded about us, so terrifying that I felt it would be better to do it absolutely alone than ask for any more assistance. Eventually we succeeded in passing the gaskets round a monstrous unseaman-like package of sail which we made up on top of the yard.

At midnight eight bells were struck by the helmsman and echoed by the look-out on the big bell forward. We mustered on the foredeck and the watches were appointed.

To my dismay I found myself transferred to the First Mate's watch – the port watch with Sedelquist. Here all the younger, turbulent Finns were housed, including the sickly but demonical Taanila. I had hoped to remain with my new-found friends, Vytautas, Kroner and the other foreign apprentices in the starboard fo'c'sle under the command of the Second Mate, to whom I had become quite attached. With the exception of Sedelquist, whose interests were of an almost academic narrowness, hardly anyone in the port fo'c'sle spoke English. In addition I had to face the problem of moving the Vuitton, now bulging with provisions contributed by my Mother and Lucy.

'Orlright,' said the Second Mate. 'Lösa av ror och utkik, in frivakt.' The 'rorsman' was relieved from the wheel and the 'utkik' (pronounced 'oochig'), having been relieved at his lookout position on the fo'c'sle head, reported 'Klara lanternor' (lights burning brightly), to the officer of the watch. The port watch, the 'babordsvakt' was now 'frivakt' and went below. Although ostensibly 'fri' until 4 a.m., we had been ordered to 'stand by' which meant sleeping in full regalia of oilskins and seaboots either on the floor or in a bunk. I elected to sleep in a bunk. The only accessible one was a cross-ship bunk with no mattress. I crept miserably into it and fell asleep immediately on bare boards.

After what seemed only several seconds I was woken by insistent cries of 'Resa upp, resa upp,' to see the stern of the last member of the watch disappearing through the doorway. Perspiring freely, yet cold and with a splitting headache, I waited miserably while the Mates counted us.

'Orlright,' came a deep disembodied voice from above, like Jehovah speaking to the children of Israel. 'Lösa av ror och utkik, in frivakt.' At this there was a pell-mell rush by the starboard watch to get below and into their bunks.

In the port watch we had the privilege of two Mates, the First Mate and the Third Mate, or 'Tria', as he was called. 'Tria' was tall and thin, with smiling Mongolian eyes and a terrifyingly deep voice. It was he who had sounded like Jehovah at the change of watch. His shoulders were so square that they almost turned up at the ends. At five o'clock, with the night nearly gone, he instructed me in my duties as look-out on the fo'c'sle head.

'Two bells, vessel to port; three bells, vessel ahead; one bell, vessel to starboard,' intoned Tria, very like a great bell himself. He then vanished into the darkness along the flying bridge. Soon I began to feel the effects of fatigue and nausea. *Moshulu* was beating into a choppy sea, making about seven knots and pitching a little; on the fo'c'sle head this see-saw motion was accentuated. I yawned twice and thought of Taanila up on the yard like an allegorical horn of plenty, prodigal with his gifts.

'This is bad,' I said aloud. 'It won't be long now.'

I saw the lights of a steamer to starboard; with laborious care I struck the bell twice, the signal for a vessel to port. I was so horror-struck at the possible consequences of this act of negligence that I forgot my feeling of queasiness and began to scan the horizon to port for some alibi. By good fortune there was a pinpoint of light almost on the port beam.

'Tria' came padding up. 'Yes,' he boomed when I pointed it out. 'Orlright. But you should have sounded one bell for the other ship to starboard – she's coming on fast.'

Both the Mates were jumpy; they had reason to be. In 1938 a big barque carrying nothing but port and starboard lights could easily be missed in the Irish Sea by steamer look-outs expecting nothing but other steamers with mast-head lights in addition to red and green sidelights.

At six o'clock the helmsman rang four bells and I rang five incorrectly in reply and went aft to report 'Klara lanternor'. This was my first brush with the Captain, who asked me if English boys ever learned to count.

Dawn was breaking and it was going to be a beautiful morning. The sea was a cold mauve colour, rising and tumbling lazily, the air was like ice. Belfast seemed in another world, not just over the horizon. I looked at the expanse of sea and thought how appropriate and beautiful were the words: 'They that go down to the sea in ships and occupy their business in great waters'.

By 6.30 we were abeam of the Isle of Man; the high peaks of the Island were covered in thick cloud; at seven we were passing the Calf of Man at the southern end with its two disused light-houses on the high cliffs and the Chicken Rock light silhouetted against the eastern sky. At sea-level visibility was very great and although it was day the lighthouse still flashed, more brightly than the early sun.

Our watch took in the inner jib; the halliard was cast off and we manned the downhaul on the fo'c'sle head where we found Taanila, who had succeeded me at look-out, sprawled against the capstan, his face exactly matching his bright yellow oil-skins.

Sedelquist offered to fetch various unsuitable dishes from the galley, which, he alleged, were being prepared for Taanila's benefit, and quite soon Taanila began to be ill again.

The sun was now shining brightly, and high in the rigging where I was sent to overhaul buntlines it seemed like the springtime of the world. I was even prepared to make the best of the port fo'c'sle. At Wurzel's I would have asked for a transfer, but here the thought of the violent reaction such a request would provoke encouraged me to be philosophical about remaining where I was. I felt quite cheerful when I descended at eight o'clock for breakfast.

'We're very lucky to have fried herring,' I remarked brightly to Sedelquist.

'Ees not feesh,' replied Sedelquist, 'ees bacon, smelly like English girl.'

When I looked again I saw that it was bacon. Ghastly and apparently putrefying, it gave off a very un-English smell. I tried it but it was so salt that my gums ached. I threw it overboard and a seagull picked it up but dropped it hastily. Before I went back to fill up on bread and margarine, I watched it sink: it was the last time I ever threw any food overboard.

It was our watch below and we slept until 12.30 and then we had dinner – a stew of fresh meat from a sack which was dripping blood on to the main deck and which was diminishing in size far too quickly for my liking. When we came on deck for the afternoon watch the Welsh coast was in view. Anglesey was on our beam, an almost imperceptible island, with the Snowdon massif rising above the clouds behind it. We were sailing as close to the wind as possible; soon the Lleyn peninsula was on our port bow, itself a breeding-ground of square-rig sailors; then Bardsey Island rising out of the sea like a great green grass-covered whale. On its western side were several cottages and farms with the lighthouse, a white tower with two red bands on it, standing at the southern end.

We would have to tack ship. Even if we weathered Bardsey we would be setting in to Cardigan Bay with St Patrick's Causeway (the Sarn Badrig Shoal) and the Cynfelin Patches to restrict our movement. The wind was blowing up the Irish Sea. If it freshened, to be embayed near these shoals with no room to go about might mean disaster.

The Captain came on deck in a leather coat and cloth cap. I heard him give the order 'Stagvända; tack ship.' The First Mate blew his 'vissel' three times, crying: 'Alle man på däck,' and the starboard watch, which had gone below, emerged unwillingly on deck, having just finished dinner.

Moshulu was beating up to Bardsey close-hauled on the starboard tack, that is to say, all her yards were braced round on the port backstays with the starboard yardarms pointing in the direction from which the wind was blowing. Whilst the lower course yards were braced back as hard as possible, each successive yard above was braced back a little less so that by watching the weather (windward) side of the royal, the helmsman would be warned when the sail began to shiver that he was bringing the ship too much into the wind, in which case she might be taken aback; a dangerous thing to happen as the wind would then be blowing on the front of the sails, putting too much strain on the relatively few fore-and-aft stays, possibly dismasting her if the wind was strong enough.

Now everyone was on deck, even the Cook, the Steward and the Pantry boy, all three dressed in white, pale and unused to the open air. The Carpenter was at the jib sheets and the Captain was standing by the binnacle with the experienced Sedelquist at the helm. The port watch were on the main deck standing by the Jarvis brace winches, with the First Mate at the lee braces which were coiled down on the deck for free running, in what used to be called 'Flemish Fakes'. Similarly the starboard watch were at the mizzen braces. The big main and mizzen course sails were already clewed up loosely to save labour when we went about, but they were not furled.

'Bidevind och fulla segel,' the Captain ordered Sedelquist. This meant that he wanted *Moshulu* kept with full sails and by the wind to keep sufficient way on her to ensure that she would go about smartly. 'Klart att vända!' (Ready about!)

'Ned med rodret!' ordered the Captain, and Sedelquist put the helm down, turning the six-foot wheel hard to starboard. The spanker sail, the big fore-and-after on the jigger mast, had been trimmed to starboard, which helped to swing the stern away from the wind and the bows into it. The Cook eased the foresheet.

Now *Moshulu* began to slam up into the wind with a great clashing of canvas and beating of blocks. On the fo'c'sle head the Carpenter was putting the jib sheets over the forestays.

'Akterhal!' (Mainsail haul) cried the Captain above the tumult. The Mates cast off the main and mizzen lee braces from their pins, the wind struck the weather leeches of the sail, forcing the yards round so that the men at the two brace winches had simply to wind furiously in order to take up the slack as it came in from port to starboard, and the rest took in the slack of the topgallants and royal braces which were not operated by the winches.

Moshulu's head was now past the eye of the wind and the headsails, which had previously been sheeted to port, were now sheeted to starboard. With the wind 4 points (45°) on the port bow, the success of the operation was assured and both watches went forward to manhandle the six foreyards round, first by winding at the Jarvis winch and then with the rope braces. When this was done the foretack of the foresail was boarded on the port side and the foresheet sheeted home aft. *Moshulu* was now on the port tack.

There were still the sheets of the topmast staysails to be shifted over the stays and sheeted home, the main and mizzen courses to be reset, and the yards trimmed to the Mate's satisfaction with the brace whips.

'Orlright, in frivakt,' said the Mate and the starboard watch went below, having lost nearly an hour of their free watch. We of the port watch were left to clear up the decks, coil down the falls and running gear, and send aloft a 'Jungmän' or apprentice to overhaul the buntlines, a heavy job with ninety to a hundred feet of wire below the blocks. *Moshulu* was on the port tack, starboard yardarms braced towards the starboard backstays, port yardarms pointing up to the wind. Each course sail had two wire ropes shackled to the earrings at the bottom corners, called the tack and the sheet. With the ship closehauled to the wind the weather edge of the sail was hauled down through a snatchblock taken to a capstan, leaving the sheet loose. On the lee side the sheet was led to the capstan and the tack hung loose. When the ship went about the positions were reversed. With the wind coming from any point abaft the beam neither tack was used, the yards being almost at right angles to the vessel and both sheets in use.

For days we staggered about the Irish Sea, now standing in to the Coast of Wicklow, now fetching up on the other tack by the South Stack light or by Bardsey. I had never been so tired in my whole life, far too exhausted to appreciate the beautiful pyramids of sail towering above me. In the watch below I would fall into a dreamless sleep so profound that for the first hour of our next watch on deck I would be like a somnambulist but without the happy facility of avoiding obstacles, so that I was always tripping over ring bolts set in the deck, bitts and of course the steering cables. Everyone, in the first days before they found their sealegs, was constantly falling down. Even the Sailmaker, 'Sails' as I now ventured to call him, emerging on deck at a 'tre vissel' call to all hands to 'Stagvända', had stepped on a patch of oil exuded by one of 'Doonkey's' cargo winches and described a beautiful parabola in the air before landing on his blue-patched behind with a crash that shook the deck.

'Aw, that goddam' Donkeyman,' Sails had roared, stumping off to get a spadeful of ashes from the galley to sprinkle on the offending place.

Life in the port fo'c'sle was far from lively, the language difficulty being almost insurmountable. For this state of affairs the others were as little to blame as I was, perhaps less, as some of them knew a few English expressions whilst I was still floundering around trying to remember that the 'övre märs gigtåg' was the upper topsail clewline. This seemed at the time more important than just talking, as I was likely to get into trouble with both Captain and Mates by being ignorant of such things. Conversations in these early days were punctuated by long hissing silences.

I was sitting in the fo'c'sle after dinner on the other side of the table to a 23-year-old ordinary seaman from Åland called Alvar, who was eating bread. Everyone else was asleep. In order to promote conversation I pushed towards him a pot of home-made jam, like a chess player making an opening gambit. When he had helped himself I began to attack:

'Alvar, have you been in a barque before?'

'Tree o'clock,' answered Alvar, his mouth full.

'Alvar,' I said, 'have you sailed in *Moshulu* before?'

'Coffee time har past tree,' replied Alvar, with the triumphant air of one who has checkmated his opponent.

'Slipping is bettair,' came an angry voice from one of the bunks.

'Shot up,' retorted Alvar. 'Coffee time har past tree, then slipping.'

When not wearing myself down in this garrulous fashion, I was being tormented by one of the older members of the fo'c'sle who had contracted a more or less loathsome affliction, and finding that I disliked it, kept his spirits up by waving a syringe and a large bottle of mixture in my face. At mealtimes, he would offer me tablets from a dark green bottle marked 'Poison'. Being young and inexperienced I began to be worried about touching the same ropes as he did. The jokes we had sniggered over behind the filing cabinets at Wurzel's seemed less funny now. I had from the first taken to standing on the lavatory seat, a precarious habit in a short pitching sea. I now redoubled my precautions, but somehow Sedelquist got wind of this. As in prisons, lunatic asylums and schools, the doors did not lock and I was caught one morning when he flung the door open crying: 'English boggert, take dose boots off.' He was the senior member of our fo'c'sle and felt that what I was doing was an affront to his authority. With or without boots I managed to maintain this custom to the end by timing my visits to take place by night or when he was at the wheel.

The watch-keeping system in *Moshulu* was a good one. It was calculated so that a man was not on watch at the same time on any two consecutive days. The ship's work painting, chipping, washing-down and so on, began at 6 a.m. and ended at 6 p.m. Sail handling, bracing, steering the ship was continuous. At any time of the day the working watch might be called upon to stop whatever work it was doing and set or shorten sail or brace up the yards on a change of wind. In cases of urgency, or for tacking ship, the watch below was also called by the Mate's use of what we knew as 'tre vissel'.

If the port watch had the watch from midnight to 4 a.m., the starboard fo'c'sle had the next one from 4 a.m. to 8 a.m. At 6 a.m the starboard watch turned to for the day's work and the daymen – the Carpenter, Donkeymen, Sailmaker and his assistant – also started. At 5.30 there was coffee for the watch that had been on duty from 4 a.m. and at 7.30 a.m. the port watch had breakfast. At 8 a.m. the watches were changed, the port watch coming on deck for five hours, the starboard watch going below for breakfast, to sleep, wash clothes, or do whatever they wanted till 1 p.m. Their dinner was at 12.30.

At 1 p.m. the starboard watch took over and worked for six hours till 7 p.m. At 3.30 both watches had coffee time, fifteen minutes for the working watch, a time which was eagerly awaited. At 6 p.m. the everyday work ceased and the daymen went below. At 6.30 the port watch was roused and ate supper before relieving the starboard watch at 7 p.m The port watch remained on watch till midnight when the whole cycle began again, but this time in reverse order with the starboard watch on deck from midnight to 4 a.m. instead of the port watch.

Thus in two days a member of the port watch spent a total of twenty-four hours out of the forty-eight on watch; twelve hours of this was devoted to day work, five hours on the first day and seven hours on the second. In rough weather this table could not always be adhered to. If it was necessary to take in a lot of sail or the mainsail or the mizzen course, the watch due to go below would be kept on deck until the job was done, sometimes for hours, but on the whole the system was both sensible and fair.

There were the jobs concerned with navigation of the vessel:

Wheel, Look-out and Police. Each was for a period of an hour. The job of look-out or 'utkik' I had already performed. The policeman or 'påpass'* (pronounced porpuss) was the fag of the officer of the watch. One blast of the Mate's whistle would bring him on deck, two whistles and he had to summon the watch. He was also required to wake up the next man relieving the helmsman; he was useful because he could be blamed for things.

By Saturday the Captain gave up trying to beat down the Irish Sea and headed back for the North Channel, hoping to reach the Atlantic that way. By supper time, except for a few cabbage leaves in which the meat balls were wrapped, there was no more fresh food. Our numbers had been augmented by two robins and a thrush which had arrived exhausted on Wednesday but were now becoming cheeky and stealing food from the chickens which were thoroughly demoralized.

That night I stood my first wheel from ten o'clock until eleven. In fact only the first three minutes were solo. When I came to the wheel the Captain was muttering abstruse calculations to himself while the First Mate gazed anxiously at the lights of the large number of vessels which seemed to hem us in. It was a wet hazy night and the air was heavy with unspoken anxiety. Jammed somewhere near the mouth of the Firth of Clyde was not a happy situation for a big sailing ship.

'Nordost till ost,' ordered the Captain, too busy to notice his greenest apprentice at the wheel.

'Nordost till ost,' I quavered, heaving the wheel in the direction which I hoped would bring *Moshulu* up to the course. Weighed down by responsibility I watched the illuminated card in the binnacle. The ship's head began to swing and NE. by E. appeared for a moment, then the card began to spin, and like a demented gambler looking through the window of a fruit-machine, I watched the process of *Moshulu* swinging off course,

* From Swedish 'passa på' – stand by.

91

through NE. to NNE., until from aloft came a terrifying crashing of canvas, blocks and chain-sheets as *Moshulu* came up into the wind.

I was paralysed with fear of what I had done. The Captain was swearing, good Anglo-Saxon stuff, heaving at the wheel, and giving the Mate a rocket for letting me come to it alone on a dark night. The Mate blew his whistle, the 'påpass' appeared, and soon Sedelquist, roused from sleep and not pleased, arrived to take over. It seemed that Sedelquist was fated to witness all my humiliations. I spent the next fifty-seven minutes on the lee side of the wheel and from him I learned not to turn it violently and also to check the ship's tendency to come up into the wind by meeting her by turning the wheel in the opposite direction to that in which she was swinging.

Very early on Sunday morning the rain had ceased, but it was extremely cold. Taanila, now a nervous and physical wreck from six days of seasickness, was sent aloft with me to furl the main royal. After half an hour we managed to heave the great lump of sail up to the yard, but just as I was about to pass the gaskets, Taanila began to be sick again and let the sail go. The sounds which rose from the midships deck showed that the officers and helmsman were not unaware of what was going on above them.

We were joined by the owner of the syringe and Taanila was sent down. By the time we had finished, the dark night clouds were rolling away, the sky was deep blue and in it the morning star shone brilliantly.

'Veree beautiful,' said my companion. 'This morning I am bettair.'

'I'm glad to hear it,' I replied, and really meant it.

Soon a big orange sun came up from behind the low ramparts of cloud and revealed a pleasant peaceful scene. The barque was landlocked on three sides, ghosting along with her topgallants set, her sails aflame in the sunlight. To the north were the islands of Jura and Islay. On Jura, the steep cliffs of Rudha Dubh flashed like burnished steel, and westwards was the Mull of Oa, its slopes covered with bright green grass and patches of purple heather. It looked the sort of place to spend a long summer afternoon sleeping and idling. Southwards was Rathlin Island with its lighthouse on a bench of rock above the sea, and behind it the cliffs of Fair head, on the Irish mainland. To the south-east was the lonely extremity of the Mull of Kintyre, where in the eighteenth century the last family of British cannibals had feasted on unwary travellers.

Sunday was a free day in the ship and after breakfast the gramophone was removed from the starboard fo'c'sle by a raiding party, but it expired as it reached our fo'c'sle and refused to play either of our two records. (Vytautas had bought 'The Post Horn Gallop' in Belfast.)

After two hours in which everyone had contributed advice, help or both, the apparatus still failed to function and lay about in pieces on the table. Once more it was reassembled, but the result was still disappointing, only one note coming from its mouth every thirty seconds. Eventually Jansson was woken. He said that the governor was not functioning properly. Very soon the gramophone was working and throughout the afternoon the dreadful sounds of the 'Post Horn Gallop' floated across the still waters of the North Channel on which, apart from the south-easterly set of the stream, we were utterly becalmed. Kroner and I lay on the hatch covers and let the October sun warm us. Twice I was called away with the port watch, once to clew up the course sails to save them slatting and banging, and later to brace the yards.

Towards evening a breeze sprang up, the still waters began to heave, and the ship began to lift to the long fetch of the Atlantic swell. At once the courses were sheeted home and in the gathering dusk the ship began to move out of the North Channel, leaving Rathlin Island behind. That night the wind freshened from the south-west. By midnight *Moshulu* was running thirteen knots and flinging a sixty-foot bow wave on either side of her. On deck it was a hard climb to windward and a wild slippery descent to the lee scuppers. At supper-time we all banged our plates and sang with sheer joy, and at the change of watch we took the upper topgallants off her as she was running heavily.

All through the night the south-west wind hurled us out into the Atlantic. From aloft came the great roaring sound that I heard for the first time, and will perhaps never hear again, of strong winds in the rigging of a good ship.

CHAPTER EIGHT

The Watch Below

THE Atlantic swallowed the *Moshulu* and her crew. From now on we received no authentic news from the outside world. The Second Mate was said to possess a wireless receiver. Occasionally I thought I heard disconnected bursts of dance music filtering from the Officer's quarters from which we were walled off by steel bulkheads and the protocol of the sea, but I decided it must be a trick of the ear like listening to a cockle-shell and hearing waves beating on the shore. Much later in the voyage the Mate produced the wireless, but I don't think that he ever had much time to tinker with it. He was engaged in making a model of *Moshulu* nearly four feet long, with running rigging and brace winches that worked. His last model had been sold for sixty pounds in Belfast and for this one he had brought aboard a surprisingly large bundle of wood. In the free watch he was already prowling around looking aloft with a yellow eye, calculating the heights of the masts and the correct proportions for the yards. For the time he was interested in nothing else.

News came to us in the form of rumour, and in retrospect showed itself to have been so fantastic that the wireless could have only worked by fits and starts, ejecting now and then the name of a place or a personage round which some disagreeable legend could be built up. I decided from the beginning that if there was a wireless then it was only picking up German stations which in 1938 were making the ether hideous on all wavelengths. We were not anxious for news. As time passed, the ship possessed us completely. Our lives were given over to it. A hundred times a day each one of us looked aloft at the towering pyramids of canvas, the beautiful deep curves of the leeches of the sails and the straining sheets of the great courses, listened to the deep hum of the wind up the height of the rigging, the thud and judder of the steering-gear as the ship surged along, heard the helmsman striking the bells, signalling a change of watch or a mealtime, establishing a routine so strong that the outside world seemed unreal.

Crossing the midships deck to leeward of the Captain on our way aft to brace the yards, touching our forelocks to him as we went, we were no longer in the twentieth century at all. Being told to go aloft and make up that gasket on the mizzen royal and look alive, we were a hundred years out of our time. Lying in our bunks fully clad, hearing the roaring of the wind and the tramp of the officer of the watch overhead, knowing by the way the ship was dragging that in three minutes or less there would be a call for hands to take in sail, we grew so close to her that for us she became everything. Neither were we particularly anxious to be at our destination. We knew that it was remote and its climate inhospitable; we also knew that we should have no money to spend when we got there. It was difficult to think about the future with any enthusiasm. We took refuge in the present.

By noon on Monday, the seventh day of the voyage, we were about 100 miles west-north-west of Tory Island, heading south by west roughly parallel to the Irish Coast. The exaltation of the previous night, when the ship stormed out of the North Channel, had passed and we were over the plate-banging stage. The wind had fallen during the morning and veered to the North, leaving a confused and heavy swell in which *Moshulu* pitched unhappily; at the same time she developed a pronounced list to port, which showed that the ballast needed trimming. Under a cold grey sky we braced the yards to the change of wind and reset the royals.

Overhauling buntlines in the main rigging I looked down into a sea as pale and cold as the sky above. Suddenly, like rockets, a great school of dolphin shot out of a slanting hillside of water, hung for an instant suspended over the valley between, and disappeared, beautifully aligned, into the next slope in bursting clouds of spray. Then they appeared again, breaking formation, and for half an hour played about the ship scratching themselves on the bows, nuzzling one another, gasping and sighing happily until by their happiness the day was transformed and we forgot how tired we were.

They stayed with us until the Donkeyman appeared on deck armed with a harpoon set in a wooden shaft with ten or twelve fathoms of rope attached to it. Then they went roistering off at a great rate towards the west and we saw them no more.

The following morning I proudly stood my first unaided trick at the wheel, heavily wrapped up, for it was very cold, whilst the First Mate, dressed in nothing but a thin cotton shirt and khaki overall trousers, circled the binnacle apprehensively, his teeth chattering, a great dewdrop on the end of his nose.

From time to time he inclined his body in the direction in which we should have been heading, and in a wheedling agonized voice, as if afraid to upset this temperamental helmsman whom he would far sooner have strangled, cried: 'Joost a liddle . . . joost a liddle . . . joost a liddle more.' The Captain, emerging from the charthouse in a leather coat, an early motoring-cap with flaps and down-at-heel bedroom-slippers, had been more peremptory. For some time he had looked at the untidy sea with red-rimmed eyes, then at the trim of his vessel. I could see that he was unsure about what was upsetting him. Then he noticed me goggling at the compass between the spokes of the wheel and, glad to find the reason for his irritation, said in the gruffest possible manner:

'Keep the course, man, keep the course.'

'Keep the course,' I replied, bearing in mind what the Second Mate had told me about repeating orders.

The Captain glared at me and I tried to hide behind the wheel. Then he moved away to windward over the heaving deck and looked sulkily at the sea.

'You shouldn't say that,' said the First Mate. 'It's not safe. Now joost a liddle more.'

At the end of a long hour I was relieved by Sedelquist, who echoed the course I gave him in a superior kind of way, at the same time putting his weight to the spokes and making a good deal of noise with the footbrake in a manner that suggested that I had been steering in an entirely wrong direction.

The Captain was gazing angrily seaward, so I repeated the course to the First Mate. As I left him to go down to the fo'c'sle I met Taanila and Jansson who were manhandling a large and rotten sack of potatoes up the ladder. Taanila was at the top hauling and Jansson was half-way up pushing. There was a terrible swell running and the ship was lurching all over the place. Taanila's face was pale green and his cheeks were bulging as if he was sucking a large sweet. When the Captain saw Taanila's face he began to shout urgently. At once Taanila let the sack go and made for the rail. There was a muffled roar from Jansson as a hundredweight and a half of potatoes fell on him, then the sack burst and he was on his back on the well-deck buried beneath a great heap.

Taanila had obeyed the Captain's command. Very correctly he was hanging over the lee rail. Unfortunately a freakish draught caught everything and whisked it upwards under the curve of the mainsail in a mass, where it flattened out and described an arc towards the weather rail. Fascinated, Master and Mate watched its evolutions until like a boomerang it began to come back at them. At this moment they took shelter, the Captain behind the charthouse, the Mate behind the main mast, and I was delighted to see them peering out from their places of refuge in the bellicose but prudent manner adopted by Mr Winston Churchill and the Commissioner of Police in the famous photograph at the Siege of Sidney Street. They were scarcely touched. It was Sedelquist, steadfastly keeping the vessel on her course, who received the whole lot on his weather ear.

There was a great deal of confusion. I was recalled to the wheel to rattle the spokes unctuously and return the vessel to its true course, from which it had not unnaturally departed. In the fo'c'sle Sedelquist hit Taanila, which was not very brave of him, and then Taanila tried to stick a knife in Sedelquist but only succeeded in biting him, having been disarmed by Sandell. I had an extra ten minutes at the wheel because Taanila had to clean up the deck.

After dinner, while the starboard watch were shovelling away at the ballast in the hold, we began a complicated jigsaw puzzle. It showed Napoleon glowering out to sea from the quarter-deck of the *Bellerophon*, with his staff twittering anxiously in the background. All except Taanila, who was asleep in his bunk exhausted by sickness and attempted murder, and Sedelquist, who sat aloof from us all, looking like a depraved Apollo.

Sedelquist could have been interesting to talk to. He had been in the *Herzogin* when she piled up on the Devon coast in 1936, but his consuming passion was women, young and old, and with none to practise on he soon became a bore to listen to. On that ignominious night in the Irish Sea when he had supplanted me at the helm, he had whispered the most hair-raising anecdotes in my ear. There was one I liked.

'Oh, you noh Donegall Square?'

'Yes.'

'Oh, you noh schoolgirl, beeg schoolgirl?' Here he rambled off into a description of the hideous uniform worn by schoolgirls of the better sort and at the same time managed to give the impression that this particular schoolgirl had altogether outgrown this kind of dress.

'I was sitting on the tram behind heem,' he continued, 'and then he got off. I followed heem, I spoke with heem.'

'And then what happened?' I asked.

'He scrimmed,' he replied simply.

Sitting next to Sedelquist was Sandell, with a great spadebeard as black as night. Completely different in appearance from the Nordic Sedelquist, he was the son of an Italian father and a Finnish mother. At sixteen, he said, he had been to the Arctic with the Martini Nordlund Expedition. After that he had been in the Baltic Schooners, and had come to *Moshulu* from the Icelandic Herring Fishery where the pay had been good. He was the only married man in the port fo'c'sle. At the moment he was pointing at the grumpy-looking Napoleon on the lid of the jigsaw box and roaring with laughter.

'Fock me,' he bellowed, slapping his leg with a hand covered with black hairs, 'jus' like Sedelquist, bloddy angry.'

Sedelquist, for once, said nothing; like him, Sandell was an able seaman, but he was three years older and the Arctic and the Herring Fishery had made a man of Sandell who could have knocked seven bells out of Sedelquist if it had ever occurred to him to do so.

'Yes, jus' like Sedelquist,' Sandell repeated happily, for he had not approved of Sedelquist hitting Taanila who was only a nasty child and who should have been left to a jungmän or apprentice to discipline. Then absentmindedly, he felt in the pockets of his dungaree trousers and turned to me.

'Here, Kossuri,' he said. (Kossuri had become my nickname. In Finnish it was supposed to signify landed proprietor and sprang from my ownership of the Vuitton trunk.) 'Here, Kossuri, have an orange – good for the vinkle.'

On the other side of the table was Alvar, with whom I had had an animated conversation about 'coffee time har past tree'. He had been a sailor for a year or so. Before that he had been a baker's assistant. Perhaps some infringement of Finnish good housekeeping rules had decided him to give up baking and take to the sea, for in affairs of toilet Alvar was not a nice man. In order to see at all in the lower cross-ships bunk which I inhabited, I had to make use of a small German paraffin lantern. Alvar, who had the upper bunk, used to complain with reason that he was being slowly asphyxiated. As he used to break wind with the monotonous regularity of a foghorn, I felt reluctant to turn down my lamp and for many weeks, until I graduated to another bunk, we made one another as uncomfortable as possible.

Next to Alvar was Johnny, who was always known as 'Yonny Valker'. Yonny Valker was golden-haired and completely chinless, with two large tusk-like teeth protruding over his upper lip so that he looked exactly like a dugon, that large herbivorous mammal of the Indian Seas. He was the oldest jungmän in the watch and was completely indifferent both to hardship and comfort. If he had been a soldier, Yonny would have slept happily in the puddle in which he had been halted. Both Yonny and Alvar had the most depressing table-manners – spitting great gobbets of meat on to the table and crouching so low over their platters that by the end of the meal they were practically hidden from view behind mounds of potato skins.

At this moment, Yonny was not eating but was engaged in picking his nose, gazing into the distance, and possibly pondering the problems with which he was to plague us in the future.

On Yonny's left sat Bäckmann, a seventeen-year-old jungmän, who looked pale and rather homesick. Next to Bäckmann sat Hermansonn, the third jungmän. Hermansonn was seventeen. He already had a tendency to corpulence but with his bull neck, bull-like voice and great muscular arms he was not the sort of person who could be ignored. Hermansonn was the complete hearty. Going up ladders in front of him you were certain to receive a nip in the bottom. Where Hermansonn was, pails of water fell off the tops of doors. Worse than this, he regarded anyone who could not speak his language as being moronic and a figure of fun. In this way he was rather like an Englishman himself and he would have been far better off as far as I was concerned laying down the law in some suburban golf club. When I talked to Vytautas about this he said: 'Not better off in golf club – better off in Stone Age.'

There simply wasn't room in the fo'c'sle for the two of us. I knew that Hermansonn constituted a physical obstacle to my peace of mind that would have to be overcome sooner or later. Unfortunately he was very strong and as I did not yet feel equal to him, I had to suffer him.

We finished our jigsaw, but Napoleon's feet and a part of the deck were missing, which gave him an air of pantomime like the demon king coming up through a hole in a stage. At coffee time I went into the starboard fo'c'sle, where most of them were engaged on a jigsaw before returning to the hold. It was less ambitious than our own, and I recognized it immediately as the best-loved jigsaw of my youth, a Great Western Railway engine, the *Caerphilly Castle*, which I could still assemble blindfold. There were fifteen pieces to go and at that stage I could tell that the vital piece with the chimney on it was missing. The person who was deriving most pleasure from the jigsaw was Karma, an aboriginal Finn from regions so remote that hardly anyone on board could communicate with him at all. Taanila had said that he was 'velly strong' and had gone through the violent motions of wrestling. None of us knew much more about him. This was perhaps his first jigsaw and he was talking happily to himself as he pressed piece after piece into position with his great thumbs.

At first he could not believe that the chimney was missing; he looked under the table, prodded his companions to make sure that they were not secreting it, and then with a roar of rage swept up the copy of *The Tatler* on which the puzzle was laid and, before anyone could stop him, was out on deck and had hurled the whole lot into the sea. Then he slammed into his bunk, pulled the blankets over his head, and lay doggo like a homicidal maniac.

'I think Finns are bastards,' said Kroner. 'Why don't they put them all together in one fo'c'sle or in one ship. That was the last picture paper, too.'

'You do not understand,' said Vytautas Bagdanavicius. 'He is not angry with us, but with puzzle. He is veree primitive man.'

Nevertheless Kroner had some reason to be angry also. The bundles of magazines put on board by the Missions to Seamen at Belfast had nearly all gone. First all the copies of *The Field* disappeared. I was not sorry, as the questions provoked by its contents were highly technical and I was not competent to answer them. Hilbert in the starboard watch had been the most persistent.

'What is polymelus of chick?' he would ask, pointing at a gloomy photograph of a young pheasant with something wrong with it. Worse still, he would pore over the autopsies of grouse: 'Look what zey found in zis von's stomoch,' he would say and began to read out a list that made me disinclined for food.

The Tatler was more fun for everybody. It even put Sedelquist in a good humour by reinforcing his prejudices against the English. I found it very difficult to disagree with his verdict, 'English rosbif, proper strongbody,' when shown a photograph of Cynthia, only daughter of some disused Major-General, posed naïvely in pink net with her vaccination marks showing up nicely on an upper arm as hefty as Hermansonn's.

The consumption of glossy illustrateds was so rapid that soon we were left with a few copies of *The Sunday at Home*, more sombre works like *The Report of the Harbor Commissioners (Biennial) Port of San Francisco 1935–1936*, and some superbly unreadable theological books. One of these dealt with the impossibility of celibacy in the Roman priesthood. The wealth of lascivious detail made it seem certain that the writer had only recently been unfrocked himself. It was 900 pages long and printed in head-splitting lower case which defeated me.

CHAPTER NINE
'Ängelskit' and 'Kabelgarn'

THE following morning it was our turn to work in the hold, trimming and securing the ballast to prevent it shifting and throwing the ship on its beam ends, an accident which happened to *Herzogin Cecilie* off the Hebrides in 1928, laying her over at an angle of 70° on her beam ends with her hatch coamings under water.

On the open deck it was cold and when we started shovelling sand and manhandling paving-stones at seven o'clock each of us was wearing at least two sweaters. By one o'clock when the port watch took over, we were perspiring in shirts and trousers. One or two with splendid torsos like Sedelquist and Hermansonn were stripped to the waist. All were mumbling about not being 'focking farmers'.

Three days later we were still securing the ballast. Having put *Moshulu* on an even keel by spreading it evenly, we covered it with railway sleepers, lashing them down with chains and making everything taut by driving in wooden wedges with sledgehammers. Those who had not yet been sick on deck succumbed in the hold, or came very near it. I myself found that waiting for the moment when the ship was rolling away from me to totter up a steep crumbling slope of sand with a tarred railway sleeper balanced on one shoulder had a curious effect on my stomach. The hold was huge, dark and mysterious, and filled with strange sounds. As the ship rolled toward me, the pillars binding the beams above to the centre keelson rose and fell before my eyes so that I felt that I was in the nave of a cathedral during a violent earthquake, an illusion heightened by the tomb-like stones which lay about everywhere.

On deck again we became ravenous for food. In Belfast we had been hungry enough but the fish and chip shops in Corporation Street and parcels from home had taken the edge from our appetites. Now, each morning, as soon as breakfast was finished, a scout was dispatched to the galley to find out what was for dinner, five hours away. There he was nearly always given a cool reception by the 'Kock'. The 'Kock' looked like Dr Goebbels, and his face had the authentic cook's death-bed transparency which was accentuated by the clean white shirt, cap and apron which he always wore. How he endured the life I never knew, for he rose at 4.30 in the morning to prepare for his day, knowing that no one would be satisfied and that his customers would be just as hungry at 8.30 in the evening when he finally retired as they had been at breakfast.

The 'Kock' slept like a dead man in a pitch-black stifling cabin with the afterguard. It was impossible to wake him, but he could be made to rise from his bunk by repeated shakings, when he would dress with deliberation and lurch to the galley, banging against bulkheads and, if he had only known it, hurting himself dreadfully. Once there he would stand before the galley fire, preparing the coffee and the breakfast, sound asleep with an extinguished cigarette stuck between his lips. In bad weather we had to rely on his good nature to allow us to dry our wet clothes and seaboot stockings near the stove, but sometimes he would lay about him in a frenzy and throw everything in the coal bucket. Then he would be 'förbannad', or 'damned', 'Kock'.

After little more than a week his repertoire of dishes was exhausted and except for the crossing of significant lines of latitude and longitude and days of rejoicing, when he always produced something good and new, he permutated remorselessly on a few basic dishes. Indeed, he had no choice, and we sometimes wondered what would have happened to us if our 'Kock' had been a bad 'Kock'.

There were two kinds of meat; salt pork and salt beef. There were unlimited supplies of both. Salt pork, which appeared in various disguises at least once a day, was like theatrical property, produced to create an atmosphere and then whisked away uneaten. In its worst form it was fried and smothered with a metallic-flavoured bean stew. Only Yonny Valker attempted to eat this and he eventually complained of pains in the head. Sometimes the pork arrived floating in a thick heroic kind of pea soup as solid as porridge, which was eaten laced with the same sulphurous-looking pickle which had been part of the night watchman's perquisites in Belfast. The pea soup was my favourite dish; the pork could be thrown away as its function was only decorative. It is said that old sailors still remember the pea soups of fifty years ago with nostalgia. I shall always remember the pea soup in *Moshulu*.

The beef was unboned and awaited our pleasure in casks of brine. Boiled, it became 'Buffelo'; hashed with potatoes and pounded ship's biscuit, it became 'Lobscouse', a famous old-fashioned sea-dish; and stewed with potatoes 'Kabelgarn', or rope-yarn, which it resembled. 'Kabelgarn' was either good or very nasty and we never discovered the reason why it was such a temperamental dish. Sometimes 'Buffelo' was given a short spell in the oven and emerged as 'Rosbif', which invited derisive comments from Sedelquist and Hermansonn on the decline of the British Empire. Potatoes appeared at every meal and were a godsend. After the first week there were no more fresh vegetables. It was not age that made the contents of the beef and pork barrels so unpalatable, but the liquids in which they were embalmed. Yonny Valker and I had been down into the after peak to fill the potato bins and had seen them. Each barrel had a red seal on the rim stating that it had been packed and tested under the supervision of the Board of Trade Marine Dept on August 22nd, 1938.

On this trip we were closely escorted by the Steward who was suspicious of us, having been round the Horn nine times. Yonny was not even allowed down the ladder and remained framed in the hatch, winking in a heavy conspiratorial way and gesticulating in the direction of some 14 lb cans of margarine and a number of curious objects with serrated edges suspended from a cord above my head. I was eager to obtain a reputation for daring but could see no purpose in stealing these objects, which resembled the clubs used by cannibals for dispatching their victims. It would not have been the slightest use if I had taken one.

'No good looking at zose,' said the Steward, reading my thoughts. 'Stockfisk. "Kock" boils zem for hours and hours,' he went on.

'What do they taste like?' I asked.

'Taste like notting – fock notting,' said the Steward.

For afters there was sometimes a pallid sweetish kind of macaroni which the boys rightly called 'Ängelskit' and a gooey kind of soup made with dried fruit which looked rather like frog spawn. With a lot of sugar it was very sustaining and perhaps more than any other food helped to keep us healthy and free from scurvy. The nickname for this was absolutely revolting. Occasionally 'Ängelskit' appeared with 'Kabelgarn', but this was never successful as the two dishes were in some way hostile to one another. Sometimes there were pancakes. Usually they were as heavy as lead. It was best to cut them into small squares and dissect each one separately to avoid damaging one's inside. There was good porridge and rice too, served with watered-down jam.

The Officers aft had some little extra luxuries, but they were not of a very exalted kind. Things like tinned salmon, tinned fish balls from Norway, and jam, but I think that during the voyage we tasted most of the cabin stores in the fo'c'sle, for the Captain was not a mean man.

There was always plenty of fresh bread as the 'Kock' baked twice a week. At coffee-time on Saturdays he produced a special loaf with an elaborate design on top sprinkled with sugar and sometimes with fruit in it. The arrival of the special loaf marked the end of the working week and always put us in a good temper.

For the watch on deck from four to eight in the morning, there was coffee at 5.30 a.m., coffee for everyone at breakfast-time and at the break at half-past three; there was enough for everyone, but it was advisable to be early, as the pot, which was a large enamel bath jug, was not often washed out; as there was tea at dinner and supper, there were alternating layers of tea-leaves and coffee-grounds below the drink of the moment. The tea bore no resemblance at all to English tea, civil or military. There were two tins of unsweetened condensed milk to last the entire watch for a week. Inevitably this was all consumed by Monday, or at the latest coffee-time on Tuesday.

In addition to the communal food each one of us had a pound of margarine each week and a pound of sugar, which he kept privately. Both the sugar and the margarine were issued in bulk but by common consent they were divided up. This came about after an awful week in which we had tried to live like civilized human beings who are only civilized because they know that they can replace any commodity they may run short of by going down to the local shop. The sugar and margarine were left on the table and after two days nothing remained.

The rations were issued on Saturday mornings. Sometimes a collective frenzy of hunger would overcome us and we would finish all our sugar and margarine by Thursday and then endure two sugarless, margarineless days. Once it was Wednesday. Two lean days before Saturday made it more difficult to start the week in an economical frame of mind. To those who have suffered real hunger we cannot appear as proper objects of sympathy. But it must be remembered that most of us were still growing and we were working like Trojans. The eating capacity of the crew was immense but they rarely had the opportunity to indulge it. One Saturday afternoon our fo'c'sle was given an 8-1b. canister of Flett's plum-and-apple jam. By supper-time on Sunday the eight of us had eaten it.

CHAPTER TEN

'Rundvask'

TEN days out from Belfast I hauled up half a bucket of rusty red water from the depths of a big tank lashed up to the stanchions on the foredeck which had held more than a hundred gallons when we sailed. It was time for a complete wash before the warm weather set in. There was a long interval before the water grew hot on the galley fire, as the Kock kept moving it farther and farther from the centre of the range. Finally, wearing a towel and a pair of wooden clogs that I had made in the free watches, I set off for the 'Vaskrum', the steel hutch next to the lavatory, for a 'Rundvask'. The 'Rum' itself was a dim, damp place illuminated by a small paint-splashed porthole and austerely furnished with a single teak bench. The floor was smooth cement, covered with a treacherous glaze of old soap. Once inside I had to choose between washing in semi-darkness with the door closed, or else with the door open in a howling draught which came up the hawsepipes in the bows. I was joined by Kroner and we decided to keep the door shut. It was not pleasant slithering about in the dark and inevitably I upset Kroner's bucket just at the moment when he was covered with lather from head to foot. There was nothing to do but share my half-bucket of water with him; this way neither of us enjoyed our first 'Rundvask'. But when on the following day the sun came out, we congratulated ourselves as everyone wanted a 'Rundvask' and there was no water.

It was now warm enough to wear only shirts and dungarees. I was very envious of Sedelquist's denims. Countless washings had faded them to a beautiful light blue. Vytautas Bagdanavicius had a set of really brilliant ones constructed by a jean-maker called Levy in San Francisco. These were the days before denim jeans became high fashion. It was nevertheless the done thing to wear faded overalls and I began to scrub mine in hot sea-water, using the ship chandler's sea-water soap. However many times I scrubbed my English trousers they remained obstinately dark blue. Finally I asked Sedelquist, who was a sort of Brummell in overalls, what to do.

'Oh you noh,' said Sedelquist, 'those trousers are focking no good, rosbif trousers. You must vash them and vash them in caustic soda, but not moch.'

I 'vashed' them in a very weak solution and they faded a little. On the day we reached Australia they were the exact shade I wanted and that day they fell to pieces.

'Too much soda,' said Sedelquist happily, 'and too much rosbif.'

The starboard watch began to shave one another's heads. With their pallid craniums shining in the sun, they looked like visitors from outer space. Soon Hilbert, an experienced Matros, was at our door with a pair of shears. Only Yonny Valker and Sedelquist refused to be treated, the one from indifference, the other from vanity. When it was my turn I begged Hilbert not to take too much off. I had seen Hermansonn and Taanila who had both been shaved to the bone. Hermansonn looked like Von Stroheim in *Greed* and Taanila exactly like a tadpole.

'Lissun,' said Hilbert, 'I am Neptune's Queen when we come to the Equator. If you have hair then I give you the Sydkryss.'

'Sydkryss? What's that?'

'You'll see,' said Hilbert darkly.

When he got to work with his shears I made my last appeal to him to leave a bit on top. All he said was: 'Newby, you are ze crazy of all ze crazies.'

Before he finished there came a great rolling of thunder from the north-east and before I could make any remark Hilbert forestalled me: 'Gons of Gibraltar,' he said with great authority. At the time we were in the latitude of Lisbon. The thunder continued for three days. By then everyone really did believe that we were listening to the guns of Gibraltar. 'Gibraltar,' said the Mate when I came to the wheel. 'Gibraltar full of rosbif,' said Sedelquist.

In the watches below I had been plagued by things running up and down my legs inside my camel-hair sleeping-bag. At first I attributed the sensation to some condition like nettle rash brought on by eating too much salt food. Then I attempted an ambush by sticking my head inside the sack and suddenly switching on an electric torch, like a hunter after big game at night, but I bagged nothing. Lastly I tried withdrawing my legs completely from the sack, but this method also produced nothing, whatever it was being brushed off in the process. I was reluctant to speak of these matters to the rest of the watch as I already had enough to live down, but when I saw Hermansonn who was clean and above suspicion searching his blankets by torchlight at two o'clock one morning and muttering to himself: 'Vägglus – bogs, bogs, bloddy bogs,' I knew that I was not alone.

On the sixteenth day, with Madeira somewhere on the starboard beam, I opened Captain Jutsum's book on Knots and Splices and out fell a big red bug, big because he had been feeding on me. I lifted the 'donkey's breakfast', the lumpy straw mattress I had bought in London; underneath it, on the bunk boards, was a small piece of canvas folded in half. I opened it and it was full of them. I lifted the bed-boards and saw that the frames were seething. Far worse, in every crack and mortice joint in the wood were thousands of eggs. Everyone else was making similar discoveries; only Yonny Valker and Alvar, those leather-skinned men, seemed unimpressed. Sedelquist borrowed a blow-lamp from 'Doonkey'. In a small first aid kit which I had with me there were some drugs in tabloid form. I wondered whether the bugs would take to morphia, but decided to keep it for myself. If things went on like this I would need it. Sedelquist went over each bunk with the blow-lamp and I followed with boiling permanganate of potash solution. We should have used caustic soda. The best thing would have been to throw all the bunks overboard and build new ones. This time we killed thousands, but the nucleus remained.

This was no new colony; perhaps it had lain dormant for eight years on the West coast of Seattle; possibly its ancestors had boarded the ship at Port Glasgow in 1904 before she was launched. In a week they were back in force. I threw my bed-boards into the sea, drilled some holes in the side of the bunk and made a crisscross netting of wire to support the mattress. Then I found that they were inside the straw, so I threw that into the sea too and slept on the wire alone. I spent long happy hours disinfesting my sleeping-bag by hand and thinking how lucky it was that I had been unable to buy a caribou skin.

The bugs grew bolder as the weather grew warmer. At the breakfast-table, they crawled up our legs. Then they started climbing up the table legs. When we built a *chevaux de frise* of tin round the bottom to prevent them, one of their number, a born leader, swarmed up the bulkhead, traversed the ceiling, and dropped on to the table. It then set off over the rim and down to the deck, wily negotiating the barrier which it had taken in the rear. Fixed defences were useless against such an enemy. We began to cast round for the materials to make hammocks.

Kroner and Anderssen, the Danish apprentice, in the starboard watch had already slung hammocks in the 'tween-decks. Their experience had not made me anxious to have one myself. Twice they had come crashing down on the steel deck after some practical joker had sawn through the ropes. The second time Kroner had bitten his tongue, and I had found him spitting blood and raging.

'Did you do it?' he screamed hopefully.

'Don't be a fool. I've got enough to do to live with Hermansonn without getting you worked up.'

'If I find the bastard I'll stick his knife where he can't cut ropes with it,' said Kroner. He never did, and hammock ropes continued to be cut. Almost all the jokes played in *Moshulu* were like this, dangerous and ridden to death.

After a long search for materials, I found an old blown-out

American topsail. With palm and needle I spent an entire Sunday making my hammock. I sewed it strongly and when I finished I found I had sewed it to the knee of my trousers. After I had put a new knee in, I sowed a bolt-rope into the side of the hammock, worked an eye splice in each end, and slung the contraption between two pillars. Swinging myself into it, I enjoyed fifteen seconds of wonderful comfort such as I had never dreamed of on my wire griddle in the fo'c'sle. Then the canvas gave way and I crashed to the deck.

It was impossible to make a hammock with such rotten material, and I eventually bought the Sailmaker's old hammock for three ounces of tobacco.

CHAPTER ELEVEN

Kroner

SOUTH of Madeira the wind backed from SSE. to ESE., blew fitfully from the African shore, and finally died away in fickle puffs. Most of our third Sunday at sea, the nineteenth day of the voyage, was spent bracing to the shifts of a largely imaginary wind, and in twenty-four hours we only logged eighty-seven miles. By two o'clock on Monday morning the wind was strong from WSW. Beating to windward in a smoking sea, the fore royal blew out and the mizzen upper topsail split at the leech. We took the upper and lower topgallants off her, sent down the damaged sails, bent new ones, and carried on with our day's work.

The more favoured of the crew, slung in bosuns' chairs, were painting shrouds, an exciting job in such a wind; others, of whom I was one, chipped rust from the decking amidships above the living accommodation. The rust had been accumulating for thirty-four years, and when Timmerman, a gentle, sad-faced giant with huge hands, ripped up the planking, it was found to be more than a quarter of an inch thick in some places. We chipped away at it with our little hammers and it came off in great flakes. The wood was as dry as tinder at the heart. It gave off a fresh powerful smell like a forest of living pines after rain, and the wind spread it through the ship making everyone homesick.

The gale died away towards evening and that night there was an eclipse of the moon which had been shining with exceptional brightness. When the earth's shadow had passed upwards over its face, it seemed that the world was dying. For an hour and a half the moon was a corroded red like an old coin and the sea, on which the ship rose and fell as if moved by some subterranean convulsion, was the same colour. It was a depressing apocalyptical scene and I was glad when it was our watch below.

At about this time I began to feel ill. At first I had a terrible headache and the sensation that all my teeth were being pressed out of my mouth. This lasted for some days. When I awoke one morning with my mouth full of ulcers, I began to wonder whether the man with the syringe, who in spite of his optimism had suffered a relapse, had succeeded in transmitting his trouble to me. After every meal I felt worse, and I knew that it would be better to give up salt food for a time. But in spite of my afflictions I was too hungry to do so. Alvar gave me some highly coloured powders: 'Finnish medicine, focking strongbody,' but for me it was no good. At last I decided to diet. Stowed in the Vuitton I had had thirty pounds of assorted home-made jams, the farewell gift of my mother and Lucy. It had sounded a lot at the beginning, but every time I wanted a spoonful the pot had to be offered to the rest of the watch who not unnaturally finished it. At first I was very glad to be popular for even the thirty seconds which it took them to do this, but when they became dissatisfied with my rate of consumption and the jam began to disappear pot by pot, I became rather stuffy about it. Our bunks were absolutely sacred and nothing left in a bunk, however tempting, was ever touched. But my Vuitton was in a sort of no-man's land where everything was free for all, so I transferred my dwindling stocks to the bottom of my bunk and no more jam disappeared.

I decided to live on bread and jam and fruit soup till my illness left me. As if by magic, fruit soup vanished from the menu and we had a week in which it seemed that the Cook had taken a vow to destroy us all by giving us scurvy. In endless succession Stockfisk, 'Buffelo' and 'Kabelgarn' issued from his kitchen. Only once we had 'Ängelskit', but even that was submerged in 'Kabelgarn'. In the middle of this week of horror, being in genuine agony, I applied through the proper channels to speak to the Captain, who was reputed to have a medicine chest. My interview took place in an informal manner at one o'clock on a very dark morning whilst I was at the wheel. Suddenly the Captain loomed out of the darkness and addressed me in what most Europeans still imagine to be American.

'So you can't take it. You're dying, are you?'

I told him that the meat made my mouth feel terrible.

'Bloody meat is it?' This rather angrily, putting my thoughts into words.

Then reminiscently, 'Ah, English boys, plenty of ice cream every day. Here we have man's food. Drink plenty lime juice. Soon you'll be better or you'll die. Don't worry – I won't.'

This rough and ready treatment combined with the remainder of the jam effected a cure. In a week my gums hardened up and I felt well again. I also began to be on better terms with my companions who, in the mysterious way of human beings, began to like me better when they were unable to take advantage of me. With the aid of the smallest Swedish Dictionary in the world, I managed to evolve a little patter of my own beyond the 'good, no good' stage. Under private tuition in the starboard fo'c'sle I also acquired one or two expressions so obscene that I was able to bring them into action in the port fo'c'sle with great effect.

The ship's work went on. Now we washed half the ship, exactly half of it, half the masts and half the bowsprit; the other half was the property of the starboard watch. I secured a post at the saltwater pump with 'Doonkey' and his assistant, Jansson. I applied for the job because 'Doonkey' was incurably idle and I was sure it would be easy. 'Doonkey' was six-foot-one, lean and squareheaded, with a brutal, heavily lined face and a mouth full of teeth like broken flints. On the dried surface of his thick hanging underlip was stuck a cigarette stub so minute that it seemed that it must have burnt itself out. He looked savage but in fact was not. He was strong and good at hauling; it was he who had encouraged us with his cries on that first night in the Irish Sea. This afternoon he had a black skull-cap on his head and was naked to the waist. He was wearing the sort of striped trousers that Moss Bros issue with their morning coats. Below them, a pair of the largest possible feet protruded from very dressy pointed shoes minus the toecaps.

Jansson, his partner, was perhaps a little dirtier than usual. He had an empty pipe in his mouth and a cigarette-end behind his ear. As they pumped, the sweat made white tracks on their grimy backs. They both leered at me in a friendly fashion and Jansson said: 'Hey, you, Kossuri, not too much horry op with the pomping.'

We worked the pump throughout the afternoon. The starboard watch, which was free, gave up the unequal contest with the bugs and retired to the fo'c'sle head deck, dressed in strange negligée with mattresses, books and packets of sweets. They remained there sunning themselves while we sweated beneath. Five minutes' hard pumping gave the washing gang enough sea water for ten minutes' work. Smoking in working hours was not permitted, and at the end of each five-minute burst at the pump 'Doonkey' and Jansson vanished briskly – 'Doonkey' into the Båtsman's Skåp' where rope-yarns, marline and small stuff were kept; Jansson into the 'Vaskrum' where, judging by the clouds of smoke that billowed through the cracks, he had kindled a good-sized fire. I was left to keep watch for the Mate and read the *New Statesman and Nation*, which I had salvaged from the lavatory. Soon there would be a cry of 'Pomp igen' and the two 'Doonkeys' would come popping out of their retreats swearing and roaring. 'Pomp igen, pomp igen'; wheels would be turned and the whole crazy contraption set in motion as we raised and lowered the horizontal bars on either side which made it resemble an old-fashioned village fire engine.

After three hours the pump began to show signs of fatigue and we encountered a resistance to our efforts which we at first put down to an improvement in the pressure. At the same time we were puzzled by the angry cries of 'pomp igen' reaching us with increasing frequency from the gang aft. Soon Tria appeared and began to berate us.

'No water, horry up with that pomping,' he said superfluously, since we were working the handles like demons.

'Tria?' said Jansson politely, as if about to ask a favour.

'Yo?' said Tria.

'Kyss din arshålet.'

Tria never corrected this lapse from discipline because the pump chose this moment to explode, hurling into the air several nuts and bolts, a large chunk of cement, some linoleum, and an impressive jet of water on which these objects danced for a moment like targets in a shooting gallery, before rattling about our ears. There was a dead silence, then it emitted a last melancholy sigh.

'Sometings fockings' said 'Doonkey' with satisfaction, 'pumpen har släppt,' as he set off to his 'rum' for tools. Whilst the Mate fumed and tried to find work for the others we started to repair the pump we had ruined. Happily I puddled cement and kneaded putty whilst Jansson cut fresh washers and gaskets from a piece of horribly patterned orange lino which he had for just such an emergency. Then 'Doonkey', who had done very little but rattle a Stillson wrench and look impressive, put the pump together. After coffee-time, work began again. Once more I secured the pumping job, only now the *New Statesman* had disappeared. I did not feel the loss very deeply. Among the more enlightened copy writers at Wurzel's it may have been required reading; in the world in which I now found myself, most of its contents had ceased to make any sense at all.

Twenty-four days out, in Lat. 23° 0′ N. Long. 19° W., we picked up the North-East Trade Wind 150 miles from Cape Blanco on the African shore. The sun had set with unparalleled splendour the night before, with *Moshulu* close-hauled on a west-south-westerly wind. At 4 a.m. when we came on deck the yards were squared up and she was running a steady eight to nine knots.

We pressed on with the sail-changing which had started two days before. There were thirty-one fore-and-aft and square sails to send down; the same number of old, patched, fair-weather sails to be rummaged for in the warm darkness of the 'tween-decks, sent aloft, and bent. These would carry us through the North-East and South-East Trade Wind belts and the Horse Latitudes until somewhere below latitude 30° S. We would again bend our storm canvas for the journey across the Southern Indian Ocean, on the parallel of 40°.

In six hours we changed a foresail and three upper and lower topgallants. When we finally got below we found the most abominable 'Buffalo' waiting for us, and no pudding. To make it equal, the Captain kept the starboard watch at it for seven hours and they bent three upper and three lower topsails in addition to helping us with the foresail. The Mates did their best to reconcile us to these arrangements by encouraging the competitive spirit, which was not difficult, as once the sails were on the gantlines, the work was a joy, with far below the sea leaping about the ship and the African sun warm on our backs. For five days the north-east wind blew. It was warm, absolutely steady, and strong enough to whip off a hat. I spent my free watches on the fo'c'sle head watching the flying fish ripping out of the water to leeward and the tiny rainbows formed when the spray curled backwards and upwards from the waves leaping towards the sun.

At night we nearly all slept on deck in our hammocks, although none of the crew would sleep in the light of the moon, preferring to hide away under the fo'c'sle head and in various odd corners. It was Hilbert who put this strange aversion into words: 'Don't slip in ze moon, it will twist you and twist you.' I thought of the *Ghost Stories of an Antiquary* and the things with faces like crumpled linen that slipped into people's bedrooms. Nevertheless I told Hilbert that it was all nonsense.

'Were you never in a crazy house?' he said. 'Have you never seen ze crazies roaring in moonshine? Moonshine moves tides, why not faces?'

'Have you seen these people, Hilbert?'

'Ze crazies?'

'No, the ones with bad faces?'

'No, I was ridding it.'

The Trade Wind took the ship close in to the Cape Verde Islands. Nine degrees north of the Equator it died away and we entered the Doldrums. The Guinea Current set us southwards but the sea was oily. As dusk came on huge dragon-flies with biplane wings purred about the ship; a small white butterfly fell into my hammock; some distance abeam two strange black birds ghosted over the sea and a school of flying fish broke from the water and glided thirty feet or so before subsiding. In the afterglow the decks still burned with the heat of the day. The wind came from the south-east, from the shore a hundred miles off, bringing with it a sweet smell like honeysuckle. The stars came out and we could no longer see the Plough, but low down on the horizon ahead the Southern Cross rose to meet us.

At four in the morning I was woken by a series of explosions followed by a torrent of water which poured through the open skylight. The light went out as the ship heeled over at an alarming angle and all the plates were hurled from the locker. My first thought was that we had hit something and were sinking. As we struggled to get out of the fo'c'sle a voice bellowed superfluously, 'Alle man på däck.'

At the door Sandell took one look and said, 'Tornado, very strongbody.' The next moment we were in it.

It was not rain that fell but a solid barrage of water that made us fight for breath. Continuous lightning illuminated the scene, which was awe-inspiring. *Moshulu* had been caught in a terrific wind from the east while in full sail with topgallant staysails and a fore royal staysail set. Now she was laid over in a sea that resembled boiling water. In spite of being in ballast, her lee rail was under water. The explosions we had heard were made when six sails blew out. The fore royal staysail, which served no useful purpose but of which we were all rather proud, had disappeared completely; the foresail had blown out of its bolt-ropes and was flailing in tatters on the fo'c'sle head; the mizzen royal had gone, together with the main and mizzen topgallant staysails, and the gaff upper topsail.

Before the tornado hit her there had only been time to let go the main and spanker sheets, but not enough to put the helm up and bear away so that the ship would run before it, and none to clew up sail.

The noise on deck was indescribable, with staysails shooting down as the halliards were cast off, blocks beating and above everything the screaming wind and the sound of canvas flogging itself to pieces. The unearthly yellow light which flickered about the ship reminded me of a lithograph of an East Indiaman on her beam ends which hung outside the headmaster's study at school.

Working desperately at the main rigging, we hauled at bunt-lines and clewlines, getting first the royals off her, then the upper topgallants, the mainsail, and finally went aft to clew up the mizzen. Relieved of this press of sail, *Moshulu* began to regain equilibrium.

When we went below at 6 a.m. for coffee, morale was high. We were all busy telling one another what feats we had performed. Even Hermansonn, like a regenerate Mr Toad, seemed pleasant and almost reticent. This elevation of spirit was succeeded by a feeling of great fatigue and dampness. In the fo'c'sle everything was slush and we bailed three inches of water from the floor before going on deck. The deck was in chaos, none of the falls was coiled down, they were tangled with one another and there were heaps of torn canvas all over the place.

All the morning the rain swished down. Squall succeeded squall and in them *Moshulu* made 12 knots. Alvar, Jansson and I bent a fresh royal and furled it. On dock Tria stitched away at a torn sail. When we had finished we rushed with buckets and tins to scoop up the rain-water that had accumulated in the lee scuppers to a depth of eighteen inches. With full buckets we crawled up the steep slope to the weather rail, poured the water into the tank, and then slid down again.

On November 19th, a Saturday, we had the good fortune to pick up the South-East Trade Winds in Lat. 4° N. – Long. 22° W. Tria was delighted; he had been in ships that had stuck in the Doldrums for two or three weeks. 'Good strong Passad' (Trade Wind), he boomed. The ship sprang to life; close hauled she ran ten and twelve knots. It seemed impossible that this lovely lively thing, its sails dazzling white against the dark blue sky, whose hull seemed scarcely to touch the water, could two days before have been a wallowing monster with slatting sails and flailing blocks.

Sunday was a great washing-day in the ship as we had hundreds of gallons of water. 'Vi ha tvätt i dag,' everyone said as they gathered round the Sailmaker on the foredeck, laughing, chattering and swearing, pummelling their filthy garments. Soon the lines rigged under the flying bridge were loaded and the scuppers were full of soapsuds. When I finished I lay in a hammock and talked to Kroner whilst the sun and wind browned us gently. Lying there we could gaze up at the sky seen through delicate traceries of shrouds and buntlines. He told me how, when he was eleven years old, living in the old part of Antwerp, he and his companions would play truant from school, go off in rowing boats, and laze for hours on the sandbanks in the Scheldt, watching the big ships go by, and when they were tired of this, would climb the steep dykes and steal apples from the orchards.

'Sometimes,' said Kroner, 'we used to write letters to the school saying we were ill. By the time I was fourteen the days in class were a slow torture and I felt I couldn't wait any more. I used to watch the white fruit-ships unloading and I hung about fascinated by the outlandish atmosphere and smells on the dockside as the crates were lifted, out of the hold.

'One day I went to the Shipping Agents. The place was full of grown seamen who laughed at me and sent me back to my mother.

'At fifteen I got away at last, to Archangel in a cargo ship in the late summer. After that I went to the Mediterranean, Egypt, Africa, the Levant, Spain and the Greek Archipelago.'

I asked him what he wanted. 'We can't go on going round the world for ever,' I said.

'I like sail,' said Kroner, 'and I'd like to stick to it. What I want is a small schooner, a partnership. I've seen just the sort of craft on the coast of Lebanon. There's an island in the North called Ruad where they build them. It's really only a fortified rock, the Templars went there when they got chucked out of the Holy Land. On the upland part there are a lot of windmills with canvas sails you can reef and furl, like ship's sails. The men on the island look just like you imagine the Phoenicians did, skin golden brown, hooked noses and striped shirts, Phrygian caps. The women look like tents with feet: everyone belongs to a very strict sect – the strictest sort of Mohammedanism. The men build the ships. It's the last home of the sailing ship in the Mediterranean. The logs are floated out, rough-trimmed, from the mainland, everything else is done on the spot: timbers steamed, bolts forged, ropes made in a rope walk, and the sails cut. There's a lot of square sail. When I was there they had topsail schooners on the stocks, they were even building a hermaphrodite brig, with a lot of square sail on the foremast and a schooner's main mast.

'Banias is the town on the mainland. It's got a whopping Norman cathedral that you'd expect to find in France and the whole town stinks to high heaven. It's got all the original medieval sewers, the main ones big enough to run a train through. There's a hotel called "Grande Fleur de Banias", built over the biggest one. It's owned by an Armenian who looks as though he was expecting to be slaughtered at any moment.'

As he spoke I listened to him with mounting restlessness until the sun was almost vertical overhead and, obscured by the jibs, left us in shadow.

First it had been Mountstewart who had unsettled me, uprooted me, and sent me into exile while he enjoyed my experience vicariously by his study fire. Now it was Kroner with his literary romantic approach to the sea who had been sent to disturb me. Listening to him it was difficult to tell at which point his memories ceased to be of authentic experience and became something created by his own splendid imagination. I never discovered the truth; everything he said reminded me of something I had read long ago but was unable to identify or put a name to.

I began to wonder whether my face had an air of guileless receptivity that invited others to flights of wild fancy. Had Mountstewart really invented the paravane, had he ever smoked his pipe at the skysail yard of a Clipper, had Sandell ever been to the Arctic, had Martini Nordlund existed, was Hilbert's story of the moonlight part of a complicated conspiracy to delude me? And finally, was Kroner's story the result of an overdose of

Wind in the Willows and *The Letters of T. E. Lawrence*? I didn't know, but I was sure that if I succumbed to Kroner's persuasion and went to his island I would encounter there someone who would tell me that the only place worth visiting was a small salt-lake in Central Asia.

The day was so beautiful that I decided to open one of my two cans of peaches, and in order to come to terms with my conscience and absolve myself from the imputation of gluttony, I decided to share them with Kroner, who was now sitting with his feet in the scuppers, washing pants. I sidled up to him and whispered in a melodramatic way out of the corner of my mouth: 'Meet me on the poop.'

'Whatever for? I'm not that kind of girl.'

'Don't be a fool. I've got some peaches.'

I went aft as innocently as possible with the tin wrapped in a shirt, but Anderssen the Dane was at the wheel and he gazed at me in a knowing way. By now the crew was so sensitive to the presence of food that they could even smell it in tins.

Hidden by the whaleback of the coaming of the emergency wheel, I unwrapped the tin. The label was even better than I had imagined. The artist was of the American Far Western naturalist school and would have been equally at home with the more inflammatory kind of magazine cover. The peach he had painted was so full of juice that it seemed about to explode and I handled the tin gingerly. I waited five minutes, ten minutes. Would Kroner never come? Better to open the tin. It took only a moment. Thirty seconds later the tin, sufficient, so the label said, for three generous servings, was empty.

I felt very guilty when Kroner appeared, full of anticipation.

'You bloody greedy bastard. Are you trying to drive me nuts?'

'It was the label. Look at it. It's beautiful.'

' – the label. What about the peaches?'

'I'll open the other tin.'

'I should – well hope so.'

Once more I made a journey to the fo'c'sle, whistling furtively as I passed Anderssen. Back on the poop, I offered Kroner first go.

'Here, steady on,' I said.

'Just a second.'

'Damn it, you've only left two slices.'

'You remember what happened with the condensed milk. You'll only upset yourself if you have too much,' said Kroner shovelling away.

'You might have let me try the second tin. After all, they were mine. You've eaten the bloody lot.'

'There's a bit of juice left.'

Full of peach we gazed astern glassily.

'Do you know,' said Kroner, 'I feel rather peculiar.'

'I hope you feel as bad as I do.'

'Much worse,' he replied. 'I'm going to turn in.'

CHAPTER TWELVE
'England's Hope'

WE crossed the Equator in Longitude 29° W. on Monday, November 21st, the thirty-fourth day of the voyage. Sitting astride the end of the bowsprit I had the sensation of flying through the air into the Southern Hemisphere. It was easy to forget the ship's existence. I grasped the tip and scratched my hands on the nails to which the fragments of shark's fin still clung.

Moshulu crossed the Line at four o'clock. As if by arrangement we were met by a big school of bonito which suddenly shot out of the depths of the sea and exploded about the bows, exhibiting remarkable changes of colour. At first they were steel blue and then, in the spray, mauve with silvering bellies.

To tempt them we lowered big hooks baited with gauze, but they showed no interest. They would zoom through the water as straight for the hooks, but when almost on them would avert their eyes and dash away joyfully ahead of the ship.

The Steward gave me his line. It was tantalizing waiting for the fish to snap the bait. Suddenly, after about ten minutes, there was a flurry of water and a flash of silver as two of them rushed for it. I lifted the hook a little more, and one of the bonito fell back but the other jumped for it and there was a tremendous jerk as he hooked himself, nearly pulling me into the water. There was a loud cheer from the onlookers who had visions of fresh fish for supper. The bonito had looked like a small silver shell in the water, but as I hauled it up to the bowsprit it both felt and looked enormous – nearly two feet long, it was like a small tunny. I had it just below the bowsprit with Hilbert shrieking instructions in my ear, when the hook slowly straightened and the fish fell back with a flop into the sea. Twice this happened and then the bonito vanished.

'You are noh good,' said Hilbert.

'At least I hooked a couple, nobody else did.'

'It is noh good to catch zem, we want to eat zem. You have frightened zem, we shall not see zem more.'

It was true. In the entire voyage we never saw another bonito.

We had crossed the Line on Monday and to honour the occasion received a bottle of Akvavit. Alvar was in charge and gave us each a quarter of a mug, keeping the rest for the Initiation Ceremony which had been put off until the following day because certain equipment was lacking.

'Beeg trouble,' said Hilbert, who was cast for Neptune's wife, 'always beeg trouble.'

'What's the matter?'

'No teets,' said Hilbert gloomily, 'som too beeg, som too small.'

I offered him my porridge bowl.

'Von's, no good,' he said.

'I *am* sorry, but it'll be all right on the night.'

'What's olrright on ze night?'

'It's an English expression.'

'You will be zorry – tomorrow,' said Hilbert.

'Why don't you ask the Captain?'

'Ugh,' said Hilbert.

At dinner-time on Tuesday all ship's work ceased and preparations for the Ceremony began. A tarpaulin was rigged up in the fore well-deck. This was to be the initiation tank, and Taanila, Backmann and I worked hard at the pump to fill it. There was a depressing lack of pressure and after twenty minutes the apparatus showed signs of collapse. The First Mate was in a bad temper by this time and sent me to see how full the tank was. It was quite dry, and he told us to use buckets.

All the time Backmann and Taanila were mumbling that it was worse than real work. We had only filled the tank to a depth of three inches, and I was gloomily calculating how long it would take to fill it to a depth of two feet when suddenly we were surrounded by a gang of pirates led by a seaman called Hörglund, a fearsome figure with a patch over one eye.

Seven of us were pressed into the stifling 'Båtsman's Skåp': the Mess Boy, Karma, Anderssen, Alvar, Hermansonn, Taanila and myself. Five more were chucked into the 'Vaskrum' on the port side. Sweating profusely, we waited. On deck there was quite suddenly pandemonium. Fifty bells were rung, the door was flung open and we were dragged out and made to kneel before Sandell, the Chaplain, who was dressed in a long oilskin, a tall green top hat made from a chart of Portland, Oregon, and a clerical collar of sail-canvas, who read a very irreverent and original lesson.

There was a pause while everyone received a stiff tot of Akvavit from the Captain, then we were thrown into the locker again. Once more we waited uneasily. Hermansonn was the first to be taken out. We heard roars, jeers, cries of pain, and then there was silence.

When it was my turn, the pirates rushed me blindfold down the deck. There was a taut rope stretched in front of me and I fell flat on my face at Neptune's feet, hurting myself badly and losing the bandage.

Neptune had a fine set of hemp whiskers and a gold crown cut from an empty margarine tin. More unpleasant was his mistress, Hilbert. He was dressed in a suit of athletic underwear, tightly fitting where two large bowls (the cause of the postponement) did duty as breasts.

At their command I was turned over to the Surgeon, the Second Mate, dressed in a shiny black rubber coat and rubber gloves, assisted inevitably by Sedelquist who whispered something to him.

'You stand on the skit hus seat! You must be ill!' the Surgeon screamed.

I remained silent, but opened my mouth to roar with pain when something like a sharp nail jabbed my behind and a pudding of engine oil, dough and nutmeg was forced down my throat. After this my mouth was held open by force and filthy-tasting liquids were poured down on top of the pudding, which I had not been allowed to eject.

'Treat him for piles,' someone suggested. I was flung down on a hatch cover, and Jansson, looking like the leader of a German Street Band, got busy. With big brushes he gave me three coats from head to foot of red lead, stockholm tar and white paint, covering every part.

'Don't forget ze Sydkryss,' said the Queen anxiously. My hair was just growing again after the shaving he had given it. Kroner, the barber, cut two furrows across my scalp with a big pair of shears and picked them out in green paint. The Queen broke her trident across my bare back. 'We christen you,' she said, 'zis lucky day, England's hope,' and pushed me into the hard shallow tank.

Karma and 'Doonkey' were the only ones to show fight, Karma going nearly mad so that it needed Neptune's entire entourage to subdue him. When I saw what they did to Karma and 'Doonkey' I was very glad that I had not resisted. The two of them went below to nurse their injuries; black and blue, they muttered and cursed for hours afterwards.

The ceremony was followed by more Akvavit and some Port. The officers tactfully withdrew and an interminable battle began with dough and buckets of water. By this time Jansson had managed to reduce himself to a state of shambling benignity, happily throwing buckets of water over anyone within range. He threw a bucket of very dirty water at me. It missed and hit Hermansonn who had already taken to his hammock. Hermansonn lost his temper completely and ran at Jansson, who had already forgotten what he had done and was gazing blearily and benevolently at nothing, and knocked him flat in the scuppers. Poor Jansson was in too good a humour and too ruined by drink to do anything and only opened and shut his mouth like a landed fish. Hermansonn stalked off to the fo'c'sle with watery dignity and the rest of us, feeling unhappy and rather ridiculous, tried to clean ourselves up. I was in a fearful state, my head full of tar and red lead, and in considerable pain.

Two hours later, with the help of Kroner and a lot of paraffin and sand, I was in slightly better shape, but very sore.

'How was the christening?' asked the First Mate when I came to the wheel.

'Bloody awful.'

'Ho, ho, English boys like girls. In *Archibald Russell* we made the jungmän drink linseed oil.'

'I had Castrol today,' I told him.

'And Tredje Styrman had never crossed the Line. My God, dose boys, what a Sydkryss they gave him – he had long hair. Ho, ho, very fonny,' he rumbled as he made off across the deck.

✣

On the night of November 23rd the island of Fernando Norohna, the Brazilian Penal Settlement, was eighty miles to starboard. The wind was veering between east-north-east and east. By now all the experienced seamen in the ship had been made daymen. Sedelquist was mending sails, Sandell and Alvar were aloft painting the shrouds or rigging fresh ratlines. Every now and then they would shriek: 'Slak upp på däck,' and one of us in the free watch would rise from his hammock cursing and allow the bosun's chairs in which they were sitting to descend a little. Some of the daymen were no artists of the brush, and Jansson received a dressing-down from the First Mate for dropping paint on the deck. In our watch Hermansonn, Taanila, Bäckmann and myself were still standing night-watches. In the starboard watch only Kroner, Anderssen, Karma, Mikelsonn and Vytautas remained. Wheel, 'utkik' and 'påpass' came round far too frequently and we craved for sleep.

On the evening of November 24th the daymen wore the ship on to the starboard tack, and we stood away from the coast of Brazil towards the East. We were crossing the main Southampton–Rio route and in the early morning we saw the lights of several ships. At seven we wore around on to the port tack once more. On that day we made only twenty-six miles on our course. Wearing ship was a method of going about, useful in an under-manned vessel, or in one whose rigging was old and weak, but it needed a good deal of sea room. We employed it now for the former reason, hauling up the main and mizzen courses to make it easier, as we had the whole of the South Atlantic in which to manoeuvre.

By November 29th we were close to the uninhabited island of Trinidad in 20° S. 33° W., 680 miles from the coast of Brazil. We saw Trinidad, and I began to think that we should never see land in the entire voyage.

We started to bend storm canvas. Aloft the daymen had done a good job. At the cross-trees there was no longer the smell of the sea. Instead there were the rich smells of hemp, stockholm tar and white lead. There were fresh ratlines everywhere and new lashings and shroud bindings picked out in black and white. A week before it had been dangerous to risk one's weight on a ratline; only one in three were in position and the remainder were rotten and work aloft had become more than usually unsafe. For the first time an albatross appeared, dropping dramatically out of the sky and gliding noiselessly on immense spread wings, disappeared as suddenly as it had come.

'With albatross,' everyone said, 'koms Väst Vind and then – Zoosh, horry op.'

On November 30th, the forty-third day at sea, while working in the rigging, we sighted a big sailing ship to the south. At first she was hull down and showed only a white splash of sail on the horizon, but we were making nine knots in the last of the South-East Trades and the stranger was coming up fast with the wind on her starboard quarter. There was much speculation and excitement about who she might be and some of the watch below came aloft to look at her. If one of our fleet, she could only be *Penang* on a long passage. *Penang* was the last of the homeward bound Erikson ships. Having been partially dismasted south of New Zealand, she had put back and finally left Dunedin for Falmouth on August 14th.[*] It was now the 30th of November. Somebody suggested that it might be either *Padua* or *Priwall*. *Padua* had been in Bremen when we sailed from Belfast and was destined for Valparaiso; *Priwall* had left Hamburg at the beginning of August for Iquique on the North coast of Chile. If she was *Priwall*, as Tria said, they would have to have made 'some big horry' to have made the outward passage round the Horn, loaded nitrate, and returned.

Seven months later I found out what had really happened to *Padua*. She had made a remarkable passage. Having left Bremen on October 15th, three days before we left Belfast, on November 12th she was already on the Equator, 28 days out against our 34. Even allowing for our misfortunes in the Irish sea, this was a more impressive performance than ours, but both *Padua* and *Priwall* carried more than twice the crew of *Moshulu*. Now, on November 30th, she was well to the south of us. On December 22nd she arrived at Corral, 68 days from Bremen. In the New Year this formidable ship sailed from Valparaiso to Port Lincoln in ballast to take part in the 1939 grain sailings, covering 9,014 miles in 52½ days. Of all the ships engaged, *Padua* seemed most likely to win.

But none of this was yet known to us, and controversy raged.

'I tink,' said Hermansonn, 'it's some bloody rosbif English schoolship.'

'For Christ's sake don't start again,' I said.

Soon we knew that it was not a barque. Whatever the ship, she had five masts.

'American five-masted schooner,' Vytautas suggested.

'None in commission,' said Kroner with tremendous authority.

'What about the *Doris Hamlin*?'

'She's got four masts, besides you'd never see her here. She runs between Virginia and the Caribbean.'

'It's a Vinnen ship,' said Tria. '*Carl* or *Werner Vinnen*. I don't

* She arrived off the Lizard on December 15th, 123 days from New Zealand.

know which. Got submarine diesels, trades with South America –
Bremen–Montevideo – bloddy looking ting.'

Soon she was five miles on our beam. An ugly hybrid, partly
square-rigged, with a curiously cut foresail, she crossed topsail
and topgallant yards on the fore and mizzen masts and fore-and-
aft gaff rig on the other two. Like us her crew were changing sail,
only they were bending fair-weather stuff, while we were far
advanced with our storm canvas. Although she had a fair wind,
the stranger made no attempt either to close with us or speak with
us. The Captain had his glass trained on her.

'*Carl Vinnen*,' he said to Tria. 'Bound for Bremen.'

'Friendly lot of bastards,' grumbled Kroner under his breath.

'And how should they be happy,' said Vytautas, 'in such an
ugly ship and going to Bremen in Wintertime?'

'Reasonable people like Vytautas make me sick,' said Kroner.
'Like a lot of bloody parsons.'

For eleven days the South-East Trade Wind blew. At the end
of that time the log showed that we had sailed two thousand
miles, from the latitude of Cape Palmas on the coast of Guinea to
a point on the Tropic of Capricorn six hundred miles from Rio de
Janeiro. Here is the meeting place of two ocean currents, the
Brazilian Current setting southwards along the seaboard of that
country, and the Southern Connecting Current sweeping across
the South Atlantic past Tristan da Cunha to the Cape of Good
Hope. South of the Cape the other part of the Connecting Current
mingles and conflicts with the Agulhas Current setting down the
eastern side of Africa and the icy Antarctic Current pushing up
from the regions about South Georgia, causing great changes of
surface temperature and sometimes fog.

Now, at the western extremity of the Connecting Current, the
Captain set his course to sail on the great circle, make landfall at
Tristan da Cunha, and pass southward of the African Continent,
to pick up the westerly winds that circle the world on the fortieth
parallel of south latitude and so run the easting down across the
Southern Ocean to Australia.

The South-East Trade Wind did not die but quite suddenly it

ceased to be a warm wind and shifted to east-south-east, from which quarter it blew steadily. At night the sky was full of clouds and we shivered in our hammocks, unwilling to return to the fo'c'sle and the bugs waiting there for us. Soon it was both cold and wet and we had to. The daymen, Sandell, Sedelquist and Jansson, returned to normal watchkeeping, and I hoped for more sleep, as in company with the other five juniors I had suffered 'utkik', wheel and 'påpass' in endless succession.

Some time before four in the morning in what I hoped would be my first free night watch, I was woken by a hand shaking me violently and a voice bellowing:

'Två vissel, två vissel, ut och mönstra.'

In terror as always when roused in this fashion, I stumbled out on deck, dragging on my clothes as I followed the retreating 'påpass', Yonny Valker, who suddenly doubled back to the fo'c'sle. The deck was deserted except for Tria looming above me on the midships deck. He regarded me curiously as I buttoned my trousers. 'Fonny,' he said conversationally, and sniggered. When I returned to the fo'c'sle the rest were emerging from their hiding places beneath the table and behind the door. This joke was played on nearly everyone except the daymen and was always well received. Yonny was already fast asleep on a bench and when I pushed him off, he fell with a good solid thud on the floor, uttered a sort of dugong grunt, but still went on sleeping. As he was 'påpass' it was necessary to wake him.

'That Yonny is a proper strongbody for slip,' said Alvar who was himself nearly impossible to wake.

'Yonny, Yonny,' chanted the horrible little Taanila. 'Yonny wants knife to his bloddy asse,' and before anyone could stop him, he had whipped out his great Finnish sheath knife and carried out his own suggestion. There was a terrible roar and an effusion of blood from Yonny, who lumbered round the table trying to catch Taanila, an agile evil flea; but what would have seriously injured a normal person really worried Yonny very little.

In the next two days I spent a happy morning and afternoon in the rigging, slung in a bosun's chair, greasing the wire braces and halliards with a mixture of oil and tallow. I never discovered why I was selected for this sinecure when there were so many more loathsome tasks to be performed. Far below I could see Hermansonn and Taanila engaged in cleaning the lavatories, a job which I had come to regard as my own peculiar monopoly. From the hold rose the muffled thud of hammers as the remainder of the watch performed 'knacka rost'. Above me, Pipinen, a kindly blond Matros, whose back was terribly scarred by boiling water, was rigging new ratlines. The wind had shifted still more, through east to east-north-east; the ship was running nine or ten knots, heeling steadily, with the wind on the beam. The sky was grey, the sea cold. Through it the barque drove, her wake curling white and blue, like the thread of a screw, almost to the horizon.

The bosun's chair was a plank seat with a rope through a hole drilled in each corner and seized round a thimble above. The rope from which this contrivance was suspended in mid-air was made fast to the stretcher of the cross-trees and a bight (loop) of it passed through the eye of the thimble, over the chair itself, and was drawn taut. In this way the chair was held in a half-hitch quite safely so long as the weight of the occupant was sufficient to jam it. To lower oneself it was only necessary to take some weight off the chair, ease the half-hitch, and descend cautiously. Tossed from side to side by the wind, buffeted by a 14-1b margarine can of tallow and oil swinging beside me, I greased the cables, using a signal flag which I had drawn from the 'Båtsman's Skåp'. On it were four red and white squares diagonally opposed.

'Joost for you,' Tria had said and roared with laughter. On the aft I looked it up in the International Code. It was the letter 'U', but used as a single-letter hoist, it read: 'You are standing into danger'.

With this warning in mind I worked carefully, but the flag material was not absorbent and soon the yards and sails were finely speckled with grease. I prayed that none would fall on the deck. It would be far better to die than to allow such a thing to happen. Although neither the Captain nor his Officers seemed likely to resort to physical violence, there were punishments of a disagreeable and repetitive kind which they could inflict, such as permanent wardenship of the 'skit hus', or perhaps worse, an indefinite period of 'knacka rost' in the darkness below. I was so anxious about my margarine can and its deadly contents that I neglected the chair in which I was sitting.

In rigging the rope to the cross-trees I had foolishly allowed the end to fall on the lee side of the topgallant staysail. Without considering what I was doing I began to overhaul fifty feet of rope to the weather side without jamming tight the half-hitch. On land a similar but more obviously dangerous effect would have been produced by sitting on the branch of a tall tree and then sawing it off close to the trunk. Suddenly there was a shrill whistle and a blurred vision of rigging rushing past, as the chair, with me in it, hugging my margarine can, descended bomb-like towards the deck. I tried to catch the rope but only succeeded in taking a great strip of flesh off my arm. As I went down I had time to wonder why I was not screaming in a conventional manner like a pirate falling from aloft in a film. I opened my mouth but only succeeded in biting my tongue, as at that moment the chair fetched up with a terrific jerk in the bight of rope which I had overhauled. I now swung like a pendulum fifty feet above the deck in this tenuous loop, only one end of which was attached to anything at all. I was shaking with terror, partly because I had had a narrow escape and partly because I was expecting to find that I had fouled the Captain's private piece of deck by the charthouse. With burnt arm and bitten tongue, I hastened to the deck.

'Lost somting?' asked the First Mate. He had not witnessed the incident, and was surprised to find me looking frantically at the deck.

'Not yet,' I said.

'Found somting?'

'Not yet?'

'Op the rigging then.'

'I'm off to the skit hus.'

By a miracle nothing had been spilt. In the lavatory, to avoid publicity, I was sick for the first time in the voyage.

When I came out Tria was waiting wearing his Central Asian grin.

'Your fadder,' he boomed, 'nearly got back his feefty poun'.'

Dinner that day was a melancholy affair of fossilized stockfish in a nasty anaemic sauce, and everyone mumbled angrily about it, but I felt like a condemned man reprieved and ate it with pleasure.

CHAPTER THIRTEEN
Inaccessible Island

THAT night, Friday, December 2nd, there was an immense halo round the moon, and the wind blew freshly, with a salt tang in it. Two albatross wheeled above the water, black shadows against the moon. It was too cold for hammocks on deck, and we were spending the night-watches in the fo'c'sle.

'Now, Kossuri,' said Sandell, as he had said every day since we cleared the North Channel, 'where's the bloddy map?'

I took the little Woolworth's atlas from under my pillow and opened it at The World.

'What's the position?' he demanded.

I handed over a slip of paper on which I had written down the position, 29° 46′ 5 S., 30° 02′ 4 W., course S. 21° E. 'Hah,' said Sandell, pointing to a line undulating across the Southern Hemisphere. 'Southern limit of Palms. No more palms.'

'Poetry,' said Sedelquist. 'Never mind, plenty icebergs. Nice for Kossuri, very romantic.'

'Wind Ostorndost,' Sandell was saying. 'Should go round to Nordost, perhaps to Nordväst, and blow like strongbody.'

Sandell was right, by the next night the ship was flying. In the first four hours of Saturday afternoon, with the wind east-north-east, force 3–4, and a light sea, she ran 47 miles. Reading was difficult in the fo'c'sle. At one moment the print was a foot from one's nose, the next it was right on it. Model-making was abandoned. Between four and eight the wind was shifting towards north-east and she logged 49 miles. The glass was falling and by midnight the wind was north-west, blowing in the very best position for a barque, on the quarter, so that she ran 54 miles between eight and midnight, and 55 more by 4 a.m. She was still carrying everything, except the jigger topmast staysail, which was taken in at 2 o'clock.

'We're making a passage and she's a bitch to steer,' said Kroner when I relieved him at the wheel at four o'clock. The night was bright and the wind was increasing; the ship looked wild and beautiful, running 14 and 15 knots to the south-east. She was beautiful, but very difficult to control with a strong weather helm, so that I had to fight the wheel to stop her coming up into the wind; and when she began to swing with increased momentum to starboard I had to meet her and check her so that she would not yaw from side to side and lose way.

At five when I was relieved the Captain sent two men to the wheel. By eight the sea was rising and the ship running heavily. In the four hours she logged 58 miles. Overhead the sun struggled to break through the masses of torn cloud hurrying before us. At nine the royals came in, together with the topgallant staysails, the gaff topsail and the flying jib. But she still dragged her heels and at eleven the upper topgallants were taken in too.

Everyone was wondering what the noon position would be. None of us had dreamed of sailing like this. At noon the wind was north-east, force 6, with the barometer still falling. The daymen were called and all hands dewed up the mizzen course, furling it in an unusually short time, because it was Sunday and because they were in good humour. On deck the Captain beamed up at us. He had reason to be happy. Between noon on Saturday and noon on Sunday we had logged 333 sea miles and made 315 between positions, the best day *Moshulu* had had since Erikson bought her.

Everyone was in excellent spirits. The atlas was carried reverently to the starboard fo'c'sle like a prophetic book, and a sort of combined general staff got to work on it . . . '35° 12′ 5 S., 20° 36′ 1 W. – Soon,' they said, 'soon we shall find the Väst Vind and then Zoosh!' Grubby fingers slurred half across the world from Tristan to the Australian Bight.

Back in our own fo'c'sle Hermansonn began to get out of hand and threw a wet pillow which hit me behind the ear.

However, this was done in a conciliatory way, and when we fought on the wet foredeck it was all very good-humoured, which was fortunate for me, because I lost. Returning battered and bleeding to the fo'c'sle, I was gratified to receive an unsolicited testimonial from Taanila who had, under the benign influence of the strong wind, at last made peace with Sedelquist.

'Soon one day,' he said, digging me in the ribs, 'you no more Kossuri – you focking strongbody.'

Between noon and midnight on Sunday *Moshulu* logged 168 miles. At five the mizzen course was reset but the wind shifted to north-north-east, blowing force 6, and at 10 o'clock, in bright moonlight, all hands were called to furl the mizzen course once again, and then the mainsail, the three lower topgallants, and the outer jib.

'Stor segel . . . bräck gårdingarna . . . tag i gigtåget . . . Ooh . . . Ooh . . . ah . . . ee . . . or . . .' This time it was the Sailmaker, cloth cap reversed like an early racing motorist, bellowing like a bull, hauling on the falls. 'Ooh . . . ooh . . . two blocks. Gigtåget . . . Ooh . . . ah . . . two blocks. Orlright, upp och göra fast . . .'

There was a scramble for the rigging, to reach the clewed up canvas crashing and banging against the yards. Eighteen of us went aloft for the mainsail and layed out to port and starboard along the yard, feet splaying on the taut foot-rope; the only sounds audible above the rushing of the wind and the sea were the little grunts and cries of immediate neighbours as they bent their stomachs over the yard and stretched down to heave the canvas up on it.

The gaskets were uncoiled and turns taken round sail and yard, a difficult job on a steel spar two feet thick. It needed two to a gasket. Hermansonn, my neighbour, with whom I was working, lowered himself to sit on the foot-rope and passed the gasket between the chain sheet of the lower topsail and the yard itself, flicking the end of it upwards until, by leaning so far forward over the yard that my legs were higher than my head, I could take it and pass it back to him again.

There was another sound now – battered hands beating the canvas, frapping and tightening the gaskets; until voices all along the yard began calling in the polyglot of the ship. 'Orlright, fast.'

Dark figures began to edge in towards the mast, a procession slow at first, dispersing more rapidly down the ratlines and backstays to the deck to clear up and coil down the tangle of buntlines and clewlines.

That night I learned what it meant to take in the outer jib near the end of a sixty-foot steel bowsprit, with no safety netting under it, alternately pointing to the sky and dipping to the tremendous boiling sea. The foot-rope on the weather side was fearfully slippery, the sail a lunatic wet thing. The wire leech of the sail was battering my head and shoulders and the sheet block was lashing about like a great conker on a string and threatening to brain us.

'Get the block, Kossuri,' said Hermansonn as it came whistling over our heads, 'quick.'

I missed it once, heard Hermansonn bellowing at me derisively, and taking a tremendous risk stood up on the foot-rope and caught it with both hands as it came at us. With the block secured, the rest was easier. Little by little all of it was snugged down on top of the yard and gasketed. 'Like creeket,' said Hermansonn. In his voice I could detect a note of approval, but I felt that I had had to behave in a foolhardy way to secure it.

'You can play by yourself next time.'

At midnight on the 4th the wind was north-north-east, force 7. Down to topsails now, her upper and lower yards naked, gleaming yellow like great bones in the moonlight, she was a terrible wild stranger to us. At the wheel a Swede and a Dane were fighting to hold her as she ran 13 and 14 knots in the gusts. I knew then that I would never see sailing like this again. When such ships as this went it would be the finish. The windbelts of the world would be deserted and the great West Wind and the Trades would never blow on steel rigging and flax canvas again.

It was already light when we went below at four on Monday morning and no sooner had my head touched the pillow than it was eight o'clock. Whilst we slept *Moshulu* logged 55 miles. The upper topgallants and the mainsail were reset and by midday we were in 36° 39′ 3 S., 14° 15′ 1 W., having made 320 miles by log in the twenty-four hours.

All through the day there were two helmsmen. The weather was fine. Four great albatross and a school of dolphins disported themselves about the ship and the sun shone in a sky banked with high cirrus. In the afternoon the weather worsened, but the glass was steady and in the first four hours we once more logged 55 miles. There were many more birds now, Cape Pigeons, varieties of petrels and albatross. I was in the Sailmaker's loft, listening to his comments as he thumbed through a book of pictures of the early clippers which he had obtained from the Captain, when the door was flung open and an excited Jansson appeared in the entrance.

'Quick,' he said. 'Tristan om babord, make horry op,' and vanished.

'Tristan – ugh,' replied the Sailmaker rather grumpily, and then as though nothing out of the ordinary had been announced, he turned another page. No doubt he had seen Tristan da Cunha hundreds of times and was no longer impressed. 'Now this,' he went on, 'is *Marco Polo*. She was a goer all right. In 52 she ran 364 miles in 24 hours south of Cape Horn – and she was deeploaded. Her Captain was Bully Forbes. He was a real – '

Whatever Bully Forbes was I never heard, because at this point the Sailmaker noticed my impatience.

'D'you want to see the Consul or something?'

'Would you mind terribly if I came back later? I rather want to see the island.'

'It'll be there the next time.'

'I may not be this way again.'

'They do it for the experience . . . Jesus!' said the Sailmaker, grumbling, prepared to go on deck himself. I did not wait.

It was an impressive landfall. Astern the sun was setting in a wild ruin of saffron, bathing the ship and the sea in a fearful light. Five miles off, the island rose into a leaden dome of dark cloud. Great seas were bursting on the sheer cliffs of the western side which were like the ramparts of some fortress.

'Are we going to land at Tristan?' I asked Tria.

'In that?' he said, pointing to the seas battering the island.

'With rollers setting in – are you crazy? Besides, landing's on the north side. If the pipple saw us and launched a boat they might never get back from leeward.'

'We could anchor for the night.'

'We could,' said Tria, who loved a delayed effect. 'There's 2,000 fathoms just here, and it's not Tristan anyway. It's Inaccessible Island and no one lives on it. Veree lonely.'

Inaccessible Island certainly was lonely; one of the three islands of the group, it was twenty miles west-south-west of da Cunha, eleven miles from Nightingale Island, 1,500 west of the Cape of Good Hope, 1,800 from Uruguay, and 1,200 miles south of St Helena.

With its tremendous cliffs a thousand feet high vanishing into the clouds, it was impossible that evening to know whether Inaccessible Island was, like Tristan, a cone 6,700 feet high with an extinct crater at the summit. In fact Inaccessible was sawn off, truncated, but with its top obscured it was easy to confuse it with Tristan in poor visibility, though actually it was much smaller.

Tristan, Inaccessible and Nightingale islands are the southern summits of a chain of volcanic mountains of which Jan Mayen Island near Iceland and the Azores are the other visible peaks. On the hidden ranges of the Atlantic Ridge the sea, in comparison with the vast deeps on either side, is shallow but shelves so rapidly that, as Tria had said, between the islands of the Tristan group there were places where the water was more than six thousand feet deep.

As we came under the lee of Inaccessible Island the wind shifted to north by east and the sails began to clatter and crash on the yards until the starboard watch, called to the braces, squared them away so that we ran dead before the wind.

'The birds,' said Tria, 'look at the birds.'

There were hundreds, thousands of them flying over or floating on the sea between the ship and land. Tiny, white-faced Storm Petrels flying weakly and erratically, long legs dangling so close to the crests that they seemed certain to be dragged down by the sea. Cape Pigeons, black and white, almost chequered – some with striking white patches on the dorsal surfaces where their feathers had moulted – floating like corks on the water or running comically over it at our approach. Another petrel dressed in black, with a grey face, which the Sailmaker said was a Cape Parson. Pediunkers – grey and white-breasted petrels – diving headlong into the sea from twenty feet up in search of food. There were numbers of other birds too, which might have been Noddys, Fulmars, Shearwaters, but with such a concourse and in the failing light it was impossible to identify them; and, lording it over all of them, the Wandering Albatross, some stopping to feed, others hanging motionless over the ship, or soaring restlessly on the wind.

Inaccessible Island was visited infrequently by the inhabitants of Tristan and was the home of a unique flightless bird of the rail family, *Atlantisca Rogersi*, whose means of arrival without wings cannot be imagined and whose future existence depends on the rats on Tristan staying where they are. The rats, which had originally come ashore from a wrecked ship, had practically exterminated the land-birds on Tristan and had even been known to eat cats. Inaccessible Island was also one of the breeding grounds of the Rockhopper Penguin, or Jumping Jack, the nickname describing his method of progression.

For these creatures life on Inaccessible Island must have been a steady round of seasonal activity: battling in August for a mate, egg-laying towards the end of September, followed by a five- to six-week hatching period, in which male and female alternated in sitting on the egg. Now, in December, the chicks would be grown, moulted, and sitting gloomily on the basalt pinnacles of the island. Between January and April they would all leave and, being migratory, might be encountered swimming in mid-ocean far from land.

It was the Rockhoppers which by their timely arrival saved the brothers Frederick and Gustav Stoltenhoff from extinction in 1872 after they had lived there alone for two years in conditions which even Germans must have found insupportable without an audience.

'I was here in *Ponape* in '34,' said Tria. 'Kapten was very merry.'

'Stinking?' I asked.

'No. Merry. He stood in close to Tristan, very close, and hove to. Pipple came out in long rowing boats. We gave them coffee and sugar for fresh meat and vegetables. Kapten had them on board. They gave us penguin feather caps, models of their boats – sort of ting, for tobacco and knives. Soon we had notting left but lots of tings made from bloddy penguin feathers. They had a priest with them; a preacher – somting like that I don' know what. Kapten made him very dronk. Styrman went ashore with someone from the fo'c'sle and a Miss.'

'Who was she?'

'A passenger from Belfast. They stayed four hours. Preacher could hardly stand when Kapten had finished with him. Then we stood out to sea. Sometimes I wonder what the pipple said.'

Inaccessible Island faded into the night. All around we could hear the splash of sea-birds continuing their feeding in water which must have been teeming with life to attract them in such numbers. In the fo'c'sle myth took control. Tristan, according to Hilbert, had been abandoned by its inhabitants and their place taken by an eccentric Indian Prince – a Rajah whose life had been so wildly irregular that even India had been unable to stomach him. Expelled, he had come to Tristan and built himself a castle in which he now lived, surrounded by a numerous harem.

To counter this legend I told Kroner about the Stoltenhoff brothers on Inaccessible.

'It's a good story,' said Kroner, as though it wasn't true. 'Better than Hilbert's. But they'll never believe it,' pointing at his companions seated round the table.

'Why ever not?'

'No sex,' he replied with the air of a producer rejecting a manuscript. 'No women in it. Now if they'd been brother and sister . . .'

At this moment Yonny arrived. For some time we had been having trouble with Yonny Valker, who maintained with remarkable stubbornness that the lines of longitude did not converge at the Poles but covered the world equidistantly, forming, with the lines of latitude, a great fish-net over land and sea. After a time the Starboard fo'c'sle, more intellectually inquisitive, got to hear of this heresy and invited him to appear before them. The noise of the controversy was deafening and in a short while everybody became bad-tempered – everybody except Yonny, who, like a vessel in the centre of a revolving storm, floated calmly and peacefully, unaffected by the uproar.

'Yonny,' said Kroner, after having endeavoured to demonstrate with diagrams, 'you're a stupid bastard.'

'Yeth,' said Yonny, whistling through the portcullis formed by his front teeth. 'You are bathtard, too.' Then triumphantly he opened my Woolworth Atlas at the double-page spread of the World on Mercator's Projection, at the same time tapping his head and winking significantly at the rest of us.

Kroner was driven nearly frantic by these manoeuvres.

'Yonny.'

'Yeth?'

'Do you think the world is round? Or flat?'

There was a long silence while we all waited, like members of the Holy Office about to catch a heretic. Yonny looked cunning but didn't answer. His expression suggested that he was not prepared to agree with either proposition. A terrifying vision of the future rose before me of Yonny, master of some frail vessel, setting off on a voyage equipped with the maps of his choice, perhaps those of an early cartographer like Cosmas Indicoplcustes, and finally arriving by their aid at the World's End – *terra ultra Oceanum ubi ante diluvium habitant homines* – with a very surprised crew. Nobody knew much about Yonny. Perhaps he had already been and come back.

Similar thoughts must have occurred to Kroner.

'Yonny. You do understand that the lines of latitude and longitude aren't real, don't you? That they're only on maps?'

'Yeth they are,' said Yonny with absolute finality. 'They *are* real. AND THEY NEVER MEET.'

We had made our landfall at Inaccessible Island on the evening of the 5th December. On the 6th, which was my birthday, the wind was NNE., force 5, and we reset the royals and all the fore-and-aft sails. With this increase *Moshulu* began to drive again, averaging 12½ knots. By noon we had run 292 miles, making a total of 923 in three days.

Besides being my birthday, the 6th of December was a Finnish National Holiday.

'Noh work,' said Sedelquist.

'Why?'

'*Själfständighetsdagen* – freedom from Russia.'

'Noh work,' said Taanila. '*Itsenäisyyspäivä.*'

'Say that again.'

Taanila mouthed it happily several times.

'What's that in aid of?'

'Freedom from Russia too, but Finnish word,' said Sedelquist.

'If I was a Russian I'd be celebrating too,' said Kroner who was passing.

'You are a focking Bolscheviki,' said Taanila, heatedly.

'I am not a focking Bolscheviki,' Kroner replied with good humour, 'I'm a focking Fascist. But if I was, and you and Karma were living next door, I'd help you to liberate yourselves.'

Nothing else happened to mark the occasion, and *Själfständighetsdagen*, *Itsenäisyyspäivä* and my birthday were celebrated without rapture.

For the next four days the wind steadily decreased in force and we suffered calms and light airs. Each dawn was beautiful but almost immediately obscured by great banks of mist rolling up from the east like clouds of gas, enveloping the ship in a vapour which settled upon everything in half-frozen globules, turning breath to steam, and making us shiver. From the sea came a cold salt smell, clearing the head after the frowsty air of the fo'c'sle. Visibility was only fifty feet beyond the bowsprit, but above us the sky was blue and the sun shone on the royals.

Every day, with the mist all round us and the foghorn mooing sadly, we scraped dried layers of linseed oil and turpentine from the decks. The scrapers were not satisfactory – they were old pieces of spring steel and broken rasps and files set in hard wood handles. After ten minutes work they were blunted and had to be put on the grindstone, and each time they were ground they were less successful. After the first hour most of us had no skin left on our knees although there were several low supports like church hassocks made of canvas and wood, but too few to go round. I tried sitting on deck but my behind went to sleep and I suffered excruciating pins and needles.

The albatross were with us constantly now, gliding out of the mist like giant bombers Their wings were immense, the colour of mushrooms, and we argued among ourselves as to their span. Their beaks were a delicate coral; their eyes swimming pools of black.

One afternoon we set out to catch one with a special apparatus made by Sandell. It consisted of a hollow triangle of tin with strips of stockfish lashed to it with thread The apex of the triangle was attached to a wooden float and was paid out over the stern on a codline. At first the albatross pretended not to notice. Then one, bolder than the rest, alighted about three feet from it and finally pecked at the bait; Sandell gave a sharp jerk and its beak was firmly wedged inside the triangle. As we hauled it in, the bird became completely submerged, its position marked by a long line of bubbles. The bubbles were too much for the crew, who began to roar with laughter, slapping one another on the back. I was afraid the albatross would drown.

We hauled it over the rail, held it upside down so that some of the water ran out of its lungs, and set it on deck. Like a swan, the poor creature was pathetic out of its element, rolling its black eyes reproachfully at us, and flapping its vast wings. We measured them: from tip to tip they were eleven feet – perhaps more for it was hard to extend them.

After we had posed the albatross for our cameras on the coaming of the after wheelhouse, the Second Mate carefully folded the wings and threw it back into the water. It floated, half-submerged, unable to fly. Its brief spell on deck seemed to have deprived it of its powers, and although it made tremendous efforts to rise, the suction of the water on the lower surfaces of its wings held it down. Soon we left it astern and the other birds clustered round it.

We caught another. It was the same size as the first, and just as full of salt water. The bird was shown to the hens and the effect was astonishing. With wild shrieks of fear they bolted from the henhouse and ran about the deck in a frenzy, one being so deeply affected that it flew right over the rail. There was nothing we could do to save her as she floated passively astern towards the waiting albatross two hundred yards away.

At two in the morning on 11 December, when we were in Latitude 39° South, Longitude 9° East in the South Atlantic, our watch was called on deck to square up the yards and sheet home the fore-and-aft sail on the port side. There was a new movement in the ship now: she was rocking slightly from stem to stern.

'Kom the Väst Vind,' said Tria as we ground away at the Jarvis winches. By noon that day the westerlies were blowing strongly, lumping the rollers up behind. This was a memorable day because we ran 293 miles, and Alvar dropped our dinner on the way from the galley.

On the 13th we crossed the longitude of the Cape of Good Hope and entered the Southern Indian Ocean in 40° 33' South Latitude. Whilst running eastward we edged south to 42° and finally to 43° 47'. Sometimes the West Wind blew strongly, sometimes we were nearly becalmed. Always the drift was carrying us eastwards, thirty to forty miles a day.

By five o'clock that evening *Moshulu* was sailing fifteen knots. The wind was on the quarter and there was a big sea running. When Sedelquist and I took over there were already two men at the wheel. (Sedelquist was helmsman and I was help wheel.)

'Going to be deefecult,' he said in an unusual access of friend-liness, as we stumbled out on deck, immense in our thick pilot coats, 'going to be von bastard.'

We took over from Hilbert and Hörglund, a wild-looking but capable team. Although it was quite cold with occasional squalls of hail, I noticed that their faces were glistening with perspiration in the light of the binnacle.

'Törn om,' said Sedelquist, as he stepped up beside Hilbert on the weather side.

'Törn om,' I echoed as I mounted the platform to leeward.

'Ostsydost,' said Hilbert and then more quietly as the Captain was close by, 'proper strongbody for vind, Kapten.'

The ship was a strongbody too, she was a fury, and as soon as we took over we both knew that it was going to be a fight to hold her.

Sedelquist was a first-class helmsman – very cool and calm and sure of himself. I too was on my mettle to give him all the help I could, not for reasons of prestige but because a mistake on a night like this might finish us all.

Being at the wheel was a remarkable sensation. It was as if the ship had wings. The seas were big, but they never caught up with her to drag at her and slow her down. Instead they bore her up and flung her forward.

Steering was very hard work; heaving on the spokes, at Sedelquist's direction, I was soon sweating. There was no time to speak, nor was it permitted. Only when I made 7 bells at half-past seven did Sedelquist shout out of the corner of his mouth:

'Oh you noh, Kryss Royal going in a meenit.'

The Captain, the First Mate and Tria were all on deck, the Captain constantly gazing aloft at the upper sails. At a quarter to eight with our trick nearly over, when I was congratulating myself that we had come through, we suddenly lost control of her and she began to run up into the wind.

'Kom on, kom on,' Sedelquist roared, but it was too late. Our combined strength was not enough to move the wheel.

Moshulu continued to shoot up, the yards began to swing, a big sea came over the waist, then another bigger still. There was a shout of 'Look out, man!' Then there was a great smashing sound as the Captain jumped at the after wheel and brought his whole weight upon it. Tria and the First Mate were on the other side. Spoke by spoke we fought the wheel while from above came an awful rumbling sound as the yards chafed and reared in their slings, until the ship's head began to point her course again.

The danger was past, but as the Captain turned away, pale and trembling, I heard him sob: 'Oh Christ.'

Suddenly I felt sick at the thought of what might have happened if she had broached-to.

'Oh Yesus,' muttered Sedelquist, his assurance gone, 'I tought the masts were coming down out of heem.'

The clock in the charthouse began to strike. Before it had finished, more than anxious to be gone, I had made eight bells, but the Mate was already blowing his whistle for all hands. The Captain had had enough, and before Sedelquist and I were relieved at the wheel the royals came in, all the higher fore-and-aft sails, and the mizzen course. It was now 8.30 p.m. Between four and eight *Moshulu* logged 63 miles, and the same distance again between eight and midnight.

CHAPTER FOURTEEN
'God Jul'

FOR many days we had been thinking of Christmas, which this year fell on a Sunday. There had been a good deal of grumbling about this in the fo'c'sle, but even Sedelquist, who knew his rights, and was always threatening to complain to the Finnish Consul over imaginary infringements, wasn't able to suggest any satisfactory plan for moving Christmas Day to the following Monday in order to get an extra day's holiday.

In the week before Christmas I was 'Backstern'* for the second time on the voyage. My job was to wash up for the twenty occupants of the three fo'c'sles whenever mine was a working watch. Kroner performed the same service when I was free. Besides being a romantic, Kroner was a great grumbler and every day he told me I had forgotten to dry the dishcloths in the galley. Every day I told him the same thing. Very often, on the occasions when we did remember to hang them over the range, they were knocked down by the coal-carrying party and trampled in the coal-dust. Kroner drew my washing-up water; I drew his.

To get sea-water for washing-up I tied a rope to a bucket, stood in the lee rigging of the foremast, and dropped it into the sea. Bäckmann had been the first person to do 'Backstern' in our watch and he had cast a new teak bucket into the sea on the evening of our spectacular dash into the Atlantic. With *Moshulu* running thirteen to fourteen knots it was lucky that he had not known how to attach the rope to the bucket in a seamanlike manner; if he had, the

* 'Backlagsman' – Mess man.

tremendous jerk when it fetched up at the end of a lot of slack would probably have pulled him over the side. As it was, the knot came undone and the bucket sank before the eyes of the First Mate and the Captain, who were interested spectators. I had been charged for a hammer. Bäckmarm was put down for a teak bucket.

With the water safely on deck my troubles were not over, for it still had to be heated over the galley fire, and if the 'Kock' didn't like you he would move it as far as possible from the hot part of the stove. Like all cooks he was subject to sudden glooms and rages. It was unfortunate that he had taken a dislike to Kroner, who had been rude to him about some bacon instead of keeping his mouth shut and throwing it over the side, but he had nothing against me. Thanks to the 'Kock's' misplaced malevolence, Kroner enjoyed a week of scalding and abundant water whilst I suffered lukewarm water one day, total loss on another, and on a third found a long sea-boot stocking stewing merrily away in a bucket topped with a yeasty-looking froth.

The washing-up basin was a kerosene can sawn in half, the sharp edges beaten down so that it looked like some revolting curio from an oriental bazaar. These were the days before detergents, and their place was taken by sand, with some rope-yarn as a scourer. The everyday work on the ship had already battered my hands beyond recognition so that they resembled bloodstained hooks; and now the salt water penetrated cuts and scratches, making them swell and split. There was a vivid and appropriate name for these sores which never seemed to heal.

It was an unspoken rule that the 'Backstern' washed up first in his own fo'c'sle in case he was called on deck by 'två vissel'. After the port side was finished, he washed up for the starboard watch. Then for the daymen amidships. Theirs was a gloomy hole, without ports and filled with stale cigarette smoke, its only natural illumination a skylight, rarely opened, shedding a permanent dusk into it. To one side was a tiny rectangular table piled high with the most ghastly debris of *après déjeuner*: islands of porridge; lakes of coffee in which cigarette ends were slowly sinking; great mounds of uneaten salt bacon; squashed putty-coloured fish-balls, and, in the tropics, almost phosphorescent herring. At other meals mountains of bones and a warm feral smell made the fo'c'sle more like a lair of wild beasts than a human habitation.

Kroner and I were nearly driven mad by the Finns. In cold weather most of them wore the same suits of long underwear for weeks at a time until, like Julian Pringle's suit at Wurzel's, it would have been quite easy to stand them up by themselves. But with plates they were as fastidious as old ladies. They would pick them up, sniff them, and if the light was bad, rush out on deck to inspect them more closely. A single drop of moisture would raise a storm of abuse.

'*Satan.*'

'*Djävala klackkuk!*'

In spite of these excessively high standards, 'Backstern' could be finished within the permitted time of fifty minutes if there were not too many model-makers and card-players cluttering the table in the free watch. They played an interminable sub-species of whist called 'Bismarck', slapping the cards down violently to intimidate their opponents and becoming very bad-tempered if interfered with by the 'Backstern'.

If the ship was rolling or driving hard close-hauled to the wind, the wash-basin might slither away across the table, bring up against the fiddle round the edge, and either decant its contents into the nearest bunk, which was very funny if some homicidal character like Karma was asleep within, or else shoot underneath. If it went in the bunk there would be a fight; if it went underneath it had to be bailed out with a cigarette tin which always yielded a harvest of things not originally in the basin at all. At first I preferred bailing, but now that I was growing stronger I preferred it to go in the bunk. Sometimes with 'tre vissel' to tack ship, brace the yards or take in sail, washing-up would never be finished, but interruptions of this sort were fairly rare.

On the Monday of Christmas week washing-up had been terrible. There was heavy rain and it had come on to blow hard. 'Like sonofabeetch, like *helvete*,' said Sandell as he came from the wheel. I was pressed for time as I had second look-out, which meant washing up three fo'c'sle in less than an hour. Kroner, the damn fool, had forgotten to put the drying-up cloths in the galley and there was only one tin of hot water instead of three. To make things worse the ship was heeling at such an angle that it was impossible to stand upright.

I tore the tail off a good shirt, wedged the kerosene can against the rim of the table, and put each wet irreplaceable piece of crockery in the locker as I washed it. When I finished I took them all out, dried them, and put them back piece by piece. Around me the bunks were full of men trying to sleep, but the ship was a pandemonium of noise, the wind roaring in the rigging, the footsteps of the Officer of the Watch thumping overhead, the wheel thudding and juddering, and the fo'c'sle itself filled with the squeaks and groans of stressed rivets. From the hold came a deep rumbling sound as though the ballast was shifting. I dropped a spoon and five angry heads appeared from behind little curtains and told me to 'Shot op.'

The same procedure went on in the squalor of the midship's fo'c'sle, but at least there was more room. The Sailmaker had moved off to his hammock in the sail-loft with his assistant, Essin, who slept at the feet of his master; 'Doonkey' slept with his engine in his own private Donkey house; only Jansson remained and he was at the wheel.

Eight bells sounded and still the knives had to be done. I agitated them in cold filthy sea-water, dried the whole lot in one movement on the shirt-tail, and hoped for the best. It was my 'utkik', the hour of lookout. I struggled into my oilskins, adjusting three deep sea lashings as I went – two on the sleeves to stop the water running up my arms, one round my middle and between the legs to prevent the coat from blowing over my head.

There was a fearful sunset. The ship was driving towards a wall of black storm cloud tinged with bright ochre where the sun touched it. About us was a wild, tumbling yellow sea. South of us two great concentric rainbows spanned the sky and dropped unbroken into the sea. At intervals everything was blotted out by squalls of rain and hailstones as big and hard as dried peas. It only needed a waterspout to complete the scene.

Soon I became clammy and forlorn, gazing into the murk. It was dark now and the rain was freezing in the squalls. Above the curve of the foresail everything was black, and from the rigging, right up the heights of the masts came the endless rushing of the wind. To warm my hands I pushed them into the pockets of my oilskin coat and found two deep cold puddles. In one of them was my last handkerchief.

After an hour of 'utkik' I in my turn became 'påpass'. During my spell on the foredeck there were 'två vissel'. Welcoming the opportunity to exercise my frozen limbs I flung open the fo'c'sle door and screamed, 'Two vistle, ut på däck' in the most hair-raising voice I could manage.

Inside, water was swirling pieces of newspaper and bread about the floor. It broke over Yonny Valker and Alvar, those primitive men sleeping down there, awash and shining like whales. The other five members of our watch were dozing perilously on the benches. Everyone was fully dressed in oilskins, too wet to get into their bunks. The oil-lamp was canting at an alarming angle and Bäckmann hit his head on it as he started up from the table. He didn't feel anything because he was still asleep. One by one the others lurched out of the fo'c'sle, and as they encountered the blast on deck they cursed the owner for owning *Moshulu*, the Captain for bringing us here, the Mate for blowing his 'vissel', and me for being 'påpass' and hearing it.

Little Taanila was at the wheel, clinging to it like a flea, while the Mate tried to prevent it spinning and hurling him over the top on to the deck.

'Två män till rors,' shouted the Mate, and Bäckmann went as help wheel to Taanila.

'Mesan,' said the Mate and we tailed on to the downhaul of the largest of the three fore-and-aft sails on the jigger mast. It jammed, but we continued to take the strain. Suddenly it broke and we rolled in a wet heap in the scuppers.

'That ploddy Gustav,' said Sedelquist, speaking unlovingly of the owner who was reputed to be very close with ropes. 'He vonts – '

By Friday the rain was wearing us all down. Breakfast was terrible. Black beans and fried salt bacon from the pickle cask. The margarine and sugar had both given out on Wednesday. We were ravenous and talked of nothing but food. But at noon Sandell reported that the hens had disappeared from the henhouse and that the Cook was making huge puddings. I saw them myself when I was fetching the washing-up water. They looked like sand castles. We were agog.

At last it was Saturday, December 24th, Christmas Eve. Christmas Eve was the principal Finnish celebration. It was our free watch in the morning and now came the opportunity for the great 'Vask' in the slimy little 'Vaskrum'; but the joy of putting on clean clothes was worth the discomfort. Even Yonny and Alvar had a 'Vask', and some of us whose beards had not been a success shaved. Then we put on our best clothes: clean dungarees, home-knitted jerseys, and new woollen caps. Bäckmann even put on a collar and tie. This was too much for the more rugged members of the watch, and a committee was formed to discuss the question. They were very serious about it and decided he was improperly dressed for the time and place. Nevertheless he continued to wear a tie, and presently I put one on myself, with a tennis shirt and flannel trousers with the mud of Devon lanes still on the turn-ups. It was wonderful to wear clothes that followed the contours of the body after so many weeks of damp, ill-fitting garments. In the splendour of our new robes we slept till noon. Then, except for wheel and look-out, work ceased for everyone.

Like the apprentices in *A Christmas Carol* preparing the warehouse for the party, we put the finishing touches to the fo'c'sle. Bäckmann washed the paint with hot water and green soap. I removed a large number of bugs from the bunkboards and drowned the eggs. Taanila scrubbed the floor; Hermansonn polished our door-knob, while the others removed horrid debris from the unoccupied bunks and shook all the blankets on deck. The floor and tables were washed with hot soda and burnished white with sand. Then we sat down and looked around at what we had done. It did seem more like home. It would need to for tonight to be a success. 'Like home,' said Sedelquist. 'Like hell.'

At half past one I threw the last lot of washing-up water over the side. My week of 'Backstern' was over for a whole month, and I was heartily sick of it. Cleaning the 'skit hus' was preferable. From three until four I was at the wheel. The wind was ENE. and the ship steered herself except for a slight touch from time to time. The afternoon was cold, the decks were deserted. Everyone was below having haircuts, shaving, trimming beards or squeezing pimples. Just before I was relieved the First Mate came on deck. A startling transformation had been effected in him. He was no longer grimy-looking; the ginger beard and moustaches that had given him so much the appearance of a Cheshire Cat had disappeared. Instead he was very stiff and self-conscious in a gold-braided reefer suit, his head bowed beneath an enormous peaked cap, also gold-braided, on which was pinned the white house badge, a white flag with G.E. in black letters on it. With dismay I realized that without the beard his was not the sort of face I cared for at all. Indecently bare, it was shorn of its strength. I think he realized this, for he giggled, almost apologetically. This moment marked the beginning of a certain coolness in our relationship.

'Coffee-time' brought the first fragments of a great avalanche of food. On Saturdays the bread was always different; today it arrived in the shape of scones. There were a great number, they were very good, and we ate the lot in seven minutes.

As the dinner hour approached the agony of waiting became almost unbearable. We roamed about the fo'c'sles like hungry lions. Outside, the rain beat down on the deck. The weather had broken up soon after five, but the wind blew steadily and we were all confident that there would be no work on deck unless it shifted. Otherwise the ship would carry topgallants and topmast staysails throughout the night. When it grew dark, at seven o'clock, 'tre vissel' summoned all hands. We crowded the well-deck. Looking on us was the Captain, all braid and smiles; the First and Second Mates, less braid and fewer smiles; and Tria, no braid but more smiles than all of them put together. I had never seen such splendid uniforms.

The Captain made a little speech. Addressing us as 'Pojkar' (Boys), he wished us 'God Jul' and told us to come aft to his saloon after dinner. When he had finished we tipped our caps to him, mumbled our thanks, and made a rush below. Two sheets were produced and spread on the table. We gathered all our lamps and lanterns and hung them round the bulkheads.

The food was brought in from the galley. Great steaming bowls of rice and meat; pastry, sardines, salmon, corned beef, apricots, things we had forgotten. A bottle of Akvavit and the set piece, a huge ginger pudding, its summit wreathed in steam.

There were maddening moments of delay while I took what proved to be a series of unsuccessful photographs. Then we made a dash for the table. From then on there were few sounds other than the smacking of eight pairs of lips and an occasional grunted request to pass a dish. We had been hungry for weeks and now our chance had come. After the traditional Finnish rice-porridge I worked through potato pastry, chopped fish, and methodically round the table to the ginger pudding, which was sublime, the zenith of the evening. Alvar, appointed wine steward, circled the table allowing us half a mug of Akvavit each, and the starboard watch, who had already eaten, came in in bunches to cry 'God Jul, Pojkar!'

When the others had given up, Sandell and I were still plugging on steadily. He turned to me, his face distorted by a great piece of pudding, a little rice gleaming in his black beard. 'To spik notting and eat, is bettair,' he said and carved himself a slice of Dutch cheese. We all loved one another now. Even Sedelquist offered me an old *Tatler* containing a photograph of The Duchess in Newmarket boots and raincoat at a very wet point-to-point.

'Oh, say you. I think he is fon in bed, yes?'

'No.'

I took a good look at The Duke gazing myopically over her shoulder before I remembered that Sedelquist always got his genders mixed.

Each of us had been given a green tin of Abdullah cigarettes. Shaped to fit the pocket, they held fifty; on the lid, in large letters, was inscribed 'Imperial Preference'. There were additional charms: each one contained a coloured picture of a girl in an inviting posture, more accessible than The Duchess. After dinner brisk business was done in exchanging one for another, and Sedelquist emerged with the best collection. Although I didn't really like cigarettes I smoked half-a-dozen in rapid succession in order not to miss anything.

From the midships fo'c'sle came the sound of a Christmas hymn being sung rather well in Swedish and we all went to listen. The singers were seated with their backs to the bulkhead near the Christmas tree which 'Doonkey' had made from teased-out rope yarns. There were five of them sharing three hymn books and they all sang with great earnestness. Among them were Kisstar the Carpenter, the light of the oil-lamp softening the deep lines on his face; Reino Hörglund with his great black beard; and Jansson, thick-lipped and tousled. Half of the fo'c'sle was in shadow and I stood in darkness by the huge trunk of the mainmast; next to me stood Yonny Valker, hands clasped before him like a peasant before a roadside altar. We were all very homesick.

At nine o'clock we queued up outside the Captain's stateroom to receive our Christmas presents from the Missions to Seamen. This was the first time I had seen the Officers' quarters, which seemed very warm and substantial compared with our own. From somewhere the almost legendary wireless was emitting dance music with the background of peculiar rushing and whining sounds that accompany music across great expanses of ocean. Whilst we waited in this unaccustomed place I noticed with envy the magnificence of the washing-up arrangements, the scullery with an elaborate draining-board, and the abundance of dry dishcloths. I thought then how easy it would be to provide something similar for the fo'c'sles, how much saving of time.

When it was my turn to enter the 'Great Hall' I felt very serflike and nervous, but my premonitions were soon dispersed.

Inside it was all red plush, banquettes, and brass rails, very like the old Café Royal. I almost expected to see Epstein instead of the smiling and very youthful-looking Captain seated at the mahogany table, his officers around him. He held out a hat to me, full of pieces of paper. The one I took was Number 7. 'Number 7 for England's Hope,' said the Captain, and the Steward who was kneeling on the floor surrounded by parcels handed me the one with 7 on it. I wished everybody 'God Jul' and backed out of the stateroom in fine feudal fashion, stepping heavily on the toes of the man behind me, and dashed eagerly back to the fo'c'sle to open it.

Inside the paper wrappings was a fine blue knitted scarf, a pair of grey mittens, and a pair of stout brown socks. When I picked up the scarf three bits of paper fell out. One of these was a Christmas card with 'Jultiden' in prominent red lettering on one side and on the other, in ink, 'och Gott Nytt År, onskar Aina Karlsson, Esplanadgarten 8, Mariehamn.' On the other two pieces was the text of St John, Chapter 20, in Finnish, and the good wishes of the Missions to Seamen who had sent the parcel. Right at the bottom was a hand mirror and comb.

I though of Aina Karlsson knitting woollies with loving care for unknown sailors in sailing ships. We all eagerly compared our presents. Some had thicker garments, some larger. Sedelquist said that the Mates had already appropriated the best, but no one paid any attention to this. Among us Taanila had the finest haul – a woollen helmet that pulled over head and ears with a long scarf attached. It made him look like a fiendish Finnish gnome.

In the midships fo'c'sle there were two miserable people, Essin and Pipinen. Essin, the Sailmaker's assistant, had broken one of his molars in the general struggle to eat everything within reach. He now lay groaning in his bunk, his face swathed in mufflers. I tried to plug the cavity with gutta-percha, which on the advice of my dentist I had brought with me in anticipation of such an emergency. It had looked easy in Wimpole Street when he demonstrated how to do it: he put a little vaseline on a plugger, heated the gutta-percha and popped it in the hole. Now, overcome with wine and food, in a swaying ship, by the murky light of a hurricane lamp I felt like a tipsy surgeon about to perform a major operation. Worse still, the patient kept flinching and I dropped a blob of bubbling hot gutta-percha on his tongue. He leapt into the air screaming and three boys had to hold him down while I tried to push a cooler piece into the hole. But it would not stay in, and I gave him an overdose of aspirin and hoped for the best. The operation had not been successful.

Pipinen, the other casualty, had cut his hand badly while opening a tin of apricots and Karma, the unpredictable Finn, was fixing it with fathoms of bandage. Hilbert told me that Karma would not cut the bandage because he had bought it for himself. When I left, Pipinen's hand was as big as a football and Karma still had yards left.

I went in search of my bunk. It was 9.45. By some miracle I was neither 'rorsman', 'utkik' nor 'påpass'. I crawled into my bag and slept dreamlessly until four in the morning, when a voice cried 'resa upp'; but Sandell closed the curtains and I slept on until half past seven. There were loud cheers when I woke. I had slept 'like sonofabeetch, like peeg in straw.' Ten hours – the longest sleep I ever had in *Moshulu*, or anywhere else. I was quite thrilled.

On Christmas morning the weather was cold and brilliant. Big following seas were charging up astern in endless succession. They surged beneath the ship, bearing her up, filling the air with whistling spray as their great heads tore out from under and ahead to leave her in a trough as black and polished as basalt except where, under the stern post, the angle of the rudder made the water bubble jade-green, as if from a spring. From the mizzen yardarm, where I hung festooned with photographic apparatus, I could see the whole midships of *Moshulu*. On the flying bridge main deck the Captain and the three Mates were being photographed by the Steward, solemn and black as crows in their best uniforms.

Rigid with cold I descended to eat Christmas dinner, for which the 'Kock' had made an extra sustaining fruit soup. For breakfast we had had Palethorpe's tinned sausages which were very well received; at 'Coffee-time' apple tarts and buns but not enough of either; and for supper, rice, pastry and jam. At four a.m. on what would have been Boxing Day in England we were setting royals once more. The party was over.

CHAPTER FIFTEEN

Into Battle

THAT night a squall hit the ship. There was a roar from the 'Kock' in the galley as the pots and pans went by the board. In our fo'c'sle everything slid downhill with a rush. Alvar's massive behind went clean through the panel of the cupboard and removed the whole thing from its hinges; a cup of hot tea upset over my hand. In pain I lifted it, knocking the glass out of the lantern. Everyone swore at me solidly for five minutes. On deck there were men at the wheel, including the Captain and Second Mate.

With the wind north-westerly the ship began to roll as she had never rolled before, thirty degrees to port, then thirty degrees to starboard. My cross-ships bunk became a purgatory: at one moment I would be standing on my feet, the next my legs would be in the air with the blood rushing to my head. At supper the table rose to meet us in a very disconcerting way. Potatoes, fruit soup and sugar rained about us, benches overturned, books and papers cascaded from our bunks and were ruined underfoot. Everyone settled down to enjoy the chaos except the unfortunate 'Backstern' who was having trouble washing-up. Just before midnight came an even more extravagant series of rolls. Both benches crashed in the darkness and seaboots, chests and buckets careered wildly about the floor. From the hold came a sound like an earthquake.

'Ballast going somewhere,' a voice observed. 'Very soon we are arse before, I tink.'

'Not before. Upwards.'

'Yo, upwards, dat's right.'

Tria and Sedelquist were sent into the hold with lanterns. They were gone a long time and we waited with gloomy foreboding. After about half-an-hour the rumbling ceased and they returned. The ballast was firm, they said. The noise had come from a number of barrels rolling about in the 'tween-decks.

With 3,000 miles to sail we ran the easting down towards Australia on the 43rd parallel of south latitude. Mostly, by day, when not employed working the ship, we were below chipping rust. By night the stars glinted with an unwinking frosty hardness and the ship was dwarfed by the immensity of the night sky. There were other days and nights when the sky seemed to close in on us and our world contracted. There would be squalls accompanied by cold driving rain that bit into the flesh, or violent bombardments of hail with the chips of ice piling against the coamings of the skylights in drifts. At such times the ship would become almost unmanageable, and the rain would drive in beneath the band of the brake on the wheel so that it failed to grip. At the height of one of these squalls, whilst helmsman, I lost control of the wheel. It began to spin furiously and seven spokes hit the point of my elbow before I managed to stop it. For some moments after the mishap I was so sick and faint that my feet would hardly support me, and I felt almost too apathetic to keep the ship on her course.

On December 30th, 74 days out, the wireless – in whose existence we had never really believed – suddenly became active and erupted with alarming news. Sails had it from the Captain, who was said to have listened in person, that Poland had invaded Czechoslovakia; war had broken out between Italy and France in Tunisia; and Chamberlain had flown to Rome. As it was known that the Captain did not possess a wireless and his solitary position as Master would prevent him from sitting in the Second cabin, he had presumably listened by applying his ear to the bulkhead as I had done when I had heard distant music in the fo'c'sle. Whatever method the Captain used, the part about Chamberlain was a remarkable piece of prescience that made it practically certain that the news was of Axis origin. I subsequently learnt that Chamberlain did not go to Rome for another eleven days. At that time only the Germans and Italians were able to order the movements of British elder statesmen so long in advance.

At first I accepted his flight to Rome quite literally and wondered whether he had taken refuge in the Quirinale, the Vatican or the Palazzo Venezia. I had to put up with a good deal of rather ill-natured chaff from various members of the crew who, in common with a good many Scandinavians at that time, were altogether too impressed with the totalitarian way of life. That we were not really very interested was shown when the news of the non-existent Tunisian war was being discussed in the starboard fo'c'sle. Mikelsonn, the good-humoured Danish apprentice, was asleep in his bunk when shouts of war woke him.

'A war,' he said in a voice full of relief. 'I thought you said *The War*,' and turned over and went back to sleep.

The last day of the year came, but inauspiciously, and to celebrate it I had an icily unpleasant 'Rundvask'. I was well covered with soap when the ship began yawing and rolling as if about to turn turtle, and my meagre supply of hot water was spilled, so that to obtain more I had to run the whole length of the foredeck, cursing the helmsman. But when it was my turn at the wheel I too found it possessed. At first the Captain was almost tolerant.

'Are you trying to tie the log in knots? Keep the course, man, Ostsydost.'

'Ostsydost it is, sir,' but it was only for a moment and then she was swinging again.

'Goddam it, man, keep the course. *Satan* and *Helvete*.' So, without humour he began; and went on repeating himself but with such variations that I listened with admiration in the intervals of struggling with the bloody wheel. All that evening squalls of gale force bore down on the ship. At eleven the glass fell rapidly and there was continuous lightning. All hands were called and I found myself with Kroner sent to furl the main upper topgallant. Going aloft was horrible, the atmosphere illuminated by the incandescent glare of electricity burning on the steel yards.

At the main top, playing for time and hoping that these phenomena would disperse, I clutched Kroner's jacket. Only after trying several times could I make myself heard above the din.

'What is it?' I shouted.

'St Elmo's fire. Götterbloodydämmerung. Nice, isn't it?'

'It's horrible.' Then as an afterthought I wished him a Happy New Year.

'Let's get on,' shouted Kroner. 'You can push 1939 right up.'

The sail was wild and untameable because someone had made up the gaskets in such a way that they could not be released. Holding the sail on the yard in a damp huge mass, we struggled to loose them while the masthead careered across the sky and the yard arms pointed at one moment into the sea and the next into the upper air. All around us the overcharged atmosphere crackled and hummed with electricity. At midnight our watch, while clewing-up the mainsail on deck, wished each other a Happy New Year.

'You noh,' said Sedelquist with more than usually happy inspiration, '1939 is going to be focking no good year.'

At dawn on the 4th January we were about 350 miles from Port Lincoln; a day-and-a-half – two days at the most, I thought. I was almost sad that the outward voyage was nearly done. By the afternoon we were becalmed and only the swell from the south set us on. We grumbled as we scrubbed the decks because the food was bad – breakfast had been salt pork and potatoes, dinner stockfish, and supper the night before salt pork and potatoes. Tempers were becoming short. First it was Kroner's vendetta with the 'Kock' that came to a head. Kroner began it, roaring 'Come out on deck, you bastard. Come out on deck and we'll settle it there.'

Nobody ever knew what it was all about, but the 'Kock' emitted an eldritch scream and in two shakes was out on the deck brandishing a cleaver. I thought that Hilbert was a friend of Kroner's so I asked him what the trouble was.

'Urrgh, that Kroner he is crazy, too much temper. If he fight that "Kock" he get somting he don' like . . .'

Then some of my own troubles came to a head. We were all

heartily sick of one another. Being an alien, and better still, English, I found myself becoming a kind of safety valve through which the port watch could give vent to their exasperation. Throughout our gruesome dinner, with the weather tropical, Taanila hissed:

'Focking boggert, focking boggert,' until I told him to shut up.

'Better *you* shot op,' said Hermansonn. 'You are rosbif boggert.'

While this conversation was going on Sedelquist had not been inactive. He had dropped a large piece of bread in my tea. Feeling very much alone and knowing the end was quite near I poured the whole mess into Sedelquist's mug. The effect was terrific. He leapt up roaring at me to remove it and at the same time aimed a powerful but inexpert blow at me, which I avoided. His fist hit a clothes hook on the inside of the door which split his knuckle open. Fortunately 'två vissel' sounded and we were called to the winches.

I felt very miserable and lonely amongst a foreign people. To jump overboard and swim away from *Moshulu* seemed the most desirable thing in the world. I knew now that I must fight someone. But who? I was slow to anger but if I didn't do something I ran the risk of being thought a coward.

The opportunity to be angry came sooner than I expected. After a tense and silent supper I turned to take a cigarette from the tin in my bunk. I opened the tin. The cigarettes were gone and had been replaced by a turd. The fo'c'sle was absolutely quiet now. I turned back to the table and decided rightly or wrongly that it must be Hermansonn. In front of me stood a large enamel bowl full of thick custard; Hermansonn was sitting down eyeing me hungrily; I stood up and poured the whole lot, about 5 or 6 pints, over his head and shoulders.

From the onlookers came a kind of roar, almost a cheer. Not for me but for the prospect of real trouble in tangible form. Then Hermansonn was over the table in a welter of plates. 'Ut, ut på däck,' came the next cry and we went out on the foredeck. Before he got his great arms round me I got in one good blow that smashed his nose. I didn't think he had ever been hit before from the way he halted and grunted, but in a second we were rolling on the deck, covered in his blood. Hermansonn could have won if he had not foolishly chosen to knee me between the legs. It was extremely painful and I saw red. All the humiliations that Hermansonn had subjected me to in the last months came to a head. Now I really wanted to smash him.

The whole crew were on deck yelling encouragement and I was gratified to hear someone yell for me. Eventually I did smash him, but it took a long ten minutes for there was a splendid monolithic quality about Hermansonn and once he got over his distaste for being hit he fought well. The end came when I laid him on the deck and alternately thumped his head on it and jabbed his face with my left fist. Then the voice of the Captain, icy and remote, cut down from somewhere above.

'That's enough. You've done enough. Stop it. Shake hands.'

The crowd dispersed. We both looked terrible but Hermansonn had lost a tooth, one eye was closed, and the other was bleeding. I had cut my left knuckle to the bone on one of his teeth and I still felt sick from the kick. We shook hands.

'You know,' said Sandell as I sat on the hatch cover licking my wounds, 'it wasn't Hermansonn.'

'Who was it then?'

'Alvar.'

'I'll bloody well . . .'

'Lissun,' said Sandell, 'don't you start anything more. You will be all right now.'

He left me. Night was coming on. The watches mustered. While we were being counted, Taanila whispered, 'Now, *you*, strongbody.'

'And you're still a horrible little Finnish bastard.'

'Orlright,' called the Mate. 'Lösa av ror, utkik på bracken, in frivakt.'

Suddenly I was very tired. There seemed too little room for Hermansonn and me in the fo'c'sle, so I lay down on the canvas of the hatch cover and fell happily asleep where I was.

CHAPTER SIXTEEN

Cape Catastrophe

THE next morning I was cleaning the brass outside the Captain's cabin with caustic soda. Suddenly he appeared.

'You spill any of that dam stuff,' he said, 'and I'll fix you like Hermansonn.'

The afternoon of that day was like a furnace – from noon to noon we had made only 59 miles. The ship was practically becalmed, the sails hung limply. Only a few albatross followed us, but these were magnificent and bold, floating at times almost at arm's length.

In the ship there was every sign of approaching landfall. While the carpenter oiled the anchor windlass, teak rails and companion ways were being scraped. Aloft three boys in bosun's chairs were washing down the masts. Suddenly the irritated voice of the Captain cut across the creaking of blocks and the slatting of sails. Someone had failed to wash the spreaders of the cross-trees . . .

While cleaning brass, I gazed at Hermansonn's disfigurements, only now blossoming. Every time I looked at them I felt a guilty pride, like an artist who has created something. I was only sorry I had picked the wrong man, but Hermansonn was as good as anyone. Later I made my peace with Hermansonn, who extended a powerful hand and grasped my own.

'No more trobble is bettair,' he said magnanimously, and was as good as his word for he never bore me any ill-will.

At 4 am on January 7th we sighted Cape Catastrophe at the western side of Spencer's Gulf. There was much joy and we all thought we should be in Port Lincoln by midday. But there was only a narrow pass between the Cape and Neptune Island to the east of it, and the wind was 2 to 3 knots straight from the entrance. By 8 o'clock we were close enough to the land to dislike the look of it. For miles the cliffs rose in bulwarks to the west.

In our first attempt to weather the Cape we landed far too leeward. All day under a molten sky with the temperature in the hundreds, we hauled and wound at the braces, tacked ship and made long slow beats to the south of it. Most inopportunely, the decks had just been oiled with linseed and as we worked we skidded and sizzled on them like frying fish. So we continued all through the day and far into the night, the sails slatting and banging, everyone covered with oil and very sleepy, while the light on the South Neptunes flashed away mockingly at us – two flashes every six seconds, then a third at twenty seconds – now to port, now to starboard, depending on which tack we were.

At seven am on January 8th we were still 26 miles from Port Lincoln, but now we were coming in, the ship flying along in brilliant weather with, overhead, a few windswept clouds in a deep blue sky. Soon, as the sun grew hotter, the South Neptunes were abeam, shimmering like jellies in the heat, with the bare iron light tower looming on the largest of them. To starboard a loaded cargo ship was running out of the Gulf and passed us heading south eastwards. We were among a great number of islands all shrouded in a haze of heat and at ten we passed Middle Island, a brown, desolate volcanic rock capped with yellow scrub. Low-lying, without beaches, it dipped straight into the sea and the rollers setting in on it broke in white columns on the south face.

To port was Thistle Island, all rock with a few bushes or what might have been small parched trees growing on it. From the low point the island rose in great terraces to the north-west, six or seven hundred feet high, while on the east side, which came into sight at this moment, a steep cliff swept down to a long golden beach on which the sea rolled white. As we rounded the island we took in the jigger topmast staysail, the gaff topsail and the upper spanker. All about the ship numbers of white birds with grey wings and delicate tail feathers fluttered aimlessly. Timid at first, some of them plucked up courage and perched on the bowsprit. When we took in the headsails, they rose, uttering queer broken sounds like the hinges of a rusty door.

Moshulu drove up the Gulf making only 6 knots but seeming to fly as we came in past a sandy rock with a light set on it. At two we squared the yards and ran before the wind, and as we clewed-up the royals and topgallants we could see ahead of us a four-masted barque at anchor. The Captain, on deck in topee, white shirt and blue trousers, had his glass directed at her. It was *Passat*.

As we closed with her and ran in to anchor, we took in the remaining fore-and-aft sail except the fore topmast staysail and the spanker; then the fore, main and mizzen course sails and finally the fore and mizzen topsails, so that *Moshulu* came in towards *Passat* in fine style under upper and lower main topsails, fore staysail and spanker, still with plenty of way on.

We were under command of the Second Mate now, the First was on the fo'c'sle head standing by for the Captain's order to drop the anchor, which two days previously we had hoisted outboard with the crane and shackled to the cable at the hawse-pipe.

The Captain gave the order 'Ned med rodret!' and Sandell at the wheel put the helm down smartly, the foretopmast staysail halliard was cast off its pin and we manned the downhaul joyfully, stamping the length of the well-deck as it shrilled down the stay. At the same time the spanker, the only fore-and-aft sail now set, was hauled to windward to help swing the ship into the eye of the wind. As *Moshulu* came up, the maintopsails came aback, the wind pressing them against the mast so that she lost way and was gradually forced astern.

'Låt gå babords ankaret!' shouted the Captain in his loudest voice; the Mate hit the pin securing the chain stop, there was a tremendous roar as the port anchor crashed into the water and the cable surged up out of the chain lockers over the windlass, where the Carpenter stood at the compressors checking its run, and through the hawse-pipes, covering our washing in clouds of bright red dust. As *Moshulu* went astern under the influence of the backed topsails, the anchor flukes began to bite. At every fifteen fathoms of chain (90 feet) there was a shackle. When four shackles had run out, the Mate signalled that it was enough, and the Carpenter applied all his great strength to the compressors. We were at anchor. It was three o'clock on Sunday, January 8th, 1939, the eighty-second day of the voyage, and we had sailed fifteen thousand sea miles.

'Orlright, bräck bukgårdingarna på kryss övre märs,' said the Second Mate, slacking away on the halliard lowering the yard as we broke the stops on the upper topsail buntlines and began to haul away. 'Hor avay . . . ee or, ee or . . . vast.'

Now we took the clewlines. 'Tag i gigtåget. Hor avay ee or . . . ooh er . . . vast gigtåget.'

After the övre märs the lower topsail: 'Undre märs gårdingarna . . . gigtåget . . . orlright, two blocks'; bunts and clews were well snugged up to the yard. 'Upp och göra fast, harbour stow.' With the two topsails in, we raced aloft to make an especially good stow of eighteen square sails and thirteen staysails and fore-and-afters, anxious to make a good impression on *Passat*'s crew, who were no doubt watching us critically. *Passat* lay half a mile astern of us. She was still in ballast, and her hull was streaked with rust, except where square patches showed that the crew had been over the side chipping and red-leading. Like *Moshulu* she flew the Finnish Merchant Flag from the upper gaff. Superficially she might have been *Moshulu*'s twin, a four-masted barque with the short poop, raised midships deck and double gaff of a typical nitrate carrier. More discerning, we noticed the netting under the bowsprit; the poop deck longer than *Moshulu*'s, and a certain indefinable difference aloft due perhaps to more taper in the yards or greater rake to the masts.

The afternoon was wonderful, with the south wind whipping up tiny waves on the surface of the water and the land dancing in the heat. As we worked we watched with envy a small boat with a lugsail detach itself from *Passat* and skim in towards the land, finally disappearing behind what looked like a long tongue of sand. We thought of food and drink and girls, but most of all, news from home. Of Port Lincoln, our supposed destination, there

173

was no sign. We were cut off from sight of it by a large island covered with sun-bleached yellow grass and desolate spiky trees plastered across the landscape.

At the back of the sandy strip where *Passat*'s boat had disappeared from view rose the parched hills above Port Lincoln, with here and there a galvanized iron roof flashing in the sun. All around us in the shimmering sea were islands, mostly mere rocks, parched and yellow. To the south-east Cape Donington, part of the mainland of the Eyre Peninsula, showed twin peaks. On the northern one was a monument to Flinders, who had first surveyed the region.

For some time we gazed from aloft on this inhospitable lunar landscape, without speaking. In contrast with the brilliant sea the land was sterile, dead.

Finally Kroner shouted across to me from the fore upper topsail yard:

'Nice, isn't it?'

'Bloody.'

'Like Aden.'

'Why Aden?'

'Nothing but sodomy and sand.'

'Ah.'

'Iss not sand,' said Hilbert severely, 'iss grass.'

I asked him what the large island was spoiling the view of Port Lincoln astern.

'Boston Island.'

'Anyone live there?'

'Rabbits and flies.'

'Where's Port Lincoln?'

'Inside, eight miles,' said Hilbert. 'And lissun, nothing for you to be excited about. If we get orders for Port Victoria we don' go to Port Lincoln. If we get no money we don' go. If it blows we sail. If it don' blow we row. Orlright?'

'Orlright,' I said.

'Zen not so much spikking and some more horry op.'

'Orlright, Hilbert.'

Hilbert was right about the flies. The moment we were anchored we were boarded by hordes of them and, far worse, great hairy indestructible bluebottles with shiny wings which took up residence forward and were soon buzzing self-consciously to and from the unprotected food in the fo'c'sle like extras in a film about camp hygiene.

✠

When it grew dark we began to speak with Passat, signalling with an electric torch. We found that Moshulu had done well, but not sufficiently well to beat the Pommern which had come out in 78 days under Captain Broman, leaving Belfast on September 24th and arriving on December 11th at Port Victoria. Three ships arrived on Christmas Eve – Viking and Passat in 87 and 91 days from Copenhagen, and Pamir in 91 days from Gothenburg.

After gaining this information we slept undisturbed by wheels and look-outs. For half an hour I remained awake while around me on top of the pigstyes, on the hatches, anywhere a mattress could be spread, lay the sleeping figures of the crew. Occasionally one of them would emit a deep sigh, another would cry out and then there would be silence once more, broken only by the light footsteps of Taanila, the anchor watchman, as he wandered along the flying bridge, watching the first part of the night through. Strange how still the ship was, the yards so naked against a sky from which the stars looked down, blurred and remote. A week ago in 40° South they had shone with a cold intensity.

CHAPTER SEVENTEEN
Port 'Veek'

WE woke with the feeling that the holidays had begun. We were far grubbier than any schoolboys and there was no holiday, but the land was near and the scent of trees and bushes came to us and filled us with expectation. At eight o'clock a white yawl, under power and with sails set, came puffing round the point of Boston Island. There was great excitement on board *Moshulu*, and 'Doonkey' rushed off to his 'hus' to put brilliantine on his hair, while the rest of us, thinking that the Customs were arriving, hid our contraband, which amounted to not more than a packet of cigarettes apiece.

The yawl was piled high with lobster pots. On board there were three wild-looking men wearing wide-brimmed hats so roughly made they might have been hacked out with a chopper. Rolling a little, the yawl circled the ship, the men eyeing us silently. Perhaps these were Kroner's sodomites. I turned to ask him but just then the Sailmaker hailed them in Swedish, to which they replied in the same tongue with a strong Australian flavour.

'Ugh,' said Kroner in disgust, ' – squareheads, you can't even get away from them here.'

'Tell those buggers on shore to hurry up,' yelled the Captain as they went on their way.

'Now you know why the Kapten don' pay,' said Hilbert. 'Dose men came out of a sailing ship and never went back. If we run Kapten pays fine to the Aussies. That's why no money.'

It never ceased to surprise me that any of us should expect any pay at all. Ordinary seamen received about 450 Fin-Marks a month (£2), able seamen 100 marks more. The Sailmaker, in a vessel like *Moshulu*, would receive a little over £6; the Captain about £20. The wages of an apprentice were 100 marks, 10 shillings a month, and I was already paying for the hammer and packets of cigarettes bought from the Captain's slop chest. Bäckmann was paying for the bucket he had lost. Some of the others, like Kroner, smoked like chimneys and were constantly visiting the Captain when he opened his shop. I began to wonder whether I should ever receive anything.

All that first day at anchor I polished brass with Vytautas Bagdanavicius, my spirits diminishing with his own, which always sank lower as he approached dry land. I had liked Vytautas from the start. I found amusing the way he flapped his hand crying ''Evening,' in the cold dawn. I liked his face when he smiled, an incredibly ugly face with a nose squashed on to it that wrinkled when he grinned. His favourite expression was 'Yerss, not so fine', when confronted by some crushing misfortune. It had been his first remark when he had fallen off the roof of the 'Doonkey Hus' and broken his arm.

Vytautas had not seen his native Lithuania for two years. In Belfast, apart from occasional porter-drinking with Kroner and myself, he had gone ashore hardly at all. Once he had gone to the Zoo and it had poured with rain; another time to a famous hill outside the city where the view was completely shrouded in mist; and he had gone twice to Woolworth's, where people had turned at this visitor from the Baltic padding down the aisles in his shiny brown leather coat, black beret perched on dark crinkly hair, in search of galvanized pails.

Moshulu had not been built to impress passengers, and superficially there seemed to be very little brass. But when we started to polish it we found there was a great deal. There were brass ports in the fo'c'sle, the galley, the poop, the Captain's saloon, the charthouse; there were dead-lights, with brass rims in the six sky-lights amidships, and brass hinges everywhere. The double wheel was plastered with brass. There were two bells, two binnacles, rails on companion ladders, and two monstrous domed light-houses – of copper, not brass, but like all the rest of it, bright green and needing polish. As the day wore on the job became tiresome and Vytautas began to play the war game, demonstrating with polish pots for Greeks and grubby pieces of paper for Persians how Marathon had been won, using a skylight for the field.

'You can polish all bloddy night. I don' care one fock,' said the First Mate, 'but finish you vill.'

At midday *Lawhill* arrived, 85 days from Copenhagen – a splendid passage for such an old ship. This was the first barque I had seen under sail. No sailing ship looks her best in ballast: *Lawhill*, cut down to topgallants for economy by some previous owner and with a curious rake aloft due to the topgallant masts being stepped abaft the topmasts, was not a pretty sight. Nevertheless she always made a good profit for Erikson because she rarely sustained any damage.

Captain Lindvall of *Passat* came aboard. He brought with him a sackful of rabbits killed with stones on Neptune Island that morning and also some depressing news.

He opened the sack first and tipped the rabbits out on the deck, but they were already stinking and had to be thrown overboard. Later we heard the news second-hand from the Mates. There were no freights and we might have to wait months. The steamers had been in before us and loaded. There were three alongside the jetty at Port Lincoln at the moment, two British and a Norwegian. For the rest the farmers were holding on to the crop, waiting for the prices to rise. Not one Erikson ship had a freight. *Pommern* at Port Victoria might have to wait six weeks for a chance. At Wallaroo, higher up the Gulf, *Abraham Rydberg* had been offered the sensationally low freight of 14s a ton. This had had to be refused, nobody could take it, not even Gustav Erikson. The lowest freight he had ever accepted was 16s 6d, and then he barely covered his expenses. Fourteen shillings, and in 1938 *Moshulu* had loaded nearly 5,000 tons at 41s 3d a ton. All this because Canada, the Argentine and, surprisingly, Britain had had record harvests.

The Harbour Master and the Doctor finally appeared on Tuesday. They greeted the Captain as an old friend and immediately went below to transact their business in a more congenial fashion, leaving a stack of letters for us over which we fought like wolves. There was none for me and none for Vytautas.

'No letters, Vytautas.'

'Yerss, not so fine.'

After a long interval, the authorities returned on deck, where the Doctor, a dark, emaciated, sinister man, wearing an immense collar like Dr Schacht, carried out a ritual medical inspection by walking rapidly down the line of boys.

'Twenty, aren't there?' he rasped, preparing to go over the side, and twenty boys hung jealously over the rail watching the launch chug away from us, carrying the Harbour Master, Doctor, and our Captain now rigged in his best blue suit.

For two days we did not see him. He was rumoured to be beating it up with Söderlund of *Lawhill*, Lindvall of *Passat* and the Captain of an English cargo ship who was later taken ashore with delirium tremens. But it was all rumour that could only have been brought by the birds, as nothing else visited us.

Almost a week passed before we were allowed ashore. Earlier we had been ordered to launch the gig, which had raised hopes that we might be going after all. Whilst three of us stood in the boat fending her off the ship's side the rest lowered away on the falls until she took the water and was moored astern under the great overhanging counter. I was wondering how we should regain the deck when the end of a long rope came whistling down. I saw the Second Mate leering at me over the taffrail in a challenging way.

'A bowline for Newby,' I heard him say in a voice that everyone could hear. Above me was a row of faces happy in the anticipation of failure, but my honour was at stake so I went up the rope like a monkey and hopped over the taffrail feeling like an advertisement for before and after – 'before taking your pills I had to be hauled aloft in a bowline.' It was the sort of thing that Leopold might have been repeating to himself at this moment before trying it out on the Manager of the Copy Writing Department.

'I am happy for you,' said the Second Mate. 'Now you can go op the rigging and make me happier still.'

'Aren't we going ashore?'

'No. Op the rigging.'

He kept me there all day cutting loose the accumulation of rope yarns and small stuff used to stop the buntlines at the blocks. A terrible off-shore wind was blowing, hotter than the hottest hair dryer. The higher I went the hotter it became. The wind, which was pouring down from the great deserts of the interior, made my lips crack and drew all the moisture out of my body so that I gasped for air like a newly landed fish. Worst of all, it brought with it hordes of horse-flies, sandy-coloured brutes that settled in swarms on the freshly varnished charthouse. By one o'clock the temperature had risen to 114° in the shade and the Mate's radio announced that it had never been hotter in South Australia. At dinner-time we tottered below to go through the motions of eating hot stew, but no one was hungry and we took refuge under the fo'c'sle table or anywhere it seemed slightly cooler.

At two o'clock the wind was so strong that *Moshulu* began to drag her anchor at five knots and was being driven down on to *Lawhill* and *Passat*, who had already dropped their second anchors. Putting my hand on one of the links of the anchor cable by the windlass I could feel the anchor jolting over the bottom. Hastily summoned, the First Mate came rushing along the flying bridge brandishing his maul and let go the starboard anchor with forty fathoms of cable. This held her, but we were now astern of *Lawhill*, a mile south of our original anchorage.

As this uncomfortable week wore on the wildest rumours prevailed. Erikson was said to be selling *Archibald Russell* and *Viking*, the first to Britain, the second to Holland. The rest of the ships were to remain at anchorage in the Gulf, await the next harvest in December, 1939, and sail back with it in 1940. Other versions had it that we were to be repatriated, or else sold like slaves with the ship to another owner. Meanwhile we grumbled, sweated, and dreamed of fresh food and cold beer, not daring to swim in a sea reputedly so full of sharks that an American writer of cowboy stories had come to Port Lincoln with a rod and line expressly to catch the world's largest.

At last Saturday came. Shaved and clean, we filled the gig. As we had feared, the Captain had not paid us. Later, when the war came, I was made to read an Army Training Memorandum. It was called *Care of Men*. By War office standards, our Captain was a deplorable officer, never wanting to see our feet or asking impertinent questions about our private lives. The compilers of the manual might have been surprised to learn that we regarded him with pure envy and a certain amount of affection.

For some time I had nursed a secret feeling of independence of the Captain, as I had managed to keep twelve English shillings for my first night on shore. I had given a lot of thought to the best way of spending it. It was not much, but enough for a bath, a bed with clean sheets, and a meal. Now, at the moment of departure, they were not to be found. In despair I rummaged the Vuitton, but without success, all the while harbouring unjustifiable suspicions of my companions. (When I finally reached England, I found the money in the lining at the bottom of the trunk.) The boat was waiting aft, and impatient cries from the poop warned me that I was in danger of being left behind. I could have wept. I dropped into the boat with 6*d* and a rusty knife which I had some idea of selling as a curio. I soon found that most of the others had some little nest egg, two or three shillings at the most, but no more. Even the First Mate had only three shillings – I remember because I tried to borrow something from him. To make all perfect there was no wind and the lugsail hung lifeless. We took it in to row the eight hard miles to the shore. It took about three hours.

I stood on the long wooden jetty at Port Lincoln where the windjammers came alongside to load, wondering what to do. I decided to find a suitable piece of ground to sleep on when I was spoken to by a long, thin Australian a year or two older than myself, wearing an American style hat on the back of his head and gold spectacles on his nose.

'Hello, my name's Jack. You're a Pommie, aren't you?' he said.

'What's a Pommie?' I asked warily, remembering my father's warnings about undesirable contacts.

'English are Pommies. You're English.'

'How did you guess?'

'You can tell 'em any place,' he said, 'by the way they look as if they own the place but don't want it.'

This, I thought to myself, serves me right. He means that I look snooty and British whereas all I'm tying to do is to look independent when I don't feel it. Australians sound terrible to us and we both look and sound terrible to them.

Jack was on the jetty to meet an American and an Englishman from *Passat* with whom he was friendly. At that moment *Passat*'s lifeboat arrived and disgorged more boys, among them Jack's friends, Eddy and 'Sweetheart'. Eddy was just twenty and full of charm and enthusiasm. After leaving Hotchkiss he had gone to Yale but was soon expelled because of his lack of application. *Passat*'s fo'c'sle seemed a strange destination for someone who had been sent down for indolence, but Eddy seemed happy enough.

'Sweetheart', whose nickname seemed inappropriate, was a determined character from Leeds, who wanted to jump the ship and take up fishing like the three Swedes in the yawl we had seen on the day we arrived. Both were mad with hunger and learning that I was broke they bore me off to a café where they ordered an extraordinary meal: cheese, scores of pickled onions, apple pie, and toast, washed down with pints of milk. (I had developed a fixation on toast which took some time to exorcise.) Jack, more civilized and squeamish than the rest of us, looked on in horror.

When we had eaten, the problem of my penury was discussed. Eddy, who had great experience in extracting money from parents, told me to cable.

'Send a collect cable. That'll move 'em!'

'I'll stand security,' said Jack. 'And in case you don't know, you're staying at our place tonight.'

In a far happier frame of mind, I drafted a cable saying that I was alive and penniless, and after finding that there was still no mail at the Post Office, sent it off with the feeling of a submarine commander loosing a torpedo at an unarmed merchantman.

We followed Jack into the dark recesses at the back of a chemist's shop on the main street facing the sea. Here he ran a developing and printing service, and in this small back room he showed us a great collection of sailing ship photographs. Every sailing ship sailor who came to Port Lincoln brought his films to Jack, who developed them and made copies of the best negatives for himself.

There seemed so little time and so much to do. It was decided that we should try to get drunk, still an exciting possibility at nineteen, but the pubs shut at six in the evening and it was now five o'clock. As we entered each bar through swing doors which showed the bottom half of the body, reminding me of a Paris street convenience and Eddy of saloons in the Far West (which neither of us had ever seen), the professional ladies of the town eyed us unlovingly, for it was the height of the holiday season. Each bar was crammed to bursting and our arrival and known pennilessness provided yet more obstacles to legitimate business.

More exciting was a hall we visited where a dance was in progress. I found the sight of so many girls terrifying and fascinating. They looked so clean and their lips seemed very red, but they eyed us with such refined hauteur that the swashbuckling air we thought proper to sailors ashore deserted us and we hung about oafishly near the entrance.

We went to a cinema of which I remember nothing except that it was called a bioscope, and afterwards when Eddy and 'Sweetheart' went off to a hotel on the other side of the town where they were quite sure not to meet any of their shipmates, I went back with Jack to his bungalow, where, although it was extremely late, his mother stuffed me with Christmas cake and coffee. Then she made me a bed on the floor and left me with the *Tatler* and *Bystander*, which seemed to follow me wherever I went.

On Sunday morning I woke at ten o'clock to hear rain drumming on the corrugated iron roof, the first they'd had for four months. I lay in bed gazing lazily at the ceiling thinking how wonderful it was to be undisturbed.

After a large breakfast at which I was once again able to indulge my morbid craving for toast, I ploughed through the rain to the Post Office with Jack. Officially it was shut, but I found a back entrance and stormed into the sorting-room bellowing for letters.

A man with a hatchet face and steel-rimmed spectacles screeched: 'Yes, four for you and there's one for a joker with a name like the wind whistling in a barmaid's fanny. For Chris' sake take it away and put me out of his misery.'

Taking my four letters and the one for Vytautas, and thinking how refreshingly different the Australian Civil Service seemed to our own, I sat down in a puddle on the steps of the Post Office and read them. There were two from my parents, one from Mountstewart, and one from Leopold.

The letters from my father had been written on several different occasions, and were highly characteristic. The first one had been written in October, at the time of Munich, and was addressed to me at Belfast. Happily for my peace of mind, it had not arrived.

'We shall have to do something about Air Raid Precautions at home as it is being pressed upon us,' he wrote. 'We have thought of turning the Hall into our Chamber and scaling up some of the cracks under the doors and windows to keep out gas, if any. We have been told that if war comes we shall have to carry our gas masks with us in case of sudden alarums. Nevertheless we do not intend to allow ourselves to be Unnecessarily Inconvenienced' (this with a hint of menace). 'We shall take every reasonable precaution, so please do not worry. It is perhaps just as well that you signed on for the Sea.'

He also mentioned the literary scene and wrote in his inimitable manner the epitaph of a best seller.

'Your Mother has been reading an American Work of Fiction called *Gone with the Wind*. It is rather a long book.'

Some time later he wrote: 'The Old Country (England) is becoming stronger every day and we shall, I think, soon be able to tell Herr Hitler and his crew to go to the Devil for whom they are apparently working. There will be Work for Strong Men to do' (this was written very prominently, for my benefit, I imagine) 'and they will confound the Prophets and Soothsayers who are always with us.'

At the end of January he continued drily: 'Herr Hitler now says that he has no particular grievance involving war so the Stock Markets are rising.' At this point I could almost hear his snort of disgust. 'I have sent you a little money,' he went on, 'but as the pound is worth 20% less in Australia, you may find yourself short. Perhaps you will be able to contrive something,' he concluded mysteriously, and enclosed a cutting about New Zealand sailors arriving penniless in England. I read the article carefully but was unable to derive much comfort from it as the New Zealanders had apparently not been able to contrive anything at all.

Rashly, before sailing, I had told him about the Man with the Syringe, and he wrote indignantly:

'The fellow with venereal disease must be a rotten blighter. I should complain to the Captain about him.'

It was plain that this was worrying him a good deal more than Hitler or Air Raid Precautions, and in the second letter written on Overseas Club notepaper he returned to the subject: 'Keep clear of his rags and drinking vessels and do not touch anything of his whatever. Buy some permanganate of potash to mix with drinking-water.' After several more paragraphs on general hygiene, the letter wound up more surprisingly. 'I am writing this on Club notepaper as it will serve as a useful introduction to any members you may encounter in your travels.'

Leopold's letter was written in a mood of high fantasy and was so peppered with italics that it resembled a letter from Queen Victoria in an impossibly frivolous mood. It bore no other resemblance to Royal correspondence, being written in an early English uncial hand on twenty-seven sheets of toilet paper on which the makers had printed rhymed quatrains at intervals, so that, while puzzling over Leopold's calligraphy and the convolutions of his imagination, I would come up against little pieces of verse such as:

> Mary, Mary, quite contrary,
> How are your tonsils today?
> If they're feeling sore you can't do more
> Than give them an Izal spray.

'My dear boy,' wrote Leopold, 'your life must be *HELL*. Here too we are having a *STORMY PASSAGE*. You will be pleased to know that we made the run up on the Central London Line in thirty-two and a half minutes *AGAINST THE WIND*. We lost one of the tail lamps in the tunnel and had to put in to Wood Lane for repairs. You can imagine how repressed we all felt after having been so completely in the dark for such a long time. I have been helping my grandmother (*A VERY LOVELY PERSON*) lay out rubber sheets in the garden under which we propose to *SKULK* when mustard gas falls. Julian Pringle joined the A.R.P. in October but they put him in charge of a macabre warehouse full of *SHROUDS* so he has applied for a commission in the Rifle Brigade because, he says, the buttons match his spectacle frames perfectly.'

The boats were reported to be sailing at half past three, but it was an hour before the crews began to arrive, making the afternoon hideous. 'Doonkey' and *Passat*'s Cook came rolling up the jetty like moving wine-bins with whisky, brandy and wine bottles protruding from their pockets. As they came, they sang a song in Finnish of hair-raising obscenity, which began promisingly:

> When Rewick's wedding was celebrated
> An accordion was played
> And lips were lubricated
> With three star brandy . . .

But it was the wine not the brandy which had been everyone's downfall. The inhabitants called it 'plonk' and our people

'ploonk'. It cost 2*s* 6*d* a bottle. On my way to the jetty I had met
Kroner and Sedelquist sitting almost naked in an open boat on the
beach. When it began to rain they had upturned it, and with the
aid of rum and 'ploonk', which they had obtained from thin air as
mysteriously as Buchmanites gather funds, had passed the night
underneath it in drunken happiness. When I met them they were
drying their clothes in the wind.

'Oh you noh,' said Sedelquist, 'here the vimmen are stronk,
like Kangaroos.'

'A fat lot of women we've seen,' said Kroner, and then to me:
'Where are you going?'

'Back to the ship.'

'You'd better not say you've seen us.'

I promised.

'I don't think that I could stand a sea voyage after this
"ploonk",' said Kroner.

Drinking 'ploonk', wearing hats that were not theirs, the souvenirs of their adventures, the crews reeled up the jetty. *Passat*'s
people were in a far worse condition than *Moshulu*'s who, penniless, had had to be content with simpler pleasures and, like
myself, live on charity.

The wind was now blowing hard, straight into the bay, and
there was a whip-round to pay a local man to tow the three boats
– *Passat*'s steel lifeboat, *Lawhill*'s boat and *Moshulu*'s leaky gig
– out beyond Boston Island to the anchorage. In our gig there
were five first voyagers, including a stray from *Passat*. Astern of
us in *Passat*'s boat was an unimaginably dissipated crew, and I
had a last glimpse of Eddy and 'Sweetheart' as they threw me
mock kisses of farewell before being submerged in a welter of
bodies.

The tow out was a nightmare. Nothing that the unfortunate
Australian did was considered right. From time to time great
drunken Finns would swarm across the intervening tow-ropes,
board his motor-boat, and threaten to beat him up. The Australian
became nervous and rightly refused to take us any farther. By this
time we were more than four miles out, the sea was white and

running heavily, and *Lawhill*'s boat and our gig began to take water on board, so that we had to bail furiously. The stage seemed set for a spectacular disaster. To avert it, he cast us adrift and turned back towards the land.

The occupants of the two other boats reefed their lugsails and sheered away from us to windward. Our gig was too frail and the sail had long ago lost any reef points it might have possessed originally. In a heavy following sea we manned the oars and steered rather than rowed a mile down wind until we reached a small island, really no more than a scrub-covered rock, and turning into the wind's eye, we beached the boat on the leeward side, where the shore was solid corrugated rock.

The island rose fifteen feet above the level of the sea and was about fifty yards wide. It was completely lacking in amenity; there was no water and no shelter, except that provided in cracks in the rock for exceptionally large numbers of snakes and lizards, which made half-hearted attempts at concealment when we approached.

Soon the 'ploonk' drinkers were in an agony of thirst, but their plight was remedied as rain began to fall in torrents. As a form of therapy we began to stone the white fluffy rabbits which, together with the snakes and lizards, infested the place, but they were so stupid and seemed to welcome death so eagerly that we soon tired of killing them. Instead, we started to build a communal bed on the foreshore, padding the sharper ridges with dried grass, as we all felt an unspoken horror of the snakes lurking higher up.

Here the five of us passed a night of misery under four oilskins with the wind, rain and spray sweeping horizontally over us. In the early hours of the morning we were so cold that to gain some little heat we mastered our repugnance and lay clammily embracing one another. At five, ravenously hungry, but without food, we staggered about the beach beating one another to revive our circulation. The wind had dropped a little during the night, leaving a heavy swell, and the rain had ceased. But the tide had run out, leaving the boat high and dry, and our combined efforts needed forty-five minutes to launch it over the rocks. After an hour's hard sailing, we came under *Moshulu*'s stern, having previously put the boy from *Passat* on board his own ship. A short rope ladder was hanging over the counter and as the gig lifted on a roller one by one we jumped for it and swung up to the deck. It was more difficult for me than for the others as I had 500 rounds of 22 ammunition for the Second Mate distributed about me.

Tria was waiting for us on deck. It was he who had taken our line and helped us on board.

'Joost in time,' he remarked, happily, 'seven o'clock.'

'Time for what?'

'Time for Breakfast, with stockfisk,' he remarked parenthetically. 'Clean the "skit hus" and then over the side for knacka rost.'

Kroner and Sedelquist remained ashore without leave for three days. During that time they met the Captain and that unpredictable man lent them ten shillings from his own pocket, and stopped their pay and further shore leave when they finally returned. For ten days we worked over the side, chipping and painting, or else down in the bilges. Occasionally we would visit *Passat*, and I saw a good deal of Eddy and 'Sweetheart'. The weather was appallingly hot. All through South Australia bush fires raged.

The next time the crew got shore leave, Kroner and Sedelquist remained as watchmen with the First Mate in command. At Sunday midnight the wind blew SSE., force 6 and *Moshulu* began to drag her anchors again. The Mate was called to stream another thirty fathoms of cable.

At last, on January 24th, our orders came to load at Port Victoria, Clarkson having secured a freight at 27*s* 6*d* a ton for us.

'You haven't seen fock notting,' said Tria, 'until you've been in Port Veck.'

'Why? What's there to see?'

'Fock notting.'

We began to throw the ballast overboard, manhandling the stone slabs into large wicker baskets and topping them up with sand. In the North Atlantic the work had been hard; under the sun it was prodigious and the hold became an inferno, the thermometer registering 120°.

On deck the two Donkeymen at last began to fulfil their proper function at the winches, winding the baskets aloft. Occasionally a paving stone would be dislodged when the baskets hit the hatch coaming and would come whistling down on us in the hold below, to be followed too late by a conventional cry of 'Stand from under.' When this did not happen the baskets were seized by the First Mate, a demon of energy, and an assistant who stood with him on a platform, who upset their contents into the Gulf with a satisfying roar.

Neither the noise nor the heat upset us as much as a terrible sickly sweet smell of decaying bodies which hung like a cloud over the hold.

'What do you think it is?'

'Kapten, perhaps, haven't seen him for some time.'

'I think it's a stowaway.'

'Oh, you noh,' said Sedelquist, 'it is a bloddy no good smell. I shall complain to the Consul.'

On the thirtieth we made sail for Port Victoria, walking the anchors out of the ground by hand, straining at the bars of the capstan on the fo'c'sle head, and, as we sailed the miles across the Gulf to the opposite shore, still continuing to shovel ballast into the wicker baskets. In two days we got rid of three hundred tons of it.

At three in the afternoon we arrived off Port Victoria and lay between the shore and Wardang Island a waste land in this hot summer.

Port Victoria, Port 'Veek' as Tria and the rest called it, seen from offshore was an idea more than a place, for the heat of the sun was enormous, destroying the substance of the land itself which swam in mirage. Avenues of distant trees loomed in the air above shimmering lakes which dissolved and vanished, and as rapidly reappeared in different forms. *Pommern*, at anchor between our ship and the shore, was an extraordinary sight with a twin projection of herself balanced upside down on top of her, mast cap to mast cap.

To reach the town we used to row past the white loading-ketches rocking at their moorings, to the wooden jetty and go up past some iron storage sheds into the main street of Port Victoria, wider than Knightsbridge at its widest, but unsurfaced. On either side was a façade of single-storeyed, iron-roofed buildings so impermanent in appearance that I never overcame my surprise when passing through the doors of the Post Office, the secretive-looking Hotel, or Kneebone's Café, at not finding myself at the back of a film lot facing the open country that extended to the horizon in every direction except to the west, where the waters of the Gulf lay. It had none of the cosy resort flavour of Port Lincoln. Port 'Veek' had a genuine air of *terribilitá* that raised it above the level of an ordinary small town.

The great main street, in which early motor-cars lay lifeless under the implacable sky waiting for owners who might never return, seemed to be expecting some world-shaking event, perhaps a procession of mindless automata to come plodding down from the wilderness and march through the calm and silent town into the sea. Sometimes, thankfully having a cool drink in Kneebone's, I used to gaze out at the whirls of dust scurrying along the length of the street and imagine them the presentiment of the event.

Perhaps for the best, this dream atmosphere was dissipated whenever the inhabitants appeared, for they were kind and hospitable to a degree. In any event Port Victoria could never be commonplace. At anchor in the roads during this February and March there were five four-masted barques: *Moshulu*, *Olivebank*, *Pamir*, *Pommern* and *Viking*, perhaps the last concourse of merchant sailing ships the world would ever see. There were no crowds of sightseers to gape at them. Here they were a part of the scenery, for the business of this town was grain. Neither was the visitor allowed to forget it. Everywhere there was bagged wheat, brought down from the back blocks and piled in great stacks until it could be run on to the jetty in open freight trucks, transferred to the loading-ketches, and taken out to the waiting ships. The stacks loomed over everything and as they

191

grew, piled up around the little church until only the tin spire and the iron roof were visible.

I was befriended by the agent in charge of shipping *Moshulu*'s cargo, John Scott-Todd, who, with his wife, entertained me whenever I came ashore. With him I visited the neighbouring farmhouses where the inhabitants introduced me to a hospitality undreamed of in England, and to a form of fox hunting by night, equally unthought of, in their vast thousand-acre paddocks. Armed with shot-guns, we stood in the backs of open trucks, sprawled precariously over the tops of the cabs, blazing away at the foxes as they ran ahead of us over the stubble, endeavouring to escape the spotlights trained on them. It would have been a source of delight to the foxes themselves and to all more legitimate hunters if they had seen our truck, when it finally hit an invisible ditch at thirty miles an hour, throwing us high into the air and breaking its front axle.

The Australians seemed a resourceful race, the young men making journeys of hundreds of miles in order to spend an hour or so with their girls, so that a young farmer would be invested with some of the splendour of a medieval paladin setting out to redeem some lofty pledge as he kicked the starter of his motor cycle in the already gathering dusk.

'Well, so long, I'm going to see my sheila in Kadina.'

'Is every girl in Australia called Sheila? I never hear anything else.'

'All girls are sheilas to us,' said the paladin, settling himself comfortably the saddle as the engine began to roar.

'How far's Kadina?' I asked him.

'Two hundred miles – a hundred each way.'

To me it sounded a lot of miles on such an errand.

'Too right it is,' he said, 'but I want to see my sheila real bad,' and vanished into the gloom in a cloud of blue smoke.

For a month and two days we lay at Port Victoria; sometimes a mile or so off-shore, so that the white ketches could come out from the jetty under power, loaded with grain; sometimes at the outer ballast-grounds, where we continued to throw ballast over the side.

In the first four days, with ballast still in her, the lumpers stowed seven thousand sacks in Nos 2, 3 and 4 holds, using the ship's own gear and winches. In language that made our own seem commonplace they complained bitterly of the smells below. What they said has not survived; if it had it would have proved meaningless robbed of the monotonous epithet which they attributed to every noun.

'I was reading somewhere,' said Vytautas, 'that Tibetans think themselves more holee if they say "Jewel of Lotus"' many times. If they say "Jewel of Lotus" enough they have vision. Perhaps lumpers think they will have mystic vision if they use that worrd.'

'My – oath, it's – hot on this – cow,' shouted one lumper to another, just at that moment.

' – ,' answered his companion, 'too – right it – is.'

'I don't think it's the right word for that, Vytautas.'

'Yerss,' he replied unexpectedly, 'not so fine that worrd for God.'

Cut off from contact with the shore, we worked for six days at the outer ballast-grounds, trying to get rid of the ballast as quickly as possible and at the same time discover what had died. On the fifth day we exhumed the liquefied remains of a large dog, and on the sixth and last, with damp cloths round our faces, we spooned up a second one which lay at the very bottom, and committed it thankfully to the sea, cursing the Belfast stevedores for their perverse sense of humour.

With the last of the ballast overside, we cleaned the bilges, cemented them, and sailed back to Port Victoria. Thenceforward, day after day, the routine was unvaried. Every morning at six the calm would be shattered by the deafening sounds of winches and donkey engines warming up for the day's work. The ketches would come alongside and the bags, each weighing about 180 lb, would be swung into *Moshulu*'s holds in slings, a dozen at a time, where the lumpers stowed them away, slitting some, allowing them to 'bleed' and bind the cargo more solidly together. The work went on every day except for Saturday afternoons and Sundays, but sometimes the wind blew force 5 and 6 from the south-west and there would be no loading. In three weeks we lost three whole days this way. For the remainder of the time the lumpers crammed grain into her, and in one working week from Monday to Saturday they loaded 16,900 bags.

Twice, at week-ends, I went to Adelaide; once with Scott-Todd in his car; the second time in a lorry as hot as a blast furnace. It was a long journey and once again I was treated to a display of the *Fata Morgana*. This time the ingredients were dead eucalyptus trees, themselves sufficiently nightmare objects without the elongations and liquefactions of the mirage.

In the city I stayed at a hotel, where I encountered the Captain who kindly feigned not to see me. It was a curious place. As I went down the corridor to the bathroom, the bedroom doors would open slightly, displaying the flushed, furtive faces of visiting business men hoping for an encounter with one of the highly developed chamber-maids with which the hotel was insufficiently staffed.

Adelaide itself was more like a cantonment than a city, with its bungalows and corrugated iron roofs. It had been laid out by an English Sapper Officer obsessed, perhaps, like Baron Haussmann, with the necessity of one day having to subdue a mob. 'Beautifully laid out,' as a visiting American said, 'like in a morgue.' More probably he had planned it to satisfy a soldier's sense of order. There was certainly no need for machine-guns to cover the long avenues of the outer suburbs beyond the public parks where, on Sundays, a preternatural silence reigned, producing a *taedium vitae* more potent than that of the most Scottish Sabbath.

Nevertheless I was delighted with everything. The bookshops, the cool drinks, even, with nothing to do, the excessive heat. The girls, too, were a delightful dream, strong bare-legged creatures who moved down the streets with the speed of kangaroos to avoid undesirable contacts, so that after a time I began to feel sorry for the males who never seemed able to halt their rapid progression. In spite of this, I contrived to fall in love, worshipping silently the object of my affection, as, happily unconscious of the fire she was stoking, she chatted remorsely on, giving me the statistical information, mileages, populations, areas, and outputs with which all Australians, young and old, seem to be born and which leave the visitor with such a woeful sense of inadequacy.

After three days of this inarticulate courtship, I returned to Port Victoria laden with Penguin books, films and souvenirs which the crew had commissioned me to buy.

Whilst unpacking the souvenirs I was greeted by Kroner, who had the air of a conspirator. But whatever he was intending to confide to me was for the moment obliterated from his mind by the objects I was unwrapping on the fo'c'sle table. 'What's this?' he demanded with distaste, holding up a long tortured object that resembled a snake struck dead in the moment of striking.

'It's an aboriginal walking-stick.'

'Since when have aborigines taken to walking-sticks?'

'I couldn't say. Fairly recently, I should think.'

'All right, that's a walking-stick. But what the devil are these?' he went on, holding up a number of flat, chocolate-coloured objects. 'You can't blame savages for these.'

'These' consisted of slices of the wattle tree, thickly varnished and inscribed: 'All the best from Adelaide'. They were a hideous testimonial to civilized ingenuity.

'I was very lucky to get them. I met the manager of the factory and he let me have them wholesale. It was very kind of him,' I said.

'You won't need them where you're going,' said Kroner with the same air of heavy secrecy with which he had greeted me in the first place.

'Why ever not?'

'You're going to the South Seas,' he replied, employing the American shock technique. 'Better come out on deck,' he said. 'I'll see you on the poop.'

There, at the headquarters of all our clandestine activity, he told me how he had been approached by the Captain of one of the ketches alongside who wanted us both to ship away with him when the loading was finished, sailing first to Sydney, then to the Pacific Islands to trade. The wages seemed tremendous, for he offered us twelve pounds a month against the ten shillings we were at present receiving.

'Which one is it?' I asked, looking over the taffrail at the two ketches moored alongside.

'Neither, he'll be out tomorrow,' Kroner said. 'He wants a sea-man and a Cook. I told him I thought you could be Cook.'

'That was thoughtful of you,' I answered, thinking of our haggard 'Kock' and the hours he kept.

'Oh, that's orlright. I mustn't always think of myself,' said Kroner generously.

The next day the ketch was alongside.

'Is that the man?' I said, pointing at a big ruffian with one eye who was at that moment discharging a stream of tobacco juice over the side of his vessel with force and accuracy.

'That's the one. His name's Jelks.'

'I'd better think it over.'

'Better decide now,' said Kroner, 'he wants to know soon.'

'There's one thing I'd really like to know,' I said to Kroner as we went forward under the suspicious eye of the First Mate.

'What's that?'

'What's going to happen to me if Jelks doesn't like my cooking?'

For days afterwards there were secret meetings, heavy conspiratorial winks, and the passing from hand to hand of grubby pieces of paper with indecipherable messages on them, but all came to nothing. My mind had been made up for me by the first sight of Captain Jelks and the thought of cooking for him.

The loading went on: Tuesday, February 28th, wind west force 6 – no loading; Wednesday, March 1st, 322 sacks in No. 3 hold, in 2,883 No. 2; Thursday, 1,627 in No. 2; Friday, 3,670 No. 2; Saturday, March 4th, 1,004 in No. 2.

'You'll be out of here in a week,' said Scott-Todd. 'We'd better have a party – a drop of beer.'

Late at night he decided that we must eat a chicken; armed with a great axe he went into the back yard to despatch one of the sleeping occupants of the roost. Soon dreadful sounds began to drift into the house, and going to his aid I found him alone in bright moonlight whirling his weapon about his head whilst the intended victim easily evaded his strokes.

'Do we really want to eat chicken?' I demanded anxiously, alternately ducking and jumping to avoid Scottie's whistling axe. 'It'll take hours to cook and there's no fire.'

'MUST have a chicken,' he repeated manfully. 'Party.' Then he sat down on the chopping-block which he had intended for the execution of the victim and began to giggle. After a bit he rose to his feet, drove the axe into the block, and marched resolutely towards the house.

'Too right we don't want chicken,' he said firmly over his shoulder. 'Well have some more beer instead.'

By Monday, March 6th, we knew that our departure could not be long delayed. The tempo of the loading increased, and that day in spite of a strong wind from the south-south-east, the lumpers put 1,620 sacks into No. 4 and 2,442 into No. 3 hold. On Tuesday they had their best day, loading 4,654 in No. 2 hold while we worked in the rigging bending sail, swinging them aloft on the gantlines with the help of the donkey engine. On Wednesday 1,650 went into No. 3 and 1,828 in No. 4. Finally, on Thursday, March 9, the last sacks went in: 2,200 in No. 4 and 828 in No. 2 holds. On the day *Moshulu* lay deep-loaded to her marks, ready to sail for home with 59,000 sacks of grain, 4,875 tons of it.

CHAPTER EIGHTEEN

The Last Grain Race

M OSHULU left Port Victoria at half past six on the morning of
Saturday, 11 March, 1939, her destination Queenstown for
orders. Three days earlier, on the 8th, *Pamir* with Captain
Björkfelt in command had left Port Victoria, while *Passat* under
Captain Lindvall had sailed from Port Lincoln on the 9th. The
exodus began on February 16th with the departure of *Viking*
(Captain Morn) from Port Victoria. Still loading wore *Archibald
Russell* (Sommarlund); *Winterhude* (Holm); the Swedish school-
ship *Abraham Rydberg* at Port Germein; *Lawhill* (Söderlund);
Norddeutscher Lloyd's *Kommodore Johnsen* (Clausen), and
Padua (Wendt) at Port Lincoln (*Padua* having only arrived on
March 8th from Valparaiso) while *Pommern* (Broman) and
Olivebank (Granith) were still at Port Victoria. Of the remaining
Erikson ships *Killoran* (Leman) was somewhere on passage
between the Seychelles and Auckland with a cargo of guano and
did not arrive at Port Lincoln until June 3rd. *Penang* was laid up
at Gothenburg and did not sail at all. Altogether thirteen ships
took part in the 1939 sailings.

Kommodore Johnsen was the only ship fitted with an auxiliary engine. An auxiliary vessel rarely made such a good passage
as a ship driven by sail alone. Perhaps the propeller slowed her
or the fitting of the engine had some effect on the morale of the
crew. Whatever the reason, no auxiliary barque ever came within
striking distance of a record passage on the Australian Grain
Run.

Priwall, the other ocean-going commercial square-rigger,
which arrived at Hamburg on April 14th, after a passage of

98 days from Iquique to Dover with nitrate cargo, also took no part in the Grain Race that year.

For two nights and a day *Moshulu* had lain ready to sail, deep-loaded, while the wind came in idle puffs. Then in the early hours of Saturday, March 11th, when the night was fading and the moon still shone overhead, the wind had begun to blow from the north and we heaved short the anchor.

I was filled with excitement. There were about us sounds half forgotten after so long: the cries of the crew as they sheeted home a jib, the ponderous clank as the cable, streaming water, came in through the hawse-pipe; and others more familiar: the sound of the donkey engine on the foredeck as it poured out sparks and soot, and the distant clatter coming from *Olivebank*, where a smother of smoke showed that her winches were warming for the day's work.

At this moment the little town was outlined against the early redness of the sun, the tin roofs and the spire of the tiny church breaking the hard, dark line of the coast. The sea was cold-looking with the sun not yet on it, and across it a ketch, the same grey as the sea, was sidling out deep-loaded towards the *Pommern*.

With the jibs cleared, the anchor aweigh, its flukes clear of the ground, the jibs were hoisted and she began to pay off before the wind until, gathering sufficient headway, the square sails were loosed. As the wind came aft, the topsails and foresails were set and sheeted home and the jibs were lowered. Passing Wardang Island to starboard, we continued to make sail aloft. The moon gave way to the sun, the light turned from red to gold. Flourishes of wind-blown cloud gave warning of heavier weather ahead. We set sail to the royals.

With the salt wind on our faces, feeling the surge of the ship as she pressed southward through the warm waters of the Gulf under the great arches of canvas springing overhead, most of us were happy to be free of the land, experiencing a sense of release and calm after the rumpus at the anchorage – the ear-shattering roar of the winches, the hoarse cries of the lumpers, the penetrating dirt, squalor and disorder which for much of the time had overwhelmed the ship.

'Beautiful, isn't she?' said the Sailmaker, coming up at this moment to look aloft at his sails.

'Yes, very,' I answered, reluctant to spoil the moment by an unseemly display of sentiment.

'Dammit, why not say so then?' he exploded blimpishly, and then added more softly: 'Sails, loveliest things ever made.'

'If this ship's ever going to make a passage it'll be this year or not at all,' he went on. 'In '38 we made a lousy passage, 112 days. Why? Because she was down by the head. This year she's down by the stern, but if there's wind and the Captain holds on, carries as much canvas as she'll take, then she'll go, you'll see!'

The wind began to have westing in it and the sky became more overcast as we hoisted the anchors inboard. They were trailing their crowns in the water beneath the bows and Sandell was slung overside to strop and secure them to the hook of the anchor crane. There he remained for some time with his body awash until, one after the other, we walked them up with the double capstan so that they hung suspended over their cradles on the fo'c'sle head.

'Orlright,' said the First Mate as we lowered the monster into its bed, cleated it down, unshackled the cables, and hauled them in through the hawse-pipes. 'Put that ting to slip.'

'And you,' he said in front of an appreciative audience, turning to me as he spoke, 'go clean dose brodders of yours.'

'Dose brodders' were four large pigs. A large white and three black ones, who lived forward in the sties beneath the break of the fo'c'sle head. The large white was female and in an all-male society never really got on good terms with us. She was eaten long before we reached Cape Horn, and unlike the three blacks never received a name. The three blacks were called Auguste, Filimon and Fabian. All three were terrific toughs and all three were almost identical. They lived in very small sties and spent a lot of time freed on humanitarian grounds. Until we grew to know them better it was very difficult to be sure which was which. At the moment they were having the time of their lives. Nothing was safe from them and they had an insatiable curiosity. Because of this, their snouts and bodies were covered with red lead, which gave them the appearance of savages in war paint. Besides being fond of red lead, they would eat sea-boots, shirts, sail-canvas and they liked to chew old paint-brushes. When they did this they looked like Russian cartoons of filthy capitalists smoking cigars. Best of all they liked lumps of coal. They used to lie in wait for the men carrying coal to the galley and when they appeared, rush on them from every side, endeavouring to upset the coal bucket. Usually they succeeded in securing a big piece and would go roistering off, punting it before them like boys with a football on a common, until it broke. Then they ate it.

In the early mornings they used to slouch around the foredeck, smelling horribly, grunting, panting and brushing against those of us who slept in hammocks. Once I awoke to find Fabian eating my sleeping-bag in a slow, ruminative kind of way. Fabian seemed obsessed by feet. He was always trying to gnaw through blankets to reach people's toes. But it was Auguste who had the most vile tricks. He succeeded in pushing Hermansonn out of his hammock by crawling underneath it and suddenly standing up. All the pigs loved fresh water. They liked the 'Kock' because he used to it trickle it into their mouths from a jug, and they liked Jansson who used to make them stand on their hind legs with their forefeet on a barrel and drink from a bottle. They liked the 'Kock' the better of the two because they were bone lazy and Jansson made them work too hard. They used to hang about for hours outside the galley, making the most loathsome noises. If the 'Kock' did not appear, they would grow bolder and charge right into the galley, from which he would drive them, furious at the profanation of his spotless quarters.

I was not at all pleased to be given the job of mucking out the pigsties. It had been coming my way far too frequently. The pigs slept on spare hatch covers which had to be extracted from the sties, for which they were very nearly a perfect fit, each time they were cleaned out. They were slippery and without handhold.

'Don' keep them vaiting,' urged the Mate.

I looked at him with unconcealed distaste, and went off to seek the necessary instruments. As I worked, with Filimon snuffling at my heels trying his best to upset me, I pondered the reasons for my ever-growing unpopularity with the Mate. Since I had first seen him beardless, he had nurtured an aversion to me. At Port Victoria the thing had come to a head when he had emerged on deck one morning after an unusually heavy night and had caught sight of me with a pot of red lead in my hand about to go over the side.

'Gloggle, gloggle, gloggle,' he seemed to say.

'I'm sorry, I didn't hear you,' I replied, doing my best to look bright and willing.

Once more there was an extraordinary collection of sounds, only this time they sounded completely different.

'Please speak more distinctly,' I said, trying not to sound like a telephone operator.

'Someting wrong op here?' he screamed, pointing to his head.

'I *am* sorry. I didn't know you were troubled like that.'

For a moment I thought he was going to hit me, but he must have been feeling terrible, for he clapped both hands to his head and disappeared below, groaning.

It was for this brief and unsatisfactory triumph that I was now making a full requital.

At three we passed Wedge Island, about five miles to starboard. It had a great brown cliff at the eastern end, and an exposed-looking light tower on its summit. Now watches were appointed and the starboard watch went below. All hands were working the ship, including the Carpenter, who looked exceedingly ill after the extraction of twenty-four teeth at one sitting, and 'Doonkey'. On the outward voyage 'Doonkey' had slouched around the deck dressed in very greasy overalls with a Stillson wrench protruding from a back pocket, oiling nothing in particular with a large oil-can. He was able to do this all the way to Spencer's Gulf, unlike the Carpenter, who worked like a slave laying new planking.

By six o'clock the wind was rising in the north-west and a great mass of exceptionally sinister-looking cloud began to loom over the ship. Alarmed by its appearance and by the rapidly falling

falling barometer, the Captain told the Mate to take in the royals. Two whistles sounded.

'Bräck gårdingarna på kryss royal and horry up,' he shouted.

'Horry op, horry op my asse,' mumbled Hermansonn. '*Satan*, Kossuri, moonkey bizness, this horry op,' he went on in an unusual access of friendliness as we went aft to the mizzen rigging.

'Gigtåget – kom on, get dem two blocks. Hermansonn, shot that big mout',' grunted the Mate, working like a demon.

'Övre bram now,' he went on, leading us to the upper topgallant buntlines, jumping at them and breaking the stops with his own weight. There was a mutinous air about us as we worked, and I thought sadly of the Captain and my diminishing opinion of him, for I had hoped that he would drive his ship, and here he was shortening sail at the sight of the first rain cloud.

Ten minutes later, the dark cloud had swept down on the ship and we were in the middle of a first-class electric storm, with continuous lightning of the sort that always made my hair stand on end when I was aloft. *Moshulu* was drawing more than 23 feet of water and the sea came bubbling into the lee scuppers and the air was filled with the melancholy clang of freeing ports as the weight of water forced them to open and allow the ship to clear herself of it. She ran thirteen knots under lower topgallants, and when we went below, ravenous for supper, we left the starboard watch making fast aloft. We were all rather chastened at supper. Like the disciples in the New Testament we were conscious of having been deficient in faith. I half expected the Captain to appear and start rebuking us for our lack of it, but fortunately that splendid man did not care what we thought, either then or at any other time.

Throughout Sunday the north wind shifted first to west then south-west, and in the night to north-west. It blew strong on the quarter and drove *Moshulu* across the approaches to the Bass Strait, west of Tasmania, southward into the Southern Ocean at ten and twelve knots. By noon we had run 247 miles. And as if to welcome us and lead us out into these remote regions, a great wandering albatross dipped out of the sky and wheeled steeply about us. Soon it was joined by another and another. In an hour there were a dozen about the ship, accentuating as they always did our feeling of isolation in the wastes of the sea, so that it was difficult to believe that a day and a night away to the north of us were bungalows with red tin roofs, bioscopes, and men who visited their sheilas on motor bicycles.

'Only five thousand more miles to the Horn,' said Kroner as we coiled down the falls on the belaying pins in a welcome interval in the constant bracing made necessary by the shifts of wind, and ducked to avoid the clouds of spray that were breaking over the midships deck. 'We're practically there.'

'Shut up,' I told him. 'You must be crazy. D'you want us to be becalmed?'

As I feared, the wind hauled to south-west again, and then fell right away, leaving the ship idling.

In the following days we prepared for the gales we expected in the high latitudes we would traverse in order to reach the Horn. All along the ship's length hawse-pipes were stopped with blocks of wood, lifelines were rigged on the maindeck, and wire rope safety nettings set up on the bulwarks by the main braces to prevent us being washed overboard, or, as Tria remarked grimly, to prevent some of us being washed back again. The hatches too needed reinforcing. As soon as the last bags had been stowed below at Port Victoria, hatchway beams of seasoned oak were fitted in the grooves in the coamings and heavy 3-inch hatch covers put on top of them. The spaces between the covers were tightly caulked with oakum. Over each hatch two new tarred canvas covers were stretched, cut and sewn by the Sailmaker to fit one on top of the other. These had been secured to the coamings by flexible steel bands, tightly wedged, the wedges being nailed together.

Now the real labour began. On top of the canvas covers great baulks of timber 20 feet long and 4 inches thick were laid lengthways; and at right angles to them, across the ship, three heavier pieces 14 feet long and 4 inches thick. The whole lot was lashed down with wire ropes to ringbolts in the hatch coamings and hauled taut with the capstan. Frequently the wire strops broke under the strain, and the work began all over again.

'You know,' said Kroner, as we went below at coffee time, 'this business of covering the hatches would be quite good if the Mate didn't get so angry. We've only broken five strops on No. 3 hatch. You'd almost think he had shares in the company or something.'

'I expect the Second Mate gives you hell because the Captain gives him hell and Gustav gives everybody hell. That's how they run all the best things in England. Schools, prisons, businesses, everything.'

'How do you know?'

'Well, I've been to school and I was in a business so I know about that, and I once met a man who'd been at a Public School and in Dartmoor and he said that he'd rather do another five years there than have his school days over again.'

'What is this Public School?' asked Kroner.

'It's just a very good sort of school. People who've been there put their children's names down for one the moment they're born.'

'But why, when they know what it's like?'

'I don't know really. Perhaps they don't want them to miss anything.'

'It's amazing,' said Kroner. 'Are they all like that, English schools?'

'Only the good ones.'

'I shall go mad,' he said, 'let's stop this conversation.' He was silent for a moment, then he asked me, 'Why are you limping?'

'I've done something to my knee. It feels as if something's bust.'

'I know,' said Kroner, unsympathetically, 'it hurts when you have to work. Perhaps it's something you picked up in Australia, like that painter who died in the South Seas. He had a bad leg for years.'

'You mean Gaugin. He had syph,' I answered rashly.

'Perhaps that's what you've got,' said Kroner enthusiastically.

'You'd better see the Captain right away. Perhaps he'll put into New Zealand.'

'He didn't have it in the leg,' I tried to explain. 'He got a bad leg tripping over something.'

But Kroner was not listening. 'Much better ask the Captain.'

'Ask the Captain what?' asked Hilbert, who appeared at that moment.

'Newby thinks he's got syphilis,' explained Kroner.

'Now you've really started something,' I said.

The pain in my leg grew worse and worse. It became difficult to hobble about at all, but as none of the ship's officers suggested I should stop going aloft, and as the syphilis story gained momentum I still continued to do so.

At last, not being on particularly good terms with the First Mate, I asked the Second to have a look at it.

'Bend it,' he said.

I bent it.

'Now stretch it.'

I stretched it.

'Does it hurt when you go aloft?' he asked.

I said it did, beginning to have a high opinion of his capabilities.

'Now,' he said. 'Does it hurt when I do this?' giving my kneecap a sharp tap.

'Yes,' I roared.

'I should wash it,' he said. 'There's no charge for the advice.'

I acted on his suggestion and applied hot compresses. In a week it was better.

Soon No. 1 by the fo'c'sle head was the only hatch still open. There was a big diesel winch just forward of the galley by No. 2 cargo hatch. 'Doonkey' was hard at work dismantling it, before joining the starboard watch as a permanent member. At intervals the whole of the foredeck would be blotted out by clouds of spray and the unfortunate 'Doonkey' would disappear from view, while from the shelter of the fo'c'sle the watch below would shout remarks of little comfort.

'You can jus' put dat vinsch ting in the 'tween-deck,' said the First Mate as he mustered us in the well-deck.

Even partially dismantled the winch was a formidable object. It had a solid cast-iron base, a massive drum and a heavy fly-wheel. Moving it forward and into the fore part of the 'tween-decks was to prove one of the most difficult operations we ever attempted.

With a block hung off from the mainstay which supported the mainmast, and double purchase tackle, we managed to lift the whole thing into the air by capstan power, swing it over the hatch coamings, and deposit it on a makeshift sled of hatch covers on which we hoped to slide it along the deck. Instead it became immovable, and horrid visions arose of the winch thundering about on deck in a gale of wind, smashing everything in its path as muzzle-loaders in ships-of-the-line had been known to do.

'Try pig skit,' said Sedelquist. 'It's slippery enough. I've just sat my asse in it.'

With rollers and levers and tackles taken to the capstan we strove to move the winch along the deck. It was a heart-breaking task, full of uncertainty, like erecting an obelisk. Every few feet obstacles blocked the way: the bitts to which the foresheet was made fast, the donkey house, the capstan itself, all producing problems which had to be met by shifting the tackles and bringing fresh ones into use, so that the sled could pursue its zig-zag course.

After five hours we got it as far as No. I hatch. With one tackle rigged to the forestay and two others to prevent it swinging side-ways, the winch was lifted over the opening, which was only eight feet square.

'Orlright, slack ava-a-y,' the Mate cried in a rather too carefree voice. The man at the capstan took him quite literally, and a ton of winch fell two feet dead, banging itself badly on the hatch coaming as it did so.

'Va-a-ast, Va-a-ast,' screamed the Mate in a frenzy as the winch bounced up and down on the tackle on the forestay, which itself was vibrating like the string of a giant harp. The rest of us, powerless and fascinated, watched the gear which was being subjected to this unfair strain and waited for it to collapse.

'Who pays if it smashes?' I asked Sedelquist, that born litigant, who seemed best qualified to answer such a question.

'Styrman,' he answered, with evident pleasure.

'I shouldn't think he'd want to do that,' I said. 'The last time I asked him he only had 3s 6d.'

'Dozzent matter what he wants,' Sedelquist replied; and went on, with impeccable logic, 'you didn't want to pay for the hammer in Belfast, but you bloody did.'

Finally, miraculously undamaged, the winch – 'dat bloddy vinsch, dat *Satan's* vinsch from *helvete*,' as the Mate picturesquely described it – was sitting in the 'tween-decks. With infinite loathing we set up our tackles for the last time, moved it aft to its appointed place, and lashed it down. The move was accomplished. It had taken ten men six hours.

✛

Monday and Tuesday of the first week at sea, there was scarcely any wind. In 24 hours we made only 91 miles on our course. By noon on that first Monday our position was roughly two hundred miles due West of Cape Grim, the north-westernmost point of Tasmania. The log gives a good idea of these uninspiring days:

> Monday, March 13. First part: Wind SW. force 3,7 knots;
> Middle: Wind SW. force 2; Midnight: Wind SE. force 1.
> Tuesday, March 14th. First part: Wind SE. force 1, bare steerage
> way; Middle: SE. by E., veering continuously; Midnight: E.,
> force 3, 6 knots.

By noon on Tuesday we had only made 76 miles in 24 hours. Wednesday was better and *Moshulu* averaged 10 or 11 knots all through the day under a cold overcast sky.

On the sixteenth the wind went round to WNW. It was a fine warm day for 45° South, with a deep blue sea and a leaping swell that from time to time jumped over the weather rail. The night that followed was beautiful, warm and clear, with a thin sliver of moon in the east. All night the ship sailed serene and unhurried and there was no work at sheets or braces. The following morning to make up for this idyll, we were set to work greasing the braces and the wire sheets of the course sails.

'Noh good,' said the Mate, when he saw that I was using a rag to apply a black filthy mixture of what seemed to be a combination of tar, graphite, grease and paint to the foresheet.

'Perhaps you'd like me to put it on like this,' I replied, picking up a black lump and applying it to the wire with my bare hands.

To my surprise he said: 'Yo, yo, yo – dat's better, joost keep on with the hands,' and left me looking rather foolish.

In the afternoon the wind went to NNW. and freshened a little. The weather began to look forbidding, with dark rain clouds everywhere, but then it cleared and there was bright sunshine with a coldness in the air, and towards evening there was a blue mistiness in the atmosphere like an autumn evening in England.

In the night that followed we came to realize the enormity of what we had done in greasing the wire sheets. In their rusty primitive state they had been difficult to manage. Now, as they jumped and writhed in our hands, they burned. With the yards squared away the foresail was sheeted home amidships and hauled taut on a small winch on the rail. The greasy wire would not grip on the small drum, slipping and shuddering as we wound away. Soon we were covered with filth and when we went below at four in the morning we transferred still more of it to our blankets and the walls of the fo'c'sle.

✝

By the eighteenth of March we were well to the south and east of Tasmania in 47° South latitude and longitude 153° East. The sky was cold and overcast but we saw little of it by day, having returned to 'knacka rost' beneath No. 1 hatch. There, dizzy from the fumes of smoking lanterns, we chipped and scraped the beams. The rust got into our eyes and blinded us, trickled down our sleeves and down the backs of our necks, setting up violent itching.

'Peety scrapers don' take so much roost off the ship as they take meat off my bloddy hands,' Alvar remarked after three days of scraping.

As always when engaged in 'knacka rost' I tried to think of nothing at all, but only succeeded in conjuring up visions of failure, bankruptcy, and death from painful diseases brought on by this monstrous occupation, all the fears that beset civilized man. Alvar's words decided us: from this moment, obeying an unspoken thought, we all did as little as possible. Tria was our slave driver. As soon as he went away all work ceased, and we lolled on a heap of sails, at the same time keeping a sharp eye on the ladder, while Hermansonn banged his scraper against the ship's side to simulate industry and allay the Mate's suspicion. Half an hour later when Tria's seaboot showed m the hatch opening, we leapt to our feet and began to scrape and hammer furiously, but our pretence was unnecessary as at that moment *Moshulu* gave a fearful lurch and began to heel violently, taken aback in full sail by a heavy squall while running before a moderate WNW. breeze.

As we struggled up the ladder to the deck 'två vissel' sounded. We could see the giant course sails buckling and flogging in a wind which was every moment increasing in violence and pressing the upper sails hard against the masts, while the helmsman, little Taanila, tried desperately to put the helm down, assisted by the Captain, who had come on deck.

'Förbrassar,' ordered Tria. He cast the long coils of the rope braces off their pins and we manned the winch. At this important moment one of the drums, decrepit after thirty-four years of alternate use and neglect, began to break up, jamming the entire mechanism.

' "Doonkey hus", horry, horry,' Tria shouted, but Sandell was on his way there.

After what seemed an eternity, during which we gazed apprehensively aloft at the canvas curling itself into strange shapes, expecting either the sheets or the topgallant stay to part, he returned with a hammer and a crowbar. With the winch cleared it was possible to brace the foreyards so that the wind was at least bearing on the proper side of the sails. Then we raced aft and braced the main and mizzen yards, where we were joined by the First Mate who had dowsed the gaff topsail at the first sign of trouble. Nothing was lost, nothing carried away. The wind settled down to blow steadily from the south and we proceeded close-hauled on the starboard tack, having had a narrow escape.

We had now been at sea a week and I was beginning to be afraid that we might not encounter the sort of impressive gale that Mountstewart was hoping for on my behalf, the sort that is the stock-in-trade of all writers of books about ocean voyages. In secret I prayed for the great winds to blow. I also showed Mountstewart's letter to Kroner and the Sailmaker. It was a letter which began with a few rather arid courtesies and then hurried on to ask a lot of highly technical questions about rivets, the composition of steel employed in the ship's construction, and so on.

'You will hardly be able to answer these yourself,' he wrote, 'but at any rate I should prefer you to ask the Master. By this time,' the letter had concluded, 'I hope that you will have had the good fortune to encounter a real "Southerly Buster" or Cyclonic Gale, with great seas, "greybeards", we used to call them, rolling up astern of the vessel – a memorable sight. I am only sorry that yours is not a long-decked ship as a Liverpool House amidships will prevent the seas sweeping her and appreciably reduce the effect.'

I had no intention of approaching our formidable Captain to ask him questions which he himself might not be able to answer. I showed Mountstewart's letter to Kroner first.

'You know,' said Kroner after reading it, 'that friend of yours, Mountstewart, seems a stinker to me. What the hell does he think this is, a film or something?'

The Sailmaker's reaction was much the same. 'Stupid old buzzard,' he snarled. 'Wants his head looked at. Maybe we get more than we can take. Hope you don't feel like that,' he said accusingly.

I tried to reassure him, but he was still suspicious and went off mumbling 'Wants his head tested.'

The weather grew colder and colder. On the night of March 20th, the Captain issued rum to all hands outside the charthouse, a large wooden spoonful to each man. This rum was like no other I had ever tasted. It was four over proof and had the same effect as a blow from a heavy stick. Going below I found the rest of the watch already turned in, drunk as lords but far less amiable.

'Light ut,' came a voice before I had even removed my seaboots. I ignored it, but half a dozen voices arose, chorusing, 'Focking light ut,' in a menacing way. Cursing, I leaned over and with a long-drawn, potent breath, extinguished it, blowing a neat hole through the lamp glass. 'Bloody, blodddy bastard,' said Hermansonn as I lay in bed chuckling and hiccupping. Just then Bäckmann arrived. Like me he had been detained on deck to finish off some task on which he had been engaged when the rum came up. He was not best pleased to find the light out, and as he stowed his oilskins his position was signalled by a glowing cigarette end. He stumbled about, demanding who had put the light out.

'Kossuri,' said Taanila, 'Kossuri, the rosbif. Kossuri put the light ut.'

I no longer cared for the opinions of the port watch or anyone else. Since my fight with Hermansonn I was independent of them. 'You have first look-out and I hope you freeze to death,' I told Taanila. 'For the rest of you, God damn and blast you all,' I said and went happily to sleep.

CHAPTER NINETEEN
Storm in the Southern Ocean

ON the 20th of March *Moshulu* was in a position near the Snares, a group of uninhabited islands in latitude 48° southward of New Zealand. At midnight on the 19th we had come on deck at the muster to find the ship under full sail, flying along at 13 knots with a NNW. wind, the seas boiling out from under her bows.

I had first wheel and it needed the greatest attention to keep the course. She had to be steady, so I kept my eyes and my whole attention on the card, grimly determined that if Moshulu was to be lost by broaching to, it wasn't going to happen while I was at the wheel.

At two bells (1 a.m.) I was relieved. Soaked through and very cold I was happily going below for a period of 'påpass' when the Mate told me to summon the watch. One by one I shook them into reluctant wakefulness whilst he roamed about impatiently on the deck above.

'Where you were all bloddy night?' he demanded when they were all finally on deck. 'Kom on. Bräck bukgårdingarna på kryss royal.'

As we stumbled aft along the slippery deck to the mizzen royal buntlines we cursed the Mate audibly and the Captain more secretly. By the time Yonny Valker and I had been aloft and furled the main royal, which was heavy and sodden with rain, and cleared up on deck, it was a quarter past two, and I was overdue for look-out. I need not have been anxious to reach it, for Sedelquist failed to relieve me at three and I spent an hour-and-three-quarters looking at nothing but rain.

At last the end of this interminable 'utkik' drew near. At twenty to four I saw the light lit in the starboard fo'c'sle where the 'påpass' was waking the other watch. At two minutes to I saw the dark figures congregating beneath the break of the midships deck for the muster. There was a short interval while the Mate counted; an interval when, finding one man short, he despatched the 'påpass' to find the missing man – in this case 'Doonkey', who had either been overlooked or was not shaken hard enough. He was greeted with jeers of disapproval when he shambled out on deck.

'Orlright,' said the Mate. 'Lösa av ror och utkik, in frivakt.' The helmsman was relieved and there was a struggle at the steel doors as the free watch went below.

'Klara lanternor,' I said to Vytautas, as he relieved me. 'It's bloody cold and you can see damn all.'

'Not so fine, yerss?' said Vytautas, who was a good deal warmer and drier than I was myself. 'She is going.'

'So am I,' I said and went off in a hurry to report 'Klara lanternor' to the officer of the watch.

Very cold and very miserable I went below resolved to do something to elevate my spirits. At 'utkik' I had decided that I would open a 5 lb can of marmalade which had cost me 3s 6d in Port Lincoln. Now I did so and cutting myself a massive slice of bread, I spread it on thickly. The marmalade looked rather insipid but I was not prepared for it to be absolutely tasteless as well. When we had reached Port 'Veek' we found that a 5-lb tin of jam was only 2s 6d, but I had comforted myself that the extra shilling was well spent in order to obtain a superior article. I thought now of all the splendid jam I might have bought instead. Bäckmann had a big tin of peach jam, one of the most delicious things I had ever tasted. Alvar had fig, Sedelquist quince, Hermansonn loganberry – all good fully flavoured stuff. Only I had managed, in a country with a vast growth of every kind of fruit, to pick on some with either taste nor smell of any kind.

I soon found that nobody was very keen to offer me their jam in exchange. One day I offered my marmalade to Sedelquist.

'Have some jam, Sedelquist,' I said, pushing my hateful marmalade towards him.

'Oh you noh,' he said, 'there's damn all oranges in your jam. It tastes of olt bolls to me.'

'Balls?'

'Yes, olt goolf bolls. You should try quince. Veree good.'

'I should like to very much – '

'It's a peety,' he went on, 'that your marmalade isn't bettair.'

✝

Thirteen days out from Spencer's Guff we crossed the 180th meridian and suffered two Fridays in succession. Two Fridays were not popular. Sedelquist was angry because he had been deprived of the two Sundays he had hoped for; I was depressed because it meant an extra day of 'Backstern'; only Yonny Valker, that rigid medievalist, was happy, secure in the knowledge that here was a problem nobody would have the patience to explain to him.

'Koms to blow,' said Tria to me on the afternoon of the first Friday as I came on deck to pour the washing-up water over the side.

'Good.'

'No, no. Not good. Koms to blow bad,' he replied anxiously.

I asked him how he knew.

'I don' know how I know. There's someting fonny, someting noh good in the vind.' There was nobody about on the bridge deck, so I asked him if I could look at the last entry in the logbook in the charthouse.

'Orlright,' he said reluctantly. 'Don' let Kapten see you.' The Captain did not like finding the crew in the charthouse. I looked hastily at the open book and read the noon position:

'24.3.39. Lat. 51° 4S, Long. 176° 37' 16W. Course East. Run 282. Barometer 4 a.m. 758 millimetres; Noon 754 millimetres. Wind WSW, Force 4.'

I glanced at the barometer. It had been falling steadily since 4 o'clock on Wednesday morning, the 22nd. On that day, except for some light northerly airs, we had been becalmed on a sea as grey and unvarying as a featureless plain. The albatross had vanished. At midnight on Wednesday the wind had been a gentle breeze from the NW. and by the afternoon of Thursday, the 23rd, *Moshulu* was logging 12 knots with WNW. wind, force 5. At 8 it had shifted to the west, the yards were squared, the spankers and the gaff topsail were taken in and she ran before it. The time was now 4 p.m. on the 24th, the wind WSW. The air was full of masses of white and grey cloud moving rapidly eastward above the ship, which was being driven and lifted forward with a slight see-saw motion on the crest of seas of immense depth and power. These seas did not seem to be raised by wind; instead they seemed the product of some widespread underwater convulsion. All round the ship the sea was surging and hurling itself into the air in plumes of spray, occasionally leaping over the rail by the mizzen braces and filling the main deck with a swirl of white water. The air was bitter; I could see Tria's breath smoking.

'It looks all right to me,' I said.

'I don' say right now,' said Tria. 'But very soon this blody ting gets so much as she can stand. Lissun when you go aloft.'

We were joined by the Sailmaker, who stood for some time looking up at the main royal with the wind straining in it, then over the rail at the mounting sea. 'Going to blow,' he said.

Hilbert came racing down the deck from the 'Vaskrum' for'ard, dressed in nothing but wooden clogs and fresh long underwear, his teeth chattering. All he said was: 'Vind,' and vanished into the starboard fo'c'sle. The First Mate looked down at us from deck. 'Going to vind a little too mooch,' he began conversationally.

'For Christ's sake,' I said, rather too audibly.

'What the hell are you doing?' he demanded, noticing me.

'Backstern, Sir.'

'Backstern doesn't take all bloddy day. Get down in the hold for babord'svakt for knacka rost.'

I went below to where the port watch were working suspended on platforms over one of the 'tween-deck hatches. The only vacant space was next to Taanila, even more gnomelike than usual in goggles. I slipped in beside him and he turned as the platform gave a lurch. 'I tink . . .' he began. In that moment I wondered exactly what he was going to think. Was he going to think that I needed a knife inserted in some delicate part? Was he going to remind me yet again of my unfortunate nationality? Or was he going to tell me his opinion of 'knacka rost'?

'I tink it is going to . . .'

'Don't tell me, let me guess – to vind.'

'Yo, yo. How you know?'

'Because I'm bloody clever.'

At 5 the heavy chain sheet to the fore royal parted on the port side. We just managed to get the sail in before it blew itself to pieces. The remaining royals had to come in, and the flying jib, then all hands went aloft for the main and mizzen courses. All through the night there were two helmsmen. The wind increased and the seas rose higher and began to pour into the ship again. In the watch below I lay awake listening to the clang of freeing ports along the length of the main deck as they opened to the pressure of water and closed as the ship rolled away, tipping the sea right across her so that the same process took place on the other side. With more apprehension I listened to the sound of water trickling steadily into the fo'c'sle through a cracked port above Bäckmann's bunk. This seemed to constitute a far greater threat to our comfort than the more spectacular effects outside.

At 5.30 on the morning of the second Friday, *Moshulu*, still carrying her upper topgallants, began to labour under the onslaught of the heavy seas which were flooding on to the deck like a mill race. It was quite dark as six of us clewed-up the mizzen lower topgallant, and although from where I was at the tail of the rope I could see nothing at all except the hunched shoulders of Jansson ahead of me, I could hear Tria at the head of the line exhorting us. The sail was almost up when the wind fell quite suddenly and we all knew that we were in the trough of a wave far bigger than anything we had yet experienced. It was far too dark to see it at a distance, we could only sense its coming as the ship rolled slightly to port to meet it.

'Hoold . . .' someone began to shout as the darkness became darker still and the sea came looming over the rail. I was end man. There was just time to take a turn with the clewline round my middle and a good hold, the next moment it was on top of us. The rope was not torn from me; instead it was as though a gentle giant had smoothed his hands over my knuckles. They simply opened of their own accord and I unravelled from it like a cotton reel from the end of a thread and was swept away. As I went another body bumped me, and I received a blow in the eye from a seaboot. Then I was alone, rushing onwards and turning over and over. My head was filled with bright lights like a by-pass at night, and the air was full of the sounds of a large orchestra playing out of tune. In spite of this there was time to think and I thought: 'I'm done for.' At the same time the words of a sea poem, 'ten men hauling the lee fore brace . . . seven when she rose at last', came back to me with peculiar aptness. But only for an instant because now I was turning full somersaults, hitting myself violently again and again as I met something flat which might have been the coaming of No. 4 hatch, or the top of the charthouse, for all I knew. Then I was over it, full of water and very frightened, thinking 'Is this what it's like to drown?' No more obstructions now but still going very fast and still under water, perhaps no longer in the ship, washed overboard, alone in the Southern Ocean. Quite suddenly there was a parting of water, a terrific crash as my head hit something solid, and I felt myself aground.

Finding myself in the lee scuppers with my head forced right through a freeing port so that, the last of the great sea behind me spurted about my ears, I was in a panic that a second wave might come aboard and squeeze me through it like a sausage, to finish me off.

Staggering to my feet, my oilskins ballooning with water, too stupid from the blow on my head to be frightened, I had just enough sense to jump for the starboard lifeline when the next wave came boiling over the port quarter and obliterated everything from view.

Swinging above the deck on the lifeline with the sea sucking greedily at my boots, I began to realize what a fortunate escape I had had from serious injury, for the alacrity with which I had leapt for the lifeline in spite of the great weight of sea-water inside my oilskins had convinced me that I had suffered no damage except the bang on the head.

The sea had taken me and swept me from the pin rail of the mizzen rigging, where I had been working, diagonally across the deck for fifty feet past the Jarvis brace winches, on the long handles of which I could so easily have been speared, over the fife rails of the mizzen mast, right over the top of No. 3 hatch and into the scuppers by the main braces outside the Captain's quarters.

'Where you bin?' demanded Tria accusingly, when I managed to join the little knot of survivors who were forcing their way waist deep across the deck, spluttering, cursing, and spitting sea-water as they came.

'Paddling,' I said, relieved to find that there still six of us.

'Orlright, don' be all bloody day,' he added unsympathetically.

'Tag I gigtåget. One more now. Ooh – ah, oh, bräck dem.'

'What happened?' I asked Jansson.

'That goddam Valker let her come up too mooch,' said Jansson. 'I bin all over the bloddy deck in that sea.'

On the second Friday *Moshulu*'s noon position was 50° 19' S., 170° 36' W. In 23½ hours she had sailed 296 miles.[*] This was the best day's sailing with cargo she ever had with Erikson. It was only bettered by the Germans on very few occasions. Twice in 1909 on a voyage from Newcastle, N.S.W., to Valparaiso when loaded with nearly 5,000 tons of coal she ran 300 miles.

At midnight the wind was SW., force 6, and in the early hours of Saturday morning I went aloft with Hermansonn in a storm of sleet to make fast the main upper topgallant. It was now blowing a fresh gale, force 8, and the yard was swinging like a mad

---

[*] When running to the east in southerly latitudes a day, noon to noon, is about 23½ hours.

thing; we had a terrible time with this sail. Some of the gaskets had been caught in the buntline blocks on the yard and were immovable, others were missing. The sleet numbed our fingers until we almost cried with cold.

Below us, in the fore and mizzen rigging, eight boys were having the time of their lives furling the lower topgallants; on the mizzen two buntlines had carried away to starboard and the sail was being clewed-up to the yard with lines taken to the capstan on the main deck, where from time to time ton upon ton of white water poured over the rail, causing those heaving at the capstan bars to abandon their efforts and leap for the lifelines.

'OOH, what bloddy cold,' screamed Hermansonn. 'Ut, Kossuri, you strongbody,. you rosbif, ut, ut på nock.'

As we reached the yardarm there was a great ripping sound that seemed to come from below, and we both hung dizzily over the yard to see whether the upper topsail had blown out. Then, in spite of the wind and our precarious situation, Hermansonn began to laugh. I knew then that I had suffered some dire misfortune as Hermansonn only laughed in that way when a disaster happened to someone else.

'Ho, ho!' he boomed above the gale. 'Ho, ho, focking fonny!'

'What?' I screamed in his ear. 'Tell me.'

'Your trousers, ho, ho. English, no good.'

It was true. My oilskin trousers, unable to stand the strain to which they had been subjected, had split from end to end.

This was an accident of the worst kind. To find myself half way across the Southern Ocean, in the stormiest seas in the world, with defective oilskin trousers, was calamity.

At the moment however there was no time to worry over such things. The wind was awe-inspiring. Not only was it so strong in the gusts that we could do nothing but hang on until it lessened, but it moaned in a way which I had never heard before, rising and falling like the winds heard about old houses in the wintertime. It seemed, in spite of its force, to be the last part of some even more violent disturbance that was taking place at a great distance. This then was what Tria had meant when he told me to listen when I went aloft.

But in this weather there were still worse jobs on deck where the Carpenter and two helpers were trying to caulk the closet. As the ship started to run downhill into the valley between two seas, she would bury her bows nearly to the fo'c'sle head, so that the water surged into the pipes and shot into the compartment in a solid icy column like the jet emitted by a whale, leaving them half drowned and spluttering.

At noon the wind was WSW., force 9, and there was a vicious sea running. We were carrying upper and lower topsails, the foresail, forestaysail and jigger staysail. I spent the morning with a sail-needle, seaming up my ruined oilskins, while overhead the starboard watch struggled to reeve fresh buntlines on the mizzen lower topgallant. The outer steel doors of the fo'c'sle were fast, but not being close-fitting they let the water in. Soon there were more than six inches of water in the compartment reserved for our seaboots and oilskins, and half as much in the fo'c'sle itself. Every few minutes I had to leave my stitching and bail with a cocoa tin to prevent the fo'c'sle being flooded still more. Everyone else was asleep. As old soldiers do before an action, they were absorbing sleep greedily like medicine, and lay snoring happily in the midst of tumult.

For the noise was unbelievable. In the fo'c'sle the shrieking of the wind through the shrouds and about the upper yards now bereft of sail, so awe-inspiring on the open decks, was here only a murmur subordinated to the shuddering and groaning of the hull under stress and to the sounds of water; water thundering over the ship in torrents, water sluicing out through the freeing ports, water trickling into the fo'c'sle in half-a-dozen different ways, and sloshing about the floor.

By the time I had mended the trousers, the free watch was nearly over. I was 'Backstern', and having made sure that Kroner had put on the washing-up water, I waited for a lull to dash forward to the fo'c'sle head from where I could look back along the ship.

Moshulu was running ten knots in the biggest seas I had ever seen. As I watched, the poop began to sink before my eyes and the horizon astern was blotted out by a high polished wall, solid and impenetrable like marble. The poop went on dropping until the whole ship seemed to be toppling backwards into the deep moat below the wall of water that loomed over her, down and down to the bottom of the sea itself. At the moment when it seemed that this impregnable mass must engulf us, a rift appeared in its face and it collapsed beneath the ship, bearing her up so that what a moment before seemed a sluggish, solid hulk destined for the sea bed was now like a bird skimming the water, supported by the wind high above the valley.

This was noon.

In the first part of the afternoon the barometer was low, 742 millimetres. At one moment *Moshulu* would be riding the crests in brilliant sunshine, the next swooping down a great incline of water peppered by rain and hailstones, yawing a little from her course and beginning to roll, taking sea as high as her charthouse. Everyone was soaking wet and none of us had any more dry clothes. Everything in the Vuitton was wet as well. All through the afternoon we were kept busy making new wire buntlines, cold work with no movement in it, but by coffee-time one of my shirts had dried over the galley fire and I put it on rejoicing. But not for long.

As soon as I came out on deck I heard a voice calling me. It was the Captain, in leather coat and tweed cap, like a huge backwoods peer I had seen in a *Tatler* that the Sailmaker had somehow saved from destruction.

'Here you,' he said. 'Take up some slack on the crojack sheet.'

I plunged down on to the maindeck, where I was immediately knocked flat by a sea coming inboard. After this initial soaking, I no longer cared whether I was wet or not, only leaping for the lifelines when big dangerous seas came aboard.

At six there was a slight easing in the wind. I happened to be coming from the wheel, when once more the Captain had something in mind for me.

'We'll see what she can stand,' he said in a speculative way, like a gambler about to stake a large sum on an uncertainty.

'Aloft and break out the main lower topgallant. Lively now.' As I went I heard Sedelquist, who had been at the wheel with me, say: 'Crazy focker.' Privately agreeing with him, I swung myself on to the pin rail and into the main rigging. Aloft the wind seemed as strong as ever, and I looked down to a deck as narrow as a ruler on which the tiny figures of the watch were clustered, waiting to perform the ticklish job of sheeting home the sail which I was about to loose from its gaskets.

A distant cry borne on the wind told me that they were ready.

I cast off the gaskets on the weather side, hauled up a good slack on the buntlines, and, scuttling into the rigging, clung to the shrouds for my life. The yard began to plunge and whip, the buntlines plucked at the blocks seized to the shrouds, making the ratlines tremble underfoot.

'She'll never stand it,' was the general verdict when I regained the deck.

With the sail sheeted home there was too much strain on the entire sail structure and at eight o'clock the upper topsail sheet carried away and the sail had to be taken in, together with the lower topgallant we had recently set.

Thus reduced, we drove on in the darkness with both topsails set on the fore and mizzen, the main lower topsail, the foresail and one fore-and-aft sail – the jigger staysail.

This was the night of the second Friday, March 24th. We were fed up and though we cursed *Moshulu* and the Captain too, we were pleased with him for pushing her to the limit.

'This Kapten is proper strongbody for vind,' said Sandell after an issue of rum and a good dinner of Lobscouse – a sustaining hash made from pounded hard biscuit, potato and 'Buffelo'.

' – the Kapten,' replied Sedelquist who was absolutely cynical about all men. 'Vonts to get his name in the papers, I shouldn't vonder.'

'We'll be in it too, if he does,' I said.

'Yes, in the bloddy paper but on the front with beeg black lines all round "missing". That's what we'll be.'

It was too cold to argue. I slipped into my bunk dressed in my

223

long underwear with two pullovers on top. On my head was a very hairy balaclava helmet, so that I looked like the subject of some hitherto unpublished photograph of a military man in the lines about Sebastopol.

The fo'c'sle no longer seemed a human habitation. There were several inches of water on the floor, and trousers, seaboots and oilskins that had slipped from their hooks were moving gently backwards and forwards the whole length of it with a sucking sound. Wedging myself as firmly as I could in a steady position, I tried to read the *Times* leader on the dismissal of Dr Schacht, but the subject seemed so remote and unimportant and the light was so bad that when Alvar said 'Light ut' I extinguished it without argument.

Just before midnight the voice of the 'påpass' woke me. My long underwear was steaming like a kettle. Outside it was fearfully cold. Because it was my 'utkik' I put on as many layers as I could: a wet hairy shirt and trousers that I had bought in the East India Dock Road, two more pullovers in addition to the two I was sleeping in, and my heavy pilot coat. Everything was dripping with water.

'Remember *Admiral Karpfanger*[*] – keep good "utkik", plenty ice around here, maybe,' screamed Tria cheerfully in my ear, and left me.

At the lookout I peered ahead of the ship and could see nothing. The air was full of spray which rose like mist about the ship. The wind was strong enough to lean on. High above in the darkness the rest of the watch was bending a fresh chain-sheet for the main upper topsail.

With the new sheet bent we started to wind the yard into position. The gearing on the winch was very low and it was a slow job to raise it. By three in the morning it was in position and we had set the sail, together with the main lower topgallant which the Captain was determined she should carry.

---

[*] German schoolship ex *L'Avenir* lost with all hands in the Southern Ocean, February 1938.

But it was no use. The barometer continued to fall, and at five the starboard watch had to furl it again. This was on the morning of March 25th.

'Going to blow, I tink,' said Tria.

'What do you think it's doing now?' I asked him.

'Notting.'

'Golly.'

After breakfast I was at 'Backstern', extremely bad-tempered because I had been washed away when crossing the foredeck to the starboard fo'c'sle and had lost all the hot water.

Suddenly Taanila appeared. 'Kom,' he said.

'Why? I'm "Backstern".'

'Styrman, he say "BRÄCK GÅRDINGARNA PÅ STOR ÖVRE MÄRS".'

'This is it,' said Kroner as I went aft. 'Upper topsails. It's going to be really big.'

'It's the blasted "Backstern" that worries me There's no water.'

'I'll put some on for you,' he answered. 'It'll be there when you come back.'

'Maybe I shan't,' I said, nearer the mark than usual.

When we were all assembled the Mate slacked away the hand-brake of the upper topsail halliard winch and set it spinning. The eighty-foot yard began to descend in its greased track on the fore part of the mizzen mast, and as the weather sheet was progressively eased we clewed-up to windward and manned the buntlines. With the weather clew up, the lee side was easier and the sail was furled without incident.

The fore upper topsail was the most difficult. All the buntlines jammed and more than half the robands securing the topsail to the jackstay had gone. The outer buntline block had broken loose and was flailing in the air, so that when we reached the lowered yard eighty feet above the sea, we hesitated a moment before the 'Horry ops' of the Mates behind us drove us out on to the foot-ropes, hesitated because the bunt of the sail was beating back over the yard. The wind was immense. It no longer blew in the accepted sense of the word at all; instead it seemed to be tearing apart the very substance of the atmosphere. Nor was the sound of it any longer definable in ordinary terms. It no longer roared, screamed, sobbed or sang according to the various levels on which it was encountered. The power and noise of this wind was now more vast and all-comprehending, in its way as big as the sky, bigger than the sea itself, making something that the mind balked at, that it took refuge in blankness.

It was in this negative state of mind that could accept anything without qualm, even the possibility of death, that I fell off the yard backwards. I was the last man out on the weather side and was engaged in casting loose a gasket before we started to work on the sail, when without warning it flicked up, half the foot of a topsail, 40 feet of canvas as hard as corrugated iron, and knocked me clean off the footrope.

There was no interval for reflection, no sudden upsurge of remorse for past sins, nor did my life pass in rapid review before my eyes. Instead there was a delightful jerk and I found myself entangled in the weather rigging some five feet below the yard, and as soon as I could I climbed back to the yard and carried on with my job. I felt no fear at all until much later on.

It needed three-quarters of an hour to make fast the weather side. Time and time again we nearly had the sail to the yard when the wind tore it from our fingers.

My companion aloft was Alvar.

'What happened?' he said when we reached the deck.

'I fell.'

'I din' see,' he said in a disappointed way. 'I don' believe.'

'I'm damned if I'm going to do it again just because you didn't see it.'

'I don' believe.'

'Orlright,' I said. 'The next time I'll tell you when I'm going to fall off.'

'Dot's bettair,' said Alvar.

At noon on Saturday, the 25th, our position was 50° 7′ S., 164° 21′ W. In the 23½ hours from noon on the 24th *Moshulu* had sailed 241 miles and made 228 between observed positions. Her previous day's runs were 296 and 282, but the violence of the sea and the necessary reduction in canvas were slowing her increasingly.

The barometer fell and fell, 746, 742, 737 millimetres. The sun went down astern, shedding a pale watery yellow light on the undersides of the deep black clouds hurrying above the ship. It was extremely cold, colder than it had ever been, blowing a strong gale force 9. Big seas were coming aboard. I felt very lonely. The ship that had seemed huge and powerful was nothing now, a speck in the Great Southern Ocean, two thousand miles eastwards of New Zealand, three thousand from the coast of South America, separated to the North from the nearest inhabited land, the Cook Islands and Tahiti, by two thousand miles of open sea; to the South there was nothing but the Antarctic ice and darkness. She was running before seas that were being generated in the greatest expanse of open ocean, of a power and size unparalleled because there was no impediment to them as they drove eastwards round the world. She was made pigmy too by the wind, the wind that was already indescribable, that Tria said had only now begun to blow.

At this moment, for the first time I felt certain of the existence of an infinitely powerful and at the same time merciful God. Nearly everyone in the ship felt something of this, no one spoke of it. We were all of us awed by what we saw and heard beyond the common experience of men.

I had second wheel in the watch till midnight with Jansson to help me. We relieved Yonny Valker and Bäckmann.

'Törn om,' I said, mounting the platform next to Yonny and feeling with my foot for the brake pedal.

'Törn om,' repeated Yonny, showing me that he was ready to be relieved.

'Othhnordotht,' he lisped, giving me the course (we were running before the storm ENE.), and then added as he relinquished the wheel: 'No more babords.'

It seemed reasonable. The ship was pointing ENE½E., but with the rolling it was difficult to keep her right on course and I supposed that he had already given her as much port helm as she needed.

I was soon disillusioned. Yonny had left me with the wheel hard to starboard and she continued to run off in that direction.

Before Tria awoke to what was happening *Moshulu* was pointing south-east. Unfortunately he lost his head; shrieking wildly he began to turn the binnacle hood towards Jansson so that he could see the card, but only turned the hood sufficiently for the card to be invisible to both of us. At this moment the First Mate arrived and, thinking Jansson was at fault, began to give him hell. Not even the fact that I was standing on the weather side convinced him that I was helmsman.

It needed the four of us to return the ship to her course, and she took some terrific seas aboard. Afterwards the Mate laid into Jansson until the latter's nose began to glow red.

'It was my fault,' I shouted, trying to make my voice heard above the wind.

'Shot op, shot op!' bellowed the Mate with such violence that I dared not say another word. 'Shot op, or by *helvete* be jus' too bloddy bad.'

I shut up.

'I'm sorry,' I said to Jansson afterwards.

'Orlright,' he said, 'not dead, but nearly. We'll make some cocoa in the "Doonkey Hus".'

As the barometer went on falling, the wind rose. At 4 a.m. it fell to 733 metres and the wind blew force 10, Beaufort notation, a whole gale of wind. The starboard watch took in the main upper topsail at three o'clock and the ship ran before the storm under lower topsails and the foresail; the whole of the after deck was inundated.

'A liddle more,' said Sandell, 'she'll take a liddle more than this.'

Day broke at last, slowly because clouds, black as night, pressed upon the ship. Hail, driving rain and flurries of snow fell. At five the watch was called. We knew the reason before the Mate gave the order.

'Undra märs skot,' said Sedelquist. 'Got to slack those lower topsail sheets before it's too late.'

The main deck was like a reef with occasionally the tops of the winches and the hatches breaking the surface, and it seemed strange to me that a week ago, when we had been securing the hatch covers with heavy timbers, the precautions had seemed superfluous, almost too adequate, and yet now I found myself wondering what would happen if one of those awful cliff-like seas caught up with the ship and pooped her.

On the deck we were caught in a roaring flood and jumped for the lifelines hanging on minutes at a time, but with her topsails eased she ran better and there was less danger of the sail blowing out.

At six o'clock, cold yet exultant, we went below for coffee.

'She's a real ship,' said Sandell. 'I've never seen a ship like this. Blows like strongbody. Mos' ships you'd have the foresail off her and heave-to. Lovs vind, lovs it. But my God if ve have to take the foresail, be someting.'

The clouds cleared and a whole gale of wind blew out of a clear blue sky. At eight the wind reached its greatest velocity, force 11 on the Beaufort scale, a wind in which a wooden ship might well have foundered, and a lesser than *Moshulu* would have hove to, drifting to leeward, lying on the wind under a storm try-sail.

All through the storm the pigs had been setting up despairing cries, as well they might, cooped in their narrow steel coffins. At six o'clock we cleaned out their sties, a difficult job in a ship running before a great gale. It took three of us to do it.

'For Chrissake don' let them go,' grunted Tria, as we levered the iron troughs through the door of the sty with crowbars.

He had no sooner said this than Auguste and Filimon, believing that the ship was about to founder, charged the barricade of hatch covers with which we had fenced them in, intent on finding a place in the boats. The barricade collapsed and Filimon, who was leading, shot between Tria's legs, upsetting him in the nasty mess we were shovelling up. Auguste followed him closely, and they both went glissading away on their behinds into the lee scuppers, from which we had difficulty in rescuing them.

'Better eat them before they go overside,' I said as we struggled with Auguste, who was threshing about under water.

'I don' care how soon we eat that Filimon,' Tria said.

✝

Moshulu continued to carry her sail and the storm entered its last and most impressive phase. We were cold and wet and yet too excited to sleep. Some stood on the fo'c'sle head but only for a short time as the force of the wind made it difficult to remain on two feet. Others stood beneath it and gazed out along the ship, watching the seas rearing up astern as high as a three-storeyed house. It was not only their height that was impressive but their length. Between the greatest of them there was a distance that could only be estimated in relation to the ship, as much as four times her entire length, or nearly a quarter of a mile. The seas approached very deliberately, black and shiny as jet, with smoking white crests gleaming in the sunshine, hissing as they came, hurling a fine spume into the air as high as the main yard.

I went aloft in the fore rigging, out of the comparative shelter of the foresail, into the top, and higher again to the cross-trees, where I braced myself to the backstays. At this height, 130 feet up, in a wind blowing 70 miles an hour, the noise was an unearthly scream. Above me was the naked topgallant yard and above that again the royal to which I presently climbed. I was now used to heights but the bare yard, gleaming yellow in the sunshine, was groaning and creaking on its tracks. The high whistle of the wind through the halliards sheaf, and above all the pale blue illimitable sky, cold and serene, made me deeply afraid and conscious of my insignificance.

Far below, the ship was an impressive sight. For a time the whole of the after deck would disappear, hatches, winches, everything, as the solid water hit it, and then, like an animal pulled down by hounds, she would rise and shake them from her, would come lifting out of the sea with her freeing ports spouting.

Opening my camera, I attached the lens hood, but the wind blew it into the sea. The mist of spray rising all about the ship made it almost impossible to see anything through the viewfinder. There was no need for the range-finder. I simply set the scale to infinity and pressed the button, and even that was difficult enough.

Later, I was standing on deck just aft of the charthouse when a monster wave reared over the main rail and exploded on the house itself. As it came I shut the camera but was too late to shut the case.

In an agony of mind I went down to the fo'c'sle. The camera was very wet. The film was undamaged. I up-ended it and a thin trickle of water ran out of the Compur shutter. The rest of the watch were observing me with interest.

'I'll have to take it to pieces or it'll rust up,' I explained.

'Good,' said everybody. 'Now.'

'No, when the storm finishes. The thing's full of springs.'

'Put it in the offen,' said Sedelquist. 'I should ask the "Kock". Dry heem out.'

By noon *Moshulu* had again run 228 miles. Since the storm began we had crossed 18 degrees of longitude. Now the barometer rose steadily. The starboard watch reset the fore and main upper topsails and all through the afternoon we were resetting sail. Big seas were still coming aboard and we frequently deserted the halliard winches for the lifelines. Sent aloft to overhaul the buntlines, I returned in a filthy temper because I had dropped my knife overboard.

By 9 p.m. the gale had passed, the wind had fallen, but there was still a tremendous sea running. The weather was clear and cold with overhead a thin crescent moon. At two in the morning of Monday, the 27th, we reset the main royal and in an hour or two more we were in full sail again.

CHAPTER TWENTY

Cape Horn

I loved the ship after a great storm. At first, as the sails were re-set, tier upon tier, upper topsails, topgallants, royals, staysails, spanker sails and jibs, the canvas would be dark and wet; and then when the whole edifice rose completed into the air it would dry quickly to a dazzling whiteness with the sun and wind playing on it.

But this time it was not for long. A day's interval and it blew hard again, this time from WNW. and NW. Between midnight on Tuesday and midnight on Wednesday, the twenty-ninth of March, she logged 297 miles with the wind force 6–8. In her best hours, from noon to eight, she logged 114 miles; at times running 15 knots with the whole lee rail under water.

Wednesday night was black and hellish cold, with wind force 8 and all hands called to shorten down, the ship buffeted but sailing splendidly.

So it went on. In nine days she sailed 2,450 sea rules from Longitude 176° 37′ W. to 119° 12′ W., which we crossed on April 1st, always to the south of the 51st parallel. We were very cold now and piled on as many clothes as possible. Even the Finns complained and appeared in wild sheepskins and black fur hats; everyone sprouted beards, some more impressive than others –mine was among the most miserable and I looked like a goose-berry. It was no good putting on a great many clothes except for wheel and lookout as work aloft was both dangerous and difficult if you were overdressed. Even at lookout it could be a disadvantage. One night Tria ordered me to trim the port navigation light.

'It's smokking like hell,' he said. 'Trim the vick.'

The entrance to the domed lighthouse was through a narrow opening in the base; inside the 'Båtsman's Skåp'. I was wearing four pullovers and an oilskin and became wedged in the hole. Unable to communicate my difficulty to anyone, I began to asphyxiate in the fumes of the light. With a struggle I managed to turn it out completely. In this position I remained, suffering acute claustrophobia, hoping that if I were rescued it would not be by someone like Hermansonn, whose Teutonic sense of humour would find ample scope in my present situation. After a long interval, somebody gripped my seaboots and pulled them off. For a moment I panicked, thinking that the soles of my feet were about to be tickled. Fortunately it was Tria who was in no mood for horseplay.

'What you tink you're doing op there all night?' he demanded when he finally managed to withdraw me. 'Förste Styrman is bloddy angry. Was eight bells and notting from you.'

The cold struck at us from the deck through the soles of our boots. Those like Kroner and myself with rubber seaboots were the worst off. The Finns and Ålanders, whose entire rig was the product of less industrialized methods, all wore leather boots which they kept greased.

'I've just been reading *Watkin's Last Expedition*,' said Kroner one bitter night as he relieved me at 'utkik'. 'Chapman says the best thing is to line your boots with grass.'

'Remind me to bring some grass next time.'

'I don't think there's going to be a next time for me.'

The Captain did his best for us. Very often after a hard night on deck both watches would get a rum ration. As the dawn was breaking, around five o'clock, we used to stand in a wet, miserable queue outside the charthouse.

'Do you take water?' the Captain asked each of us as his turn came, in the same way as my mother on the other side of the world was probably saying 'Milk? Sugar?' Nobody ever did.

With the Captain's rum inside me the rest of the watch on deck would pass like a dream and I never minded cleaning the pigs who were considerably chastened by the desolate regions we were traversing and gave no trouble. It was when the effect of the rum wore off and I looked about me at the damp unheated fo'c'sle over which a cold blue fog hung permanently that I wished myself elsewhere. The cold and the need to restore circulation made us fight in the free watches, otherwise life in the fo'c'sle resolved itself into a routine of eating and sleeping. As a variant of the rough and tumble, Yonny Valker made a rope grommet and challenged us to a tug of war. It began as a straightforward competition, with two opponents holding the grommet and pulling from opposite sides of the table, until Hermansonn had the idea of dispensing with the hands and putting the loop round our necks instead. A large audience assembled for the preliminary heats in the hope that someone would be garrotted. To my great surprise I emerged victorious. The port fo'c'sle immediately began to a organize a championship match, but a complication arose as none of the starboard watch would recognize or take part in a garrotting competition, preferring the old-fashioned single-handed tugging, so for the moment the whole thing lapsed.

In the brief intervals of calm, when the ship was stable enough, I tried to re-assemble the Compur shutter. I kept all the pieces in a cigar box and worked on it for hours on end, crouching on my bunk, almost crying with vexation. It was a nightmare. Sometimes the shutter mechanism opened and stayed open, at others it remained resolutely shut or whirred like a cuckoo clock and winked continuously. I thought sadly and enviously of the technicians at Jena, half the world away, to whom a Compur shutter was an open book. Finally, after a week of effort, I managed to obtain an exposure of something like 1/25th of a second, and with this I had to be content.

We had four more days of abnormally fine weather for such high latitudes, with strong beam winds and high barometer. Sometimes there were squalls of rain. For the most part the night air was icy cold and the sky was full of noble masses of white and black cloud with occasional rifts through which the moon shone. Once there was a rainbow in bright moonlight.

At 'utkik' we kept good lookout, both for ice and in hopes of seeing *Pamir*, *Passat* and *Viking*, who were all somewhere in this wilderness. There were few albatross, far fewer than we had seen in the Southern Indian Ocean.

Finally on April 4th, in 51° S., 107° W., with the wind SE., close-hauled on the starboard tack, we began to stand towards Cape Horn.

On the 6th the large white pig was executed. While she was happily munching a lure of potatoes, the Steward hit her behind the ear with a sledge hammer and she went down scuffling. In a moment her throat was cut and pints of blood shining like bright new paint were being decanted into a bucket.

All hands turned out to watch this gruesome spectacle.

'Good, pancake tomorrow,' Jansson said.

How do you make pancake from pig?'

'With blods and jams. Real strongbody.'

The following day was Good Friday, April 7th, the 27th day of the voyage. It was cold and stormy-looking with a tremendous sea running and incessant squalls of rain. The noon position was 54° S., 88° W. and we were closing the coast of Patagonia rapidly. Dinner was an immense orgy of roast pork and bloody pancakes. They were very nasty to look at. We ate them with melon jam and on top of the pork they were more than sustaining. Afterwards we lay about lifelessly, discussing dictators.

'They ought to give Hitler a meal like this every day,' I said to Kroner. 'That would shut him up. You can't do anything when you're full of pork.'

'You can still have filthy thoughts, though,' Kroner said, 'I've got some now.'

'I know, but that's different. You wouldn't get rid of people, Jews and so on.'

'I'd get rid of almost everyone. I'd destroy everyone who wasn't fit and young. Then I'd burn everything down, houses, libraries, museums, the whole lot, and with my few perfect human specimens start breeding again.'

'In the open air? You've just burned down all the buildings.'

235

'Whoever else I get rid of,' Kroner said, 'I'd start with you. You're typical of England. You don't take anything seriously and you're weak-minded. You've ceased to justify what you've got, so you'll go under.'

'I've changed my mind about Hitler since listening to you,' I said. 'I don't think he lives on nut salads at all. I think he's a secret pig-eater.'

'You know,' said Kroner, after we had gone on like this for some time. 'I don't care a goddam either way. But I do like a really bad-tempered argument.'

There was more pig for supper. The night was black and cold with soft rain. The wind was SW., force 5; great heaps of water were coming on deck and the ship was running 13 knots. Full of pig, I stood on the fo'c'sle head looking wanly at the sea surging under the bows, wishing that I had not lost the knack of seasickness.

The following day, Saturday, the weather cleared and the wind shifted to SSE. There were two helmsmen. By noon we were in 80° W. 55° S. *Moshulu* had sailed 283 miles in 23½ hours and crossed eight degrees of longitude.

'He looks pleased,' Sails said, indicating the Captain, who was standing on the poop, looking along the length of his ship. 'Says he's going to sail in sight of land if he can.'

We were finishing dinner when the door of the fo'c'sle was flung open and Pipinen appeared. He was in old, patched yellow oilskins and his face was white with dried spray.

'All hands stand by,' he said, and vanished into the darkness.

'What is it?' I asked as we came out on the fore deck.

'Jagare – flying jib,' someone answered as we went forward to the fo'c'sle head.

Twenty of us congregated forward. Pipinen eased the sheet of the flying jib, the Mate cast off the halliard, and the rest of us manned the downhaul on the foredeck. As it started to come down, the sail boomed like a cannon and the sheet block clanged on the lee rail. Then it came down with a rush. A torch snapped on for a moment.

'Orlright,' came the Mate's voice. 'Newby, Taanila, Bäckmann, out there and mek fast. One arm for the ship. Babordsvakt, bräck bukgårdingarna på kryss royal. In frivakt.'

We lay out along the bowsprit guys to the flying jib. We could not see it yet but we could hear it beating. The ship was going like a mad thing, making fourteen knots with her lee rail dipping and her bow wave breaking in spray which shone red in the rays of the port navigation light. As she ran she surged into the sea so that it came up at us on the bowsprit as if it was trying to lick us off. We reached the sail and as it swished towards us, fell on it. The Mate's instruction about one arm for the ship was impossible with such a sail. It needed two hands or none at all. We got the bolt-rope under our stomachs and smashed the wind out of the sail, at the same time struggling with the gaskets that had been too well made up. Once the gaskets were loose they had to be passed.

'Kossuri, take my bloddy byxor,' Taanila yelled in my ear.

I put my hand under his oilskin coat and took a good hold on his belt and trousers as he got down on to the footrope to take the gasket that Yonny Valker and I were swinging towards him over the sail and under the bowsprit. At that moment it was fortunate that Taanila's mother could not see him. It was fortunate, perhaps, that none of our mothers could see us.

The royals were in, the upper topgallants were coming in when we regained the deck. It was time for my wheel. The Mates had rigged up a tarpaulin in the weather rigging and were crouching in the lee of it. They were cold, I was hot. Furling a sail as full of life as the flying jib was like a couple of sets of brisk squash rackets. After a while a rift appeared in the gloom overhead and the weather cleared. The moon came up behind a wild bank of storm cloud and shone eerily on the water. I thought of the *Admiral Karpfanger* and the sixty members of her crew who only a year ago had disappeared somewhere in this desolation. These thoughts were to some extent dispelled by an issue of rum at midnight. Wet but warm we went to our bunks hiccuping happily.

About ten o'clock on Sunday morning a curtain of cloud lifted to the north of us and we saw the four masts of a barque about fifteen miles on the port beam. Apparently she was on the same course as ourselves, close hauled and beating to the south, but to leeward of us.

The wildest excitement prevailed. It could only be one of three ships: *Passat*, *Pamir* or *Viking*. *Viking* had left Port Victoria on the 16th of February, three weeks before us, and by now she should have been clear of Cape Horn well into the South Atlantic. *Pamir* had sailed before us on March 8th; *Passat* had left Port Lincoln on the 9th.

'Skepparen will be happy,' was the general verdict.

It was an understatement. The Captain was delighted. His glass already told him that she was carrying topgallants, but the crojack was furled. 'We'll set the royals,' I heard him say to the Second Mate, who at once sent three jungmän aloft to cast off the gaskets while the rest of the watch stood by the royal halliards.

The remainder of the morning I spent with the Sailmaker. We discussed a remarkable variety of subjects, with all of which he was perfectly at ease. My diary records what we spoke about.

'Spent the morning with the Sailmaker in his cabin under the poop' (he had moved there when the weather grew too cold for the sail-loft). 'Discussed Neolithic Britain, Runes, Sailing Ships, and Homosexuality, in that order.'

From time to time I left him and climbed to the jigger top to watch the progress of the other barque.

'She's almost in full sail now,' I said when I returned from one of these expeditions. 'They've just set the royals and the crojack and they're carrying topmast staysails. I can't see much of her hull but she looks bigger than *Viking*.'

At each fresh bulletin Sails had said, 'Good.' Now he said: 'She'll never get near us. Hasn't a hope. Nobody's going to call this a slow ship, not after this voyage, not after Mike's had her. Why she's run 27 miles in two hours, 57 in four, 114 in eight, and 296 in a day, a twenty-three-and-a-half-hour day, too. All deep-loaded. We've shown 'em. Especially that bugger X' (here he named one of the more conceited and less amiable of Erikson's captains).

My audience was at an end. 'Get off now,' he said, fixing his spectacles on his nose. 'I don't want to waste my time with you all day. I want to get on with some reading.' He flourished a book.

'What is it?'

'*People's History of England* – read it three times.'

'Good God. Why?'

'I'm trying to find out why Limeys are such stupid buggers.'

☦

It was Easter Sunday and the 'Kock' had made an extra effort. There was tomato soup so hot that it was undrinkable, more pork, and a big bowl of custard and plum jam. The pork looked like getting cold so we started with that and went on to custard. After the custard we had some of the soup, which was cooler by now, and so on to pork once more; then it was time for my wheel. With stomach protesting, I put on my pilot coat and went on deck. As I relieved Hilbert, the First Mate came down the rigging. He had a pair of binoculars round his neck. 'It's *Passat*,' he said. 'I joost seen her from the crosstrees. Old Lindvall must be vild. Keep some life in dat main royal.' And went below, chuckling, to tell the Captain.

Moshulu was making ten knots on the starboard tack, close-hauled, with the yards braced hard round on the port backstays. At first she sailed well, pointing E. by N. The wind shifted a little and she pointed E. by S. A rain squall drove down on us with smoking ragged edges. As I dragged at the wheel the wind blew on the fore part of the sails, and the Captain who had just come on deck swore aloud. As if in deference to him, the squall passed, the rain ceased instantly, and was succeeded by a blue sky with tufts of white cloud like cotton wool in it.

'Watch what you're doing, Glory of the Seas,' said the Captain with powerful irony.

Passat was a magnificent sight now with a great bone of white water between her teeth. Our passage took on a new significance. It became a trial of seamanship, a real race. I thought of Eddy in *Passat*, and how much he would be enjoying this.

'I'll be seeing you in London,' had been his parting words. 'I've just got to come. And when I do I'm going to buy a great big badger shaving brush in the Burlington Arcade.'

The wind shifted a point or two on the beam. We eased the braces a little. The ship responded at once and flew in a smother of white sea.

'Can they beat us?' I asked Sedelquist.

'Beat us,' he said in triumph, but without his usual arrogance. 'Nobody can beat us.'

That day in *Moshulu* everybody felt like that. Whatever happened now the voyage had been worth while.

By four o'clock *Passat* was far astern, and as night came down she was blotted from view by a squall of hail. We never saw her again. At half past two on Monday morning the main royal sheet parted and we had other things to think about. At three the wind shifted to SSW. It was free. We no longer sailed close-hauled.

'Today,' said Tria, 'we shall pass Cape Horn.'

Tria was my only contact with reality. Of the afterguard, he was the only one I could approach for information. The others, the First Mate, the Second and the Captain, occasionally dropped a word to the helmsman, an Olympian crumb, to feed his abysmal ignorance. Otherwise we fortified ourselves with conjecture and my minute atlas.

After Tria had given me this news I made my way cautiously to the charthouse. By this time I was well practised in evasion. With one ear for the Captain's tread on the companion way and the other for the Mate on deck, I made a rough estimate of our noon position. The day before we were already south of the extreme tip of South America, south of Tierra del Fuego, south of Cape Horn. It seemed unlikely that we would sight the Horn at all. I was disappointed. Sometimes listening to Mountstewart in his fantastic study I had imagined when he had spoken of 'Rounding the Cape' that there was some compulsion on the Captains of sailing vessels to pass within what he would have described as 'a biscuit's toss' of the high black cliffs, so close that visiting Indians could squinny down into the ship as she roared past. At the moment we were sixty miles to the south of it, and I gazed at the waters expecting to see buoys floating at intervals bearing banners with 'You are now in the Mountstewart country' inscribed on them.

I was also sorry to be rounding the Cape on a Bank Holiday Monday. It somehow rendered the whole venture more prosaic, and I would not have been surprised if we had encountered motorboats with notices 'Round the Horn and Back' chugging merrily into the prevailing wind loaded with Fuegians.

In spite of everything, as the day went on, the place triumphed and refused to be prosaic. Perhaps there had been too many poopings and dismastings, too many ships embayed in ice. The weather changed constantly. It was cold with low cloud and bad visibility. Frequently the ship was swept by heavy rain. At eight o'clock snow began to fall. The sea was not rough but there was a tremendous see-saw motion of the water as though it was being slopped from one end of a bath to the other.

As at Inaccessible Island sea and sky were filled with birds. Inquisitive black-faced mollymauks with white bodies and dark brown wing surfaces; Wandering Albatross; Silver-Grey Fulmars shining like pearls; black and brown Wilson's Petrels, Mother Carey's Chickens, fluttering aimlessly and weakly in the troughs of the sea, seeming too fragile and small for such a place.

At ten I was sent aloft.

'Put some more robands in the kryss undra märs and keep a lookout for Diego Ramirez,' Tria had said.

It was bitterly cold at the lower topsail yard in the mizzen rigging and my pilot coat felt like paper in a wind that was coming straight off the Polar Ice. I was just about to descend to the deck when I saw an island, a long way to the north of us.

The Captain was on deck when I got down. From there the land was invisible.

'Land, Sir,' I said, half hoping that he would reward me with a bag of gold . . . Perhaps he would increase my pay.

'Islas Diego Ramirez,' he answered and went on, leaning heavily on the *South American Pilot* (Part 2), 'the peak is 587 fleet high and covered with snow. The islands are usually inhabited in the season of moderate weather.'

With this, a feeling of Bank Holiday, that had been dissipated with such difficulty, returned. The Captain seemed more like a Beefeater saying his piece to a crowd of sightseers. He would have looked well in the uniform, and I could imagine him saying: 'This is the Traitors' Gate. Prisoners were formerly conveyed by water and then up them steps to the Bloody Tower. It is now disused.'

At five we passed Cape Horn well to the south in latitude 56° 50'. In the thirty days from Port Victoria we had sailed more than 6,000 sea miles.

Just two days later we were off the southern part of the Falkland Islands, having run 450 miles, with the wind WNW. for the most part.

'We're going to make a record passage,' said Kroner at one of our brief encounters. We spent most of the free watches in our bunks now, for the days were cold and the nights colder in the fo'c'sle, where everything had the chillness of death on it. He proceeded to demonstrate. 'Thirty days Port Vic to the Horn. Orlright?'

'Orlright.'

'Two days to the Falkland Islands. Orlright?'

'I suppose so.' I found myself reacting unfavourably to a form of interrogation which I had so often put up with in public houses.

'Cape Horn to the Line's been done in eighteen days – the Laeisz ships have done it, so can we but we'll allow twenty. That makes fifty,' Kroner said. 'The Equator to the Lizard, that's been done in sixteen. We could do the whole voyage in sixty-six days. *Swanhilda* did it in sixty-six.'

'You'd better allow thirty to Queenstown.'

'Orlright, thirty then. That's still only eighty, better than *Parma*.'

'You're a seely focker,' interrupted Sandell who had been passing and stopped to listen. No conversation was private. 'If you think you're going to do that you're seely. She's not a bloody tramcar, she's a sailing ship. If we're lucky we'll be 95 days to Queenstown, not much less.'

CHAPTER TWENTY-ONE
'Like Spreeng after Vinter'

A S far as most of us were concerned we had made it. Once in
the South Atlantic our relationship with the Mates deterio-
rated. For all of us Cape Horn had been a *memento mori*, a skull
on the study table.

'No more knacka rost,' said the First Mate soon after we had
passed the Falklands.

'Good,' I said enthusiastically. He seemed to be seeking conversation. 'I'm glad.'

'Yo, yo, yo, good, good,' he replied in a parody of my own
voice. 'Now you can start robbing.'

'Who?'

'All dose skylights,' indicating all the teak in the ship with a
comprehensive wave of his hand and watching me closely for any
laughter. 'Robbing down dose tik tings.'

'You know,' I said to Kroner, 'I believe he does it on purpose.
I don't believe he really speaks English like that. I think he's trying to make me laugh so that he can put me in irons for insolence.'

'I think he's in your Secret Service,' Kroner said. 'I think he's
an Englishman really, giving an imitation of a Swedish-Finn imi-
tating an Englishman.'

We washed the teak with caustic soda and burnished it with
sand and a 'bible' (the old name for a block of wood wrapped in
sail canvas). My hands never recovered from the caustic soda.

The Mate, always assiduous, became finicky. 'Är dot färdigt?
Is it finished?' he used to shout, no sooner had he set us a task.

'Fock off,' some sturdy individualist would whisper loudly,
without moving his lips.

Even Tria became impossible.

'Peety,' he said one day. 'Peety bloddy wind changes in day.'

'Why?'

'Too mooch bracing. Not so mooch work.'

'It's all work. You trying to win a medal?'

✠

As the days passed the First Mate became intolerable, setting us tasks and then moving us to other parts of the ship before they were properly finished. Eventually he had a tremendous row with Tria who was our foreman and slave-driver combined. We absorbed it with the awful fascination of children listening to their parents quarrelling. The argument was plain enough because most of it was carried on in English. I wondered if they argued in English for practice. Perhaps one of the stock questions in the oral examination for Master in the Finnish Merchant Marine was: 'Carry on an argument for fifteen minutes in English about any subject. Grammatical accuracy is not essential but marks will be given for violence.'

'Dot stonchion,' said the First Mate with deadly calm, looming over Hermansonn who was chipping, 'HAS NO BLODDY ROOST on' (suddenly bellowing). Tria was exasperated. In his hand he held a scraper which he used rather as a conductor uses his baton.

'VOT DE BLODDY HELL,' he roared, hurling it to the deck and stalking off.

'KOM HERE,' screamed the Mate.

Tria took no notice and continued to walk towards the midships deck.

'KOM HERE,' said the Mate again in a terrible voice.

Tria turned. 'I'm going to sheet,' he said. 'You make me want to sheet too much,' and disappeared without another word into the officers' quarters.

✠

On Saturdays the Captain opened the 'Slop Chest'.

'1s 9d for feefty Capstan out of bond, miserable old boggert' was the verdict on the Captain, who showed a business acumen second only to that of the great Gustav himself.

Every Saturday we tried to find out the proper prices of his tobacco. 'Those are cheaper and those are dearer' was all he would say. The truth eventually came out at the end of the voyage in the form of enormous debits to our pay. There were three sorts of cigarettes: Capstan, Imperial Preference, and Three Bells. There were Finnish cigarettes too, which came in boxes of fifty complete with wooden cigarette-holders. Like Taanila, they were small and deadly.

'It's not surprising the birth rate's going down in your country if you smoke cigarettes like that,' Kroner said to Karma.

Besides cigarettes there was Australian and Dutch tobacco; the Australian kind was called Town Talk ('Toon tolk'); cigarette papers (Le Coq d'Or), Goliath matches and Sunlight soap. That was all. There were no delicacies like jam, no necessities such as knives. The Captain showed an appreciation of stock control that would have won him success in more sheltered fields.

As the officers became more bad-tempered, the crew's relationship with one another improved. Conversation was carried on mostly at mealtimes in a polyglot of Swedish, German, Finnish and English, vigorous and obscene. There were none of the double meanings we had bandied with Miss Reidenfelt at Wurzel's, it was all full-bodied Rabelaisian stuff bellowed out by men with their mouths full of potatoes. There was no abnormality. Perhaps we were too tired, perhaps we smelled too bad. For the most part we thought of food. Nevertheless, pin-ups from magazines were greatly prized. The choice was not left to the individual but was governed by a Committee as strict, unpredictable and completely illogical as the Hanging Committee of the Royal Academy, but unlike that body, far more demanding. If the verdict was 'proper strongbody', then the picture could be stuck, with a paste made from boiled potatoes, on the bulkhead inside the owner's bunk, where it would

245

be raped in the imagination then immediately forgotten until the time came for the bunk to be repainted, when the owner would begin to find it indispensable.

We were really hungry now, hungrier than we had ever been. The pig-eating and the biting winds had both given a tremendous edge to our appetites. On the Saturday of Bank Holiday week we finished three tins of condensed milk within a few hours of receiving them. A gloomy prospect of seven milkless days rose before us. In the night watches we made ourselves miserable by composing and eating imaginary banquets.

Fortunately the weather was becoming warmer every day. Seven days after rounding the Cape there was a remarkable transformation and we were able to loll about the deck in the free watch dressed in dungarees instead of shivering under layers of damp wool. The sea was no longer wild and grey. Now it was brilliant blue, laced with white, and the ship looked fresh and young, full of sunshine and shadow in the early morning.

'Like Spreeng after Vinter,' said Sedelquist.

In these conditions we bent a 1934 foresail for the Trade Winds. With the foresail set, the weather immediately worsened, the wind shifting for east to east-south-east and then to SE.

'Beeg storm komming op,' Sandell said, making a circular movement with his right hand. 'Reevolving.'

'How do you know?'

'How? Because vind's moving to right and blowing like helvete. Sydost now. Be Väst before we finish.'

This was the night of April 20th. First the wind blew SE. and we were sent aloft to make fast the fore upper topsail. Then it blew SSE. and we had to take in the main upper topsail. At ten at night when it was blowing from the south, force 9, the lower topsail sheet parted and the sail blew out. At once it became a flailing shapeless wreckage that needed all hands to furl it. Clewing up the remnants, with big seas coming aboard, the port watch was engulfed and six of us were swept away from the mizzen rigging. Once again I was turning over and over under water with other bodies milling about me.

The wind went on shifting to the westwards and it blew SSW., force 10. Mercifully the rain had ceased and we ran before the storm with the wind on the port quarter under three sails only, two lower topsails and the 1934 foresail which surprisingly stood up to the strain. At eleven the starboard watch went below. They had been on deck for eleven hours. At midnight they relieved us once more. After another hour the wind went round to south-west and continued to shift from south-west and then to west-north-west.

All through the dark early hours we re-set sail. Because 'Doonkey' had tightened the bearings, we had to wind away at the halliard winch for half an hour to raise the topsail yard. We finally got below at about five. On the fo'c'sle table we found an entire bottle of rum.

'Kapten vonts to be lovved, you noh,' Sedelquist remarked unkindly, seeing this welcome sight.

'Don' need to drink it, do you?' said Sandell. 'But go easy with that bloddy cork if you're not wanting any.'

All the afternoon the sky had a sinister threatening appearance and the barometer was down to 757 millimetres. At one o'clock on the morning of the 22nd the wind was variable. We wore the ship to the starboard tack, a tremendous job for one watch. At three it began to rain with tropical intensity.

Suddenly the wind dropped away completely and the rain ceased. The ship was so quiet that I could hear men speaking at the poop.

'I jus' carn remember,' said Sandell, 'I jus' carn remember the name.'

'What name?'

'The name of the bloddy ting that's going to happen to us in a meenit.'

At that moment the Captain's voice came urgently through the murk.

'Bräck gårdingarna på kryss över bram.'

One moment we were hauling the sail down to the yard with the winch spinning, the next the whole of the ship fore and aft of the charthouse disappeared in a sea that swept her. The fore upper topgallant exploded noisily and in a moment had blown away to leeward, a tattered rag of canvas.

'I jus' remember,' said Sandell four hours later, after we had bent another topgallant and reset all the sail we had taken in. 'It's Pampero, beeg vind, South American vind.'

On April 22nd we picked up the SE. Trades in latitude 28° S., 30° W. Once more Kroner and I could spend the free watches in our hammocks, allowing the warm strong wind to make us first brown, then black, while we lazily discussed a future that seemed so remote as to be impossible.

'You know,' said Kroner, one more than usually perfect day, as we watched the flying fish skidding over the surface of a sea whipped white by the strong wind, 'if they put Hitler and Mussolini in charge of a lightship and anchored it somewhere near here, they wouldn't give any more trouble. They wouldn't want to do anything, they'd just sit and sit, happily, until they starved to death.'

'Just like us. There's "Buffelo" for dinner and I'm starving, but I'm not happy,' I said, disinclined to start a pseudo-philosophic discussion.

'It's impossible to talk seriously with you,' Kroner answered testily. 'You only think of your stomach.'

At night it was difficult to keep awake at all. In an hour at the 'påpass' I used to fall asleep half-a-dozen times. To keep myself awake I used to smoke one cigarette after another, carefully shielding them from the Mates amidships. But it was no use. Only the cigarette burning my fingers would jerk me into sufficient consciousness to light another from it.

Far worse was the wheel. Once, after an hour in which I had repeatedly gone to sleep, I went into the charthouse to report the course to Tria. I found him bent over the table with his head on a chart of the South Atlantic, snoring. After bawling 'Nordnordost' in his ear several times without making any impression, I left him.

The bugs came back with the fine weather, this time in greater force. After a night or so of torment we once again left the fo'c'sle to its aboriginal inhabitants.

Four days later, on the 26th, the Trades were still blowing strongly. At the change of watch at midnight the Second Mate called out:

'Whose utkik?'

'Mine,' I said.

'Keep good lookout.'

Thinking that we must be crossing a shipping lane, I went to the fo'c'sle head to relieve Kroner.

'Nobody told me anything,' he said. 'All I know, it's bloody dark.'

It was a sinister night, difficult for the lookout. Great banks of rain cloud were streaming diagonally across our course. I gazed earnestly into the darkness until my eyes were full of black spots and coloured lights and I began to imagine that they were great liners tearing down on us. In an effort to dispel these illusions, I tried an idea of Mountstewart's, 'an old trappers' dodge he had called it. First you had to pretend disinterestedness, and then suddenly swing round and glare at the prospect like someone playing grandmother's footsteps.

I was becoming tired of this when I saw something that seemed darker and more immovable than the cloud itself, low down towards the level of the sea. After some moments of indecision I decided that it was better to be taken for a fool than bear the responsibility alone. As I turned to strike three bells I found the First Mate at my elbow.

'Vot's the matter, seen a ghost?' he asked nonchalantly.

I pointed dead ahead of the ship, where there was now visible a solid mass.

'Martin Vas,' he said. Then he was gone, haring along the flying bridge to the midships deck. I heard him shouting 'Hårt babord' to the helmsman and *Moshulu* began to turn away to port. In ten minutes they were abeam, three solitary rocks rising out of the sea, two close together, the other an aloof pinnacle. In an hour they had vanished completely.

'Lokky. Been joost into them in half an hour,' said the Mate.

This unexpected landfall of three rocks suddenly in the waste of the South Atlantic made an impression on me.

'It's strange, isn't it?' said Kroner, putting my own thoughts into words the next day. 'One moment those three islands were alone absolutely. Suddenly the ship appears, filled with lights and people, for a moment only. Then the ship goes by, the lights and the noise die away, the wake subsides, and a cigarette-end thrown overboard falls to pieces, and disappears, and once more the wind blows over those three rocks. I wonder how long it'll be before another ship passes them'

The Trades blew, and the West Wind, the cold, and the wetness became a distant memory. The helmsman's work was easier now. On coming to the wheel he settled himself comfortably and only needed to shift it a spoke or two to port or starboard in a whole hour. At night the 'påpass' could lie on the hatch cover smoking his pipe, gazing up through a dark jungle of rigging to the tiers of sails dazzling white against the clear night sky his only problem to find and wake the other watch at the end of four hours and get them on deck in time for the muster. It was difficult, because they were hidden all over the forepart of the ship: in the 'tween-decks among the sails, on the roof of the Donkey house, in huts made from hatch-covers, in hammocks slung seven feet high.

On such a night I had second wheel and Alvar forgot to wake me. Suddenly he appeared and began to swing my hammock violently to and fro roaring 'Ut, ut, horry op,' in a great voice. In the dark I panicked and was unable to find my trousers. I decided to take a chance and go without them, relying on the darkness and the wheel to shield me.

All was well for twenty minutes, until the First Mate began to prowl around. When he saw me he immediately blew his whistle for the 'påpass'.

'Byxor till rorsman,' he shouted.

Very soon Yonny Valker appeared with my thickest West Wind trousers and held them out to me like a Lord of the Bedchamber robing the Monarch.

'Put dose tings on,' said the Mate in a voice strangled with fury.

'I can't put those on, they're six inches thick, I'll die,' I protested.

'PUT ON DOSE BYXOR,' he screamed. 'PUT 'EM ON, OR BY *HELVETE*, YOU'LL BE PUT AVAAY.'

I put them on and passed a most unpleasant forty minutes.

'Silly of you to leave your trousers in the bunk?' said Alvar, winking heavily at the others when I went below.

'I wonder what happened to make you so horrible?' I said.

The South East Trades blew strongly. Finally we lost them in latitude 5° S. 29° W., on May 1st. The crew felt that May 1st should be a holiday.

'If we don' ask the old boggert we'll get fock notting,' said Sedelquist, and at once set about arranging a deputation from the port watch and the daymen.

'Shouldn't we ask styrbordsvakt to come too?' I asked.

'Lissun,' said Sedelquist, 'if styrbordsvakt want a holiday they can ask for it. This is babordsvakt.'

We found the Captain leaning against the door of the chart-house, dressed in spotless white ducks and a topee. He regarded us with mild curiosity.

I stood as far back in the deputation as possible, feeling like a mutineer while Sedelquist said his piece. '. . . holiday general in Finland . . . always had one in other Erikson ships . . . if not granted would have to notify Finish Consul in order port . . . double pay . . .'

The Captain listened patiently to all this, without looking at us, tracing imaginary circles on the deck with his foot. When Sedelquist had finished I expected him to call his officers and the other watch and have us clapped in irons. Instead he looked up and said, 'Orlright, feefty-feefty . . . Halv fridag.'

So it was arranged that everyone should work till dinner-time. In this way we gained a free afternoon and the starboard watch got nothing, as they would have been free in any case.

That night I was woken for wheel in a tropical downpour. The crew were careering about the deck with buckets. To add to the confusion Filimon and Fabian had got loose and were sliding down the decks to the scuppers, screeching madly. In a few moments the rain ceased and the ship was becalmed on an oily sea. We were in the Doldrums.

We wore ship at midnight. The air was stifling and once more the rain fell in torrents. For four long hours we braced the yards to every idle puff of wind.

All the next day the ship lay becalmed. The rain beat down unceasingly, the air was steamy and left us gasping like landed fish. As if this was not enough, the Mate set me to 'knacka rost' in the officers' lavatory, where the smell of drains and stale soap was too much for my empty stomach (breakfast had been inedible beans and bacon). Respite came at midday. Feeling green and ghastly, I stood apathetically at the wheel of a ship without steerage way, on which rain descended in endless torrents.

The sky cleared but *Moshulu* still lay becalmed among her own garbage, the only sounds being the clattering of the blocks, the slatting of the sails, and the sucking sound as she lifted and plunged on the swell. Towards evening we had the finals of the garrotting and individual tug-of-war. To my own and everyone else's surprise I had emerged from the preliminary rounds. The finals were to take place before the Captain and Officers, for no other reason than that they were on deck and had nothing better to do.

The Captain looked spotless as usual and was wearing his ceremonial topee. By contrast the First Mate was as dirty as the Captain was clean and made a most unpleasant contrast – together they looked like an advertisement for washing powder; the second Mate was dressed in nothing but a bathing-slip and looked like an emaciated early Saint. In the background hovered Tria in fearfully ragged trousers through which a rather spotty bottom showed. The rest of us looked much like him.

Attracted by the noise on dock the Carpenter appeared and was invited to take part in the competition, which he had modestly shunned. 'Timmer' was one of the best-hearted men in the ship (he used to let us fool about for hours in his workshop with his pet chisels and generally get in his way). He was also the strongest member of the crew, and with his deep chest and muscular arms he looked like a big tree. He came out with his squinting smile and gripped the strop with a great hand, from which the top joints of both first finger and thumb were missing.

I wrapped my right arm round a stanchion and held on. He wound his leg round one of the iron dock bitts, and we pulled. Even after what seemed an eternity there was nothing in it. He was streaming with sweat and his eyes were bulging. Mine were doing the same.

'Timmer' slipped so that his body was parallel to the deck. We were in a deadlock. I watched my hand. I still felt strong enough to hold him, but the strop was cutting deep into it and it was beginning to turn an alarming shade of blue. 'A few more seconds,' I thought to myself, 'and it'll be dead for good.' The Sailmaker was bellowing encouragement in my ear, the noise was deafening.

'Orlright, stop, you win,' I cried out.

'I can't' said 'Timmer'. 'Somebody cut the rope. Quick.'

Our hands were too close to use a knife, so they lifted him up. There was no life in my hand at all. The boys beat it and massaged it but it was dead. Four days later there was still a deep blue depression across the wrist and still no feeling in my fingers.

'Proper strongbody, that "Timmer",' everyone said. 'Dozzent know how strong.'

Another night and another day we lay becalmed, the mizzen yards squared, the fore and main braced up to starboard. In 24 hours we only made 24 miles. By day the sea reflected the fierce light of the sun, astern of the ship a pair of birds fluttered, not daring to approach. Before breakfast we rigged a gantline and bent a royal. Breakfast was again uneatable, the meat stank, the bread dried up, and the margarine was liquid. The drinking-water grew hot in the tanks.

We dared the sharks. With the Captain keeping watch, we lowered a painting-platform over the side and dived from the rail. The water, 6,000 feet deep, was quite cold in the shadow of the hull, but beyond it, in the sunshine, it was like a warm bath. We kept close to the side, all except Jansson, who struck out, but even he returned when someone swam beneath him and nipped his leg. For fifteen minutes we swam and sat on the platform as it rose and plunged on the swell, pitying the starboard watch who were working aloft bending sail, sick and giddy with the heat.

Dinner was a name. The 'Kock' had given up the struggle. We cursed him heartlessly, and went aloft to relieve the starboard watch.

A ship of about 5,000 tons, white amidships with a black funnel, passed us about eight miles to starboard.

'Bastards,' we said malevolently when they ignored us.

Far below, the starboard watch lay on the cover of No. 2 hatch, playing cards, sleeping or reading, looking clean and cool.

On Thursday a little wind sprang up from ESE. The Captain was in a good humour. He told me that *Olivebank*, under upper topgallants, had once dropped *Herzogin Cecilie* astern off Cape Horn when the latter was in full sail with royal staysails set, and his old ship, *Archibald Russell*, though not really fast, was to both *Herzogin* and *Moshulu* in light airs.

With Hermansonn I was act to work washing down the paint on the afterdeck with caustic soda, using a fine new teak bucket. Hermansonn dropped it over the side. Immediately there was a denunciatory roar from the Captain, who went below to make the debit entry against his account. It was fortunate that he went when he did as I was so unnerved by his anger that I dropped some caustic soda on the deck.

'Let's fock off and have a smoke,' said Hermansonn miserably.

✝

Fifty-five days out and twenty-five from the Horn we crossed the Line. We received such a large rum ration that we could not get through it. It was a sweltering night and we gave six tots to little Taanila. Soon he was reduced to gibbering idiocy, running about the decks with no clothes on, and had to be restrained.

We were still level with *Parma*'s 1933 voyage of 83 days. That year she had been 30 days from Port Victoria to Cape Horn; 26 days to the Line and 27 to Falmouth.

The next day we caught a shark. The mess boy raised a cry of 'Haj om babords.' There was a rush for the fo'c'sle door, 'Doonkey' only stopping to grab a great hook which he had forged, while Jansson begged a big piece of pork from the 'Kock'.

The shark was about five feet long, twisting and turning deep in the clear water, sometimes lost in a sudden swirl, then appearing again, always below the surface, half turning on his back to show a hideous mouth.

It was a disturbing sight. Brought up on cheap fiction about sharks ('the sinister vee-shaped fin cutting the surface'), I had not imagined that they night be invisible to a swimmer and yet right beneath him.

'No more swimming for me in this ship,' said Kroner. 'I'll wait till I'm back in the Scheldt.'

The hook was really stout, and on a chain trace. A moment later the sharp snapped at the bait. Three men hauled it in. Twenty more offered encouragement from a discreet distance. Once out of the water it hung lifelessly, clean hooked, its open mouth revealing a sickly bilious-looking throat.

To its side clung several small black fish, remora. We tried to haul it over the teak taffrail, but it clashed its teeth on it, taking out a sizeable chunk, and began to thrash with its tail. I thought of Mountstewart again; he would have been in his element here. None of us really wanted the shark on deck, and although we expressed our regret when it straightened the solid iron hook and got away, we all felt secretly relieved. Only the Sailmaker was disgusted.

'Bloody lot of farmers,' he said. 'You should have slipped a running bowline over his tail, slacked off the line and hauled him up tail first. We used to take fifteen-footers that way.'

'What the hell do we want with a fifteen-footer?' said Kroner. 'You're welcome to them any day.'

CHAPTER TWENTY-TWO
North of the Line

NORTH of the Line the NE. Trades began to blow. We painted the fo'c'sle light grey and white, and tore down a couple of bunks, throwing them overboard. All our belongings were out on deck and we decided to jettison the worst of them. Everyone was happily running backwards and forwards to the rail with other people's possessions, shouting: 'År de din? År de din?' If the owner did not respond immediately they were thrown into the Atlantic.

'I jus' trowed your Vest and Vind trousers into the bloddy sea,' Sedelquist said airily 'Your name vas on them.'

'You'd better speak to Alvar about them,' I said happily.

'Why Alvar?'

'Because I've just sold them to him for a pot of jam.'

Later Alvar approached me. 'About those trousers . . .'

'If it's about the jam, I've already eaten it.'

☩

As we sailed north with the Trades humming in the rigging, the days and nights merged imperceptibly, varying only in the moods they produced. Each night the Plough rose higher out of the sea, while the Southern Cross sank correspondingly lower and finally disappeared completely.

Having painted the fo'c'sle we were set to remove the myriad paint splashes left by the enthusiastic decorators. I spent an uncomfortable morning in pools of caustic soda beneath the bunks, scraping away at immovable spots.

Every few minutes the First Mate put his head round the door to see if I had finished. With his unkempt beard, wild hair, cheap topee several sizes too large for him, and grubby khaki overalls, he fulfilled my idea of a keeper on Devil's Island.

'Är det färdigt? Horry op.'

'Grr.'

I was proud of the fo'c'sle when I had finished scraping and oiling, and began to speak of 'My floor'.

Once more the Mate appeared. 'You can joost . . .'

'I know,' I said.

'Vot's dat?'

'Scrape the midships fo'c'sle.'

He seemed mollified. 'Dat's it,' he said, softening a little. 'You can take Alvar too.'

There was so much paint under the Carpenter's bunk that nothing would shift it.

'Old "Timmer" pisses paint,' said Alvar. 'Dose scrapers are noh good.'

On May 18th, 68 days out, we were in 26° N., 46° W. on the outer fringes of the Sargasso Sea. Possibly because the wind was strong we did not meet with great beds of weed but only isolated patches of a yellowish-brown bladder wrack with circular berries.

The Second Mate was fascinated and spent a long time fishing for weed with a grapnel made from frayed-out wire rope. I used a boat-hook. Neither of us was successful. The sea smoked white, the barque rolled and plunged, and after a time we abandoned the attempt.

'I put some of that weed in a bottle in '94,' said Sails, 'and corked it up. Every year it blooms.'

'I should have thought the water would have lost its strength,' I said.

'Not if it's his own,' said Kroner.

On the 20th and 21st we were becalmed. By now we should have been in the Westerlies. The noon position was 32° N. 47° W. There seemed little chance of beating *Parma* now.

Over the side the sea had a slick on it like oil, but looking down into it, it was absolutely clear. While I was shaving off my miserable beard I dropped my mirror over the side. I watched it sink for almost half a minute before it ceased to flash.

Floating down to the ship came the most interesting variety of sea-creatures. There were legions of Portuguese men-of-war, exotic, vivid-coloured masses of translucent matter with swirling antennae. We hauled one big one on deck in a bucket. The glorious mauves and pinks swelled and contracted as the creature went through its complicated reefing operations. In the manner of counterpoise weights the chain-like tentacles were lowered on one side and hauled up on the other, the translucent comb-shaped bubble that was the sail began to heel and capsize and reduced itself to a streamlined hump. I watched these evolutions spellbound. Most of the morning I spent hauling up men-of-war. On them I found tiny, frantically struggling crabs which apparently existed in a perilous fashion by moving from one flimsy island to another. Next I caught a baby octopus. It was recently dead but a crab already inhabited the gaping hole where its ink sac had been.

Before dinner a huge yellow plate-like thing floated past. It was a turtle, taking a sunbath, drifting where the current took it. Occasionally it would poke its head out and warm that too.

Alvar came rushing on deck with a ·22 rifle, and took aim at it, mouthing something about soup. Surprisingly it was Sedelquist who knocked the barrel up.

'Don' be bloddy silly,' he said. 'Hasn't hurt you dat tottle, has it?'

Later we saw another one. Some freak of the current was taking it in circles. It was turning over and over, moving its flippers, luxuriously content.

☩

These were days of maddening delay. On the 21st we only made 38 miles; on the 22nd 78 miles; 80 on the 23rd; 70 on the 24th. On these days we bent sail and endeavoured to keep out of the Captain's way.

Filimon was executed on the 23rd and the next day there was pig for breakfast. Dinner was pig. At supper-time we sat down to an entirely pig meal – rather gingerly, like members of the public being tested for consumer reaction. There was roast pig, tinned sausage, and pig's blood pancakes.

'Eat more pig. A pig a day keeps the doctor away,' I said aloud.

'What's dat?' said Alvar suspiciously.

'Nothing.'

'Bettair notting.'

☩

Saturday, May 27th, the 77th of the voyage, was a day of incidents. The wind, which had been more or less steady from SW., shifted to north by east and caught us aback, carrying away the upper top-sheet sail. For a time, to everyone's disgust, we headed SSE.

We continued to eat Filimon. We ate him throughout Saturday and Sunday, and he wreaked havoc with our stomachs. When night came the wretched lookout was unable to leave his post and had to answer a persistent call perched far out on the bowsprit guys in driving rain with the ship running ten knots. 'Tink you're Errol Flynn or someting,' Tria shouted to him. 'Horry op, it's two bells.'

' – off,' came an agonized voice.

☩

We were heading SE. now and late that night we tacked ship to star-board, first preparing everything, coiling down the royal and top-gallant braces clear for running, trimming the spanker boom amid-ships. At 11 p.m. the daymen were mercilessly roused, but with the other watch below there were still only three men to get the fore yards round. By the time everything was coiled down it was mid-night and we were exhausted but the new course was N. 15° E.

Whit Monday was a holiday. We tacked ship at 10 and 11, but the Captain looked thunderous and there was no talk of deputations.

By Tuesday the 30th the voyage seemed nearly over. Even my little Atlas could not dishearten us.

'With this wind,' we said foolishly, 'we can reach Falmouth or Queenstown by Saturday.'

Even the Captain looked happier and exchanged his topee and ducks for a cloth cap and leather coat.

There were other changes. The sea was no longer blue, it was light green, once again it rose angrily and hurled itself at the ship in clouds of spray. The roar of the wind and the oilskins of the crew brought back distant memories of the West Wind. In these conditions we holystoned the decks on all fours, moving the great bricks about with rain running down our necks.

We were in a frequented part of the Atlantic now. A Jugoslav steamer, the *Duea*, passed astern of us and reported us at Lloyds. Two days later we saw another. She was a Norwegian tanker, with her name *Sommerstad* in glaring letters a yard high on her side. She came rolling down from the east in ballast, and altered course to pass 200 yards astern of us. Everyone who could ran to the poop, and those who were painting ceased work and simply gazed at her. We could see a man running along the flying bridges, and somewhere on board a dog was barking excitedly. As she passed we dipped our flag to her, then the Captain put his binoculars back in the rack and the painters went on painting. In the afternoon a large Italian ship, the *Belvedere*, came up with us.

'*Si mangia bene in quella barca*,' said Sandell, as we watched her go. 'Bloddy great pastas all day.'

While the officers' cabins were being painted, the Second Mate rigged his wireless on deck.

'English news,' he said pleasantly to me as I hovered within earshot. 'Want to hear i?'

'Yesterday,' said a nasty voice that could only have been cultivated in Milwaukee, 'a band of marauding Poles violated the frontier zone. In a cowardly attack on an isolated German post, one of our soldiers was shot in the back.'

He went on for a long time like this, dealing only with the most depressing news. The gayest thing was a description of an hysterically enthusiastic torchlight procession in Madrid put on by General Franco. I was terrified by this recital.

'Can't we have some dance music?'

'You don't like the news?'

'It isn't news, it's German propaganda.'

'You tell me the difference and you're bloody clever,' said the Second Mate.

When night fell Jansson and I stood and shared a cigarette as we listened to a South American station churning out rumbas. It was a perfect evening. *Moshulu* was running a steady seven knots under a high cold moon. A heavy dew had fallen and the whole ship sparkled and glittered. The long afterglow that had covered the whole of the western sky with a combination of blues and yellows had vanished. I was content.

'Not long,' said Jansson, 'and then plenty trouble.'

'What? Wind?'

'No. Vor,' he said. 'Let's get some slip, always plenty slip, that's the best.'

The ship models were coming on fast. The voyage was nearly done and the builders redoubled their efforts. The Second Mate's model was magnificent. One day whilst he was working on it the First Mate came up. 'It's not bad but it could be better,' he said grudgingly.

'Aw, shit, what does he know about it. I'd like to see him make a model like that,' the Sailmaker said angrily.

I was sitting in the sail-loft as he put the finishing touches to his own model of *L'Avenir*. She was rather like *Herzogin* with a tremendous bridge deck 170 feet long. The wheel was on a high platform that could only be reached by a ladder.

'It wouldn't do for me,' I said, and told him about the night with Yonny Valker and how we had nearly broached-to.

'Ugh,' he said and swore. 'That's what happened to *L'Avenir* when the Germans had her, I'm sure of it. I was Sailmaker in her when she was Erikson's. You see that wheel platform? If the officer of the watch wanted to see how she was heading he had to climb that ladder, not like *Moshulu* where he can keep an eye on

261

the course all the time. I think she was lost on a dark night with a big following sea and two bad helmsmen, like you and Valker at the wheel, perhaps worse, though I don't see how that'd be possible. Before anyone knew what was happening she could've broached-to, turned turtle, *kaput.*'

I was not anxious for him to enlarge on my helmanship, which I secretly thought much improved, so I asked him if there had ever been passengers in *L'Avenir*.

'Yes, and they were nearly all crazy. You have to be crazy to pay for this,' he said. 'Once we had an old farmer who lived aft. We were outward bound and the "Timmerman" was worried because someone was taking the wooden wedges for the hatches. As soon as he put new ones in, they disappeared. The old man left the ship in Australia and when he'd gone the Steward discovered that the cupboards in his cabin were full of wedges. The steward said that he found him once taking a picture of one. Isn't that crazy?'

'It's worse,' I said. 'It's unwholesome.'

'What's that?'

'Never mind, tell me some more.'

'Well, we had a girl once. She was a Canadian and she paid £100 for a round voyage. The boys didn't like her because she was dirtier than the dirtiest of them.'

'Not dirtier than Alvar?'

'You should have seen her washing her drawers,' said the Sailmaker. 'She used to put a pail of water on the fire for five minutes, just long enough for nothing to happen to it. Then she'd take her pants like this and then . . . in, out . . . squeeze.'

'No soap?'

'No soap. Then she'd hang them in MY sail-loft to dry. She didn't do that for long,' he said, grunting.

'Why? What happened?'

'I had two boys working for me then. One of them got a chunk of wood and made a dam great thing and stuck it inside her drawers. When she came to fetch 'em out it popped. It gave her a nasty shock, she never came in again.'

'But if she was dirty, surely she wouldn't mind a thing like that?'

'She was only dirty in one way, you understand,' said the Sailmaker. 'But the boys wouldn't have liked her if she'd been the biggest whore on the ocean. Nobody likes women in ships except in port and then they're better in a bed than a bunk. They're a bloody nuisance, they wander all over the place. The crew can't take their trousers off to wash, and they're always getting ill.

'There was only one girl I ever liked in a ship,' he went on. 'She was a young lady of seventeen. She sailed with her mother once on the short passage from Ipswich to Copenhagen. I used to tell them a whole lot of stories, the sort of thing I tell you sometimes,' he nodded. 'She used to come up behind me and imprison me in her soft white arms and say: "Guess who it is, you old darling, you." When she did that I felt there was still life in me.'

'You ought to stick to Blackwood's magazine at your age,' I said. 'It's less disturbing than some of this other stuff.'

But he wasn't listening to me. 'There was a reporter on the same voyage,' he went on, 'who wrote a lot of goddam stuff in the papers about me being "an old man full of kindly philosophy towards the two lady passengers".'

✠

Hopes of beating *Parma* had vanished. It was the 1st of June and we were 82 days out. *Parma* had been 83 days to Falmouth. The baffling calms north of the line had been too much for *Moshulu*.

'Six hundred and fifty miles to go and we're logging nine knots,' said Sedelquist when he came from the wheel at noon.

As if by magic the wind fell away and we logged 7, 4, 2 knots. At midnight we were almost becalmed. The Captain was sulphurous.

'I should think you had better keep the course,' said Vytautas as I took over. 'He's veree angry man today.'

I cowered behind the spokes. The Captain swooped down on the binnacle, hoping to find me off course. He was disappointed in this and I did not think he could find much else to complain of but with incomparable ingenuity he succeeded. In an unguarded moment I put my hand in my pocket to find a handkerchief. He was on me like a flash.

'Boy, is your hand cold?'

'No, sir.'

'Take it out then. Behave like a white man. Only damned dagoes put their hands in their pockets.'

In the night a ship came up astern and passed us close to starboard. As it swept past a hoarse and indescribably funny voice hailed us from her bridge. When she was abeam Sandell shone a torch on our faces as we lined the rail. 'They'll think we're a lot of focking madmen,' he said roaring with laughter.

'Well, what do you tink?' said Sedelquist.

✟

All through Friday, 2nd June, there was hardly any wind. The courses were clewed up and from high aloft came squeals and screeches as if the ship was bemoaning her powerlessness, while the lower yards groaned disapprovingly against the backstays and a hundred blocks rattled against masts and yards.

'It's funny you know,' said Kroner. 'A lot of people you meet on land think a sailing ship's quiet. If this noise goes on much longer I shall go nuts. I don't really think there's anyone in this ship I want to see again for a long time.'

'Not even me?'

'Not even you.'

Saturday. The wind was coming on the ship from all sides. You could watch its variations as it played with the black smoke from the galley chimney, hurling it first in the helmsman's face, the next moment blowing it in a plume ahead of the ship.

Two swallows, both completely exhausted, flew on board. We scattered crumbs for them but they were too tired to feel afraid and allowed themselves to be picked up. The noon position was 49° N., 18° W. If they had flown unaided they had had a long journey of it.

A carrier pigeon with a lean look about him lighted on board. On one leg was a numbered ring with an empty message-clip on it. The Cook scattered some oatmeal for the pigeon, but it was wary and preferred to rest on the yardarm.

After the arrival of the pigeon one of the swallows became so exhausted that it fell overboard. Tria tried to save it by fishing for it with a pail, but it drifted out of reach. This incident depressed us still further.

Sunday came. There was still no wind. A first-class passage was being changed into a commonplace one by a freakish succession of calms.

'Three hundred miles to bloody Queenstown,' we groaned on Monday, poring over the now filthy and dog-eared atlas.

Tuesday came, gradually the wind came back, became a force 1 air, shifted W. by N. to NNW. to NE. until we were making four knots on the port tack. At last at midnight on Wednesday the wind rose and *Moshulu* began to run at nine knots. The cloud of gloom that had hung over the ship dispelled.

One hundred and fifty miles to Queenstown. There were cormorants and gulls about the ship. The remaining swallow departed, only the pigeon, as always aloof, remained.

TWENTY-THREE

The Race is Won

THE night was succeeded by a wild and beautiful dawn, in which great black storm-clouds reared up against an impossibly green sky. As the sun came up the wind rose with it and the ship took wings; the sea was alive with white horses charging north-west. Up in the fore rigging we bent and set a fore upper topgallant with reef points that had been a lower topsail in the *Star of England*, one of the ships of the Alaska packers. The date 1922 was stencilled on the lower leech, but it was probably much older. It was my job to shift blocks along the jackstays to conform with the buntlines of this sail. It was a good job and I was perfectly content up there with a coil of wire round my neck and a shackle spike and a pair of wirecutters attached to my belt. Below me Jansson and Taanila were perched on the cap of the topmast arguing happily about something. The First Mate came out of the charthouse and shouted at them, but the wind was sufficiently strong for them to be able to pretend not to hear.

The day was completely ruined by dinner which was an enormity.

'We should complain. We should go to the Captain,' Sedelquist said. 'But you boggerts are all the same, you complain like hell behind his back and all way "Yes, Sir; No, Sir; Oh, Sir" when he spiks.' This was so true that nobody answered.

☩

On Thursday, June the 8th, *Moshulu* was eighty miles from the Irish Coast. The day before there had been only two gulls following the ship; now there were a dozen or more hanging motionless above the main yard with their beaks to the wind as if suspended by invisible cords.

This was a wonderful day for us. For the first time we could smell the land, a blending smell of beechwoods after rain, bracken in the early morning, the gorse on a hillside. It seems unbelievable now, but to us with our senses sharpened by months at sea, it came strongly.

The weather was glorious, the sea a dark blue, with leaping white horses all about the ship. But with the wind north and northeast as it was we might spend a week beating off the Western approaches.

When we came on deck in the afternoon land had already been sighted, the faint etching of mountains away to starboard.

At the change of watch we tacked ship and *Moshulu* went blazing away to the eastward, throwing a great bow wave. Watching her from the wheel, I realized that in spite of everything I should be sad to leave her.

Now that we were on the port tack the land loomed up fast; hazy masses of rolling hills, the hills of County Cork. It was a beautiful evening. The hills grew out of the sea, brown and dancing in the haze, and as the sun set were channelled with long shadows.

At 8 o'clock we raised the Fastnet Rock 15 miles to the northeast of us. As night came down, the wind fell away and the light on the Fastnet flashed mockingly at us every five seconds. The ecstasy of the day had passed, leaving us with the knowledge that although we were only half a day's sailing with a favourable wind from Queenstown it might still take a week to reach it.

By the next morning there was still no wind. We were closer in towards the land, making a lot of leeway. The air was full of haze, and what we at first took to be a dredger with a white funnel resolved itself into the angularities of the Fastnet seen in strange perspective with the white lighthouse on top of it. To seawards were several drifters with long screws of smoke twisting lazily upwards from them, while inshore the white sails of a yacht shone in the sunlight. Beyond it were the miraculous greens and browns of Ireland; a multi-coloured patchwork of cultivated land, with here and there a splendidly simple white farm-house and, far away, a great flat-topped mountain, blue in the distance.

At nine we drifted down to within four miles of the Fastnet. We tried to wear the ship around, but there was no steerage-way to do it.

All day we hovered near the Fastnet. Later in the afternoon a rowing boat with five men in it rowing like demons was sighted coming out to us from the mainland. At the same time a fishing smack under power appeared. The two craft converged on us.

About coffee-time the rowers came alongside with a lot of shouting as they shipped their oars. They were tired, as they had rowed nine miles from a village called Crookhaven on the isthmus of Mizen head. In the stern sheets was an old man who looked like Coleridge's Ancient Mariner, with great stooks of white hair pushing out from beneath a sailor's cap. He came up the Jacob's ladder we threw down to him, with difficulty. The others followed him. We gave them water, which they drank gratefully, then some powerful plug.

Over coffee one of them told me something about himself. He might have been speaking for all Ireland.

He was a fisherman, he said, but he owned the local pub and also had a plot of land under cultivation. Ever since returning disillusioned from the States in 1932 he had lived quietly at Crookhaven with his wife and four children.

'Are you contented?' I asked him.

'I am not.'

'And how are the crops?'

'Poor,' he replied, and added like a stage Irishman, 'for there's been divil little rain these six weeks.'

Another of the men was striking. Young, with red hair, a high forehead, and a determined chin, he looked the double of T. E. Lawrence. All of them were quiet fellows, behaving with a natural dignity. After a quarter-of-an-hour they said they must leave. The wind was freshening and already there was a two-knot breeze.

The patriarch was the last to go. As he went down the ladder holding a bottle of the Captain's rum, the Sailmaker said:

'Take care of that stuff. Four over proof.'

'Yes, yes,' wheezed the old man, who neither knew nor cared about proof but knew about good rum. 'Four per cent, four per cent.'

Meanwhile the smack had come alongside to starboard with lobsters for us and we hung over the rail looking down at the men on board.

'The last barque we came out to was the *C. B. Pedersen*, but she's gone now,' one said. 'Run down and sunk near the Azores, I heard.'

Presently, supplied with rum, they too cast off from *Moshulu* as she began to rustle through the water. We last saw the rowing boat drifting into the sunset towards the New World with the Ancient Mariner sitting erect and very drunk in the stern, while among the rowers a minor orgy was in progress.

'I've learnt something today,' said Kroner with great melancholy. 'People will never take me for an Englishman, however well I speak English. They pick you out straight away.'

'Since when have you wanted to be English? It seems an extraordinary ambition, especially in this ship.'

I too thought about this meeting and how difficult it had been to talk to strangers after ninety days in a foreign ship.

✝

Now we were past Cape Clear, with the Irish mainland abeam. A big Royal Mail ship came steaming past us from the west, doing 17 knots, an imposing sight. I thought how much more imposing *Moshulu* must have looked logging 16. The steamer carried a sinister deck cargo: eight big planes like troop carriers, wingless, with the orange, white and red roundels of the Free State Air Force on their sides. From the passenger decks women waved handkerchiefs to us.

'Not long now,' said Sedelquist happily.

'There's fires for velcom,' said Sandell.

It was true. As we sailed along the coast we could see long drifting columns of smoke rising from fires burning on the cliffs. It was as if they were signalling our approach: 'A ship is coming. *Moshulu* is coming.'

As the sun went down the sea shimmered gold. Inland the hills and valleys seemed to surge on for ever. The fires and the battered shapes of old forts and chapels made a timeless scene. The gold turned to red, mists rose from the valleys and were tinged with the sun's dying colour; the forts and chapels took on a grim air, darker than the darkness of the shore, and the smell of burning peat filled the ship. The lights on Galley Head and the Old Head of Kinsale further to the east began to flash. The remains of the sunset became a golden glow which was absorbed finally into the deep blue of the night sky. The stars came out, the cry of the waves was subdued. The silence was so complete you could hear it, a paradox only made possible by the nearness of Ireland.

✝

Apart from the land to port, Saturday the 10th of June began in much the same way as any other, with the filling of water-tanks and what were to prove the last ablutions of Auguste, who was slaughtered later. The Old Head of Kinsale was looming up now with the black and white striped lighthouse on the highest point. At five the wind shifted NNW., then to W., and finally to WSW., the finest wind we could wish for.

'Square away for Queenstown,' was the cry.

Our watch went below – but not to sleep for we knew we should be needed. That morning, after nine months of successful evasion, the Captain caught me looking at his logbook in the charthouse, but he no longer cared and neither did I.

'If you go ashore at Queenstown they'll eat you. They don't like Englishmen,' he said. 'Not that I'll let you,' he added as an afterthought.

'Why don't they like us, Sir?'

'Because you're dam' soft and silly. Giving them Queenstown.' Here he snorted in disgust. 'No one thinks anything of a country that does a fool thing like that. When this war starts you'll miss it. You'll see.'

At ten the yellow and blue striped pilot flag was bent at the foremast and the Finnish flag was run up at the gaff. Soon the pilot cutter appeared, under power, tailing a rowing boat aft with the Pilot in it. We clewed-up the main and mizzen courses and backed the main yards, heaving-to for him to come aboard. The cutter stood in ahead of us, cast off the Pilot's rowing boat and let it drift down on us. Two villainous-looking men brought him alongside, a little man with a face the colour of rawhide.

'The Fastnet reported you and we've had you in view since nine o'clock, but we didn't know whether you were coming in,' were his first words to the Captain.

We went to the forebraces and boarded the foretack. The Sailmaker and his assistant, who between them had cut and sewn two royals, an upper topgallant, an upper topsail, a gaff topsail, and almost completed a mainsail; the 'Kock'; the Steward and his boy; 'Timmerman' and 'Doonkey'; all put their backs into the work with the knowledge that the voyage was nearly done.

There was a race between our watch at the mainyard and the starboard at the mizzen to furl the courses, and the port watch won. All up the height of the ship we began to 'bräck gårdingarna', haul in the slack and make fast again.

Although the Pilot leaned over the rail and said little, somehow the news spread about the ship: we were first home. *Viking* had been sighted at the line, 90 days out from Port Victoria; the same Jugoslavian steamer that had reported us had also reported *Passat* but she had not yet arrived.

Moshulu came up to anchorage under a couple of topsails and staysails. The deck was a forest of ropes – clewlines, buntlines, downhauls and halliards. Occasionally the hands would lose their bearings and it would need the Mates from amidships to tell them whether they were bearing on bunt or clewlines. At last came the cry we had waited for:

'Styrman, låt gå babords ankaret.'

Once more the Mate hit the pin of the patent release gear. With a roaring and a clattering the anchor went down. It was 12 o'clock ship's time, Saturday, June 10th, 1939. *Moshulu* was lying off the entrance to Queenstown with the steep glacis of the English forts above its narrow mouth. We were first home, 91 days from Port Victoria, and although we didn't know it then we had won the Last Grain Race.

✣

The rest of the story is quickly told. For 9 days we remained at anchor in the outer roads. Somehow Kroner and I got ashore for a hair-cut, but that was all. For the remainder of the time we went on painting and scraping the ship.

During this time news came of the other ships:

Pamir arrived at Falmouth on June 12th, 96 days out, and *Passat* reached the Lizard on June 15th, 98 days out, together with *Viking*, 119 days. *Olivebank* arrived at Queenstown on July 17, 119 days out and went to Barry to discharge. She sailed for the Baltic and on September 12th struck a mine in the German field south-west of Esjberg. She sank immediately and Captain Granith and 13 of the crew lost their lives. Among them was our splendid Steward, Arno Strömberg, who had served in *Moshulu* ever since Erikson bought her. *Lawhill* and *Archibald Russell* both arrived at Falmouth on August 2nd, 140 and 121 days out respectively. The formidable *Pommern* was 117 days to Falmouth. *Winterhude* was 134 days. The auxiliary *Kommodore Johnsen* was 107 days, *Killoran* 139, arriving long after war was declared, and *Abraham Rydberg* 115.

Our most formidable rival was *Padua*. She had made one of the fastest passages ever recorded to the West Coast of South America from the Elbe and had been only 53 days to Spencer's Gulf from Valparaiso.

If any ship could have beaten *Moshulu* it was *Padua*. In the event she failed. She was 93 days to Falmouth. So ended the Grain Race.

✠

On the 19th June *Moshulu* was ordered to Glasgow and a tug was sent to tow us. It seemed an ignoble end to such a venture. On the 21st the tug appeared. 'Kommer bogserbåten,' everyone said. The 'bogserbåt' took us out into a nasty sea with a head wind in which we only made 5 miles in an hour. Steering behind the tug on a dark night in the Irish Sea was as bad as anything in the West Wind and much more dangerous.

By day we washed paintwork and painted the rigging in the rain. I was too ill with hay fever, which I had miraculously contracted far off shore, to care what happened to us.

At 4 a.m. on the 23rd the Tuskar Rock was 2 miles abeam. By this time the tug had signalled that she was out of coal and returning to Queenstown for bunkers and a fair wind. Derisively we waved goodbye and set all fore-and-aft sail, happy to be rid of it. By the afternoon we were back at anchor off Queenstown. We sailed again on the 24th at 5 in the morning. We passed the night of the 26th at anchor off Tail of the Bank. I still had hay fever.

'Soon cure that,' said the Captain. 'Down in the chain-locker.'

As the cable came in over the windlass and straight down into the vertical locker deep in the ship I coiled it down link by link. The bottom of the Clyde at Tail of the Bank was very muddy.

At last on the 27th of June we were warped with infinite difficulty into Queen's Dock.

'Coming again?' asked the Captain some days later, after some good parties, as he inked in my discharge as Ordinary Seaman and handed over some fragments of pay. 'Make a man of you next time.'

'I'll think it over,' I answered.

The Vuitton was loaded on to a taxi. Suddenly those of the crew still on board seemed remote and once more strangers.

'I'll write to you,' said Kroner. 'We'll try to get to the Grand

Banks.' It was a project we had discussed all through the home-ward voyage. Now it seemed absurd.

'Central Station,' I said to the taxi-driver. He was even more villainous-looking than the one at Belfast.

'You'll be glad to get out of that bitch,' he said, jerking a thumb over his shoulder.

'You think so, do you?' I said.

'I do.'

'Then you don't know what you're talking about.'

Now we were turning through the dock gates into the main road where the trams rattled and swayed. I looked back at *Moshulu* whose masts and yards towered above the sheds in the June sunshine.

I never saw her again.

Ship and Captain	Outward 1938			Homeward 1939			
	Sailed	Arrived	Days	Sailed	Arrived	Days	Discharged
Moshulu Sjögren 4-masted barque	Belfast 18 Oct.	Port Lincoln 8 Jan.	82	Port Victoria 11 March	Queenstown 10 June	91	Glasgow
Padua Wendt 4-masted barque	Valparaiso 14 Jan.	Port Lincoln 8 March	53	Port Lincoln 3 April	Fastnet 5 July	93	Glasgow (96)
Pamir Björkfelt 4-masted barque	Gothenburg 24 Sept.	Port Victoria 24 Dec.	91	Port Victoria 8 March	Falmouth 12 June	96	Southampton
Passat Lindvall 4-masted barque	Copenhagen 24 Sept.	Port Victoria 24 Dec.	91	Port Lincoln 9 March	Lizard 15 June	98	Belfast
Pommern Broman 4-masted barque	Belfast 24 Sept.	Port Victoria 11 Dec.	78	Port Victoria 20 March	Falmouth 15 July	117	Hull
Olivebank Granith 4-masted barque	Greenock 28 Oct.	Port Victoria 2 Feb.	97	Port Victoria 20 March	Queenstown 17 July	119	Barry
Archibald Russell 4-m. barque Sommarlund	Falmouth 5 Nov.	Port Lincoln 2 Feb.	89	Port Germein 3 April	Falmouth 2 August	121	Hull
Viking Mörn 4-masted barque	Copenhagen 28 Sept.	Port Victoria 24 Dec.	87	Port Victoria 16 Feb.	Lizard 15 June	119	Cardiff
Winterhude Holm 3-masted barque	Gothenburg 21 Oct.	Port Lincoln 2 Feb.	104	Port Germein 22 March	Falmouth 3 August	134	Barrow
Lawhill Söderlund 4-masted barque	Liverpool 15 Oct.	Port Lincoln 8 Jan.	85	Port Lincoln 15 March	Falmouth 2 August	140	Glasgow
Killoran Leman 3-masted barque	Auckland 13 May	Port Lincoln 3 June	21	Port Lincoln 13 July	Queenstown 29 Nov. (via Cape of Good Hope)	139	
Abraham Rydberg 4-m. barque Malmberg	Rivofjord 24 Aug.	Wallaroo 10 Dec.	108	Port Germein 18 Feb.	Lizard 15 June (via Cape of Good Hope)	115	Ipswich (120)
Kommodore Johnsen Peters Clausen 4-m. aux. barque	Auckland 11 Feb.	Port Lincoln 2 March	19	Port Lincoln 26 March	Queenstown 11 July	107	Cork

SAILING VESSELS TAKING PART IN 1939 GRAIN RACE

Ship	Reg. Gross Tonnage	Length B.P.	Builders	Original Owner	Owner 1938	Passages in Grain Trade Australia to UK
Passat 4-m. steel barque	3137	323	Blohm and Voss Hamburg 1911	Laiesz, Hamburg	Gustav Erikson bought 1932	1933 – 110 days; 1934 – 106; 1935 – 99; 1936 – 87; 1937 – 94; 1938 – 98
Pommern ex Mneme 4-m. steel barque	2376	310	Reid of Glasgow 1903	B. Werke und Sohn until 1906 then Laiesz, Hamburg	Gustav Erikson bought 1923	1933 – 98 days; 1934 – 110; 1935 – 95; 1936 – 94; 1937 – 94; 1938 – 199
Pamir 4-m. steel barque	2799	316	Blohm and Voss Hamburg 1905	Laiesz, Hamburg	Gustav Erikson bought 1931	1933 – 92 days; 1934 – 118; 1935 – 109; 1936 – 98; 1937 – 98
Lawhill 4-m. steel barque	2816	317	Thompson, Dundee 1892	Capt. Barrie of Dundee	Gustav Erikson bought 1919	1933 – 121 days; 1934 – 122; 1935 – 124; 1936 – 118; 1937 – 107; 1938 – 131
Viking 4-m. steel barque (Wireless Transmitter)	2670	294	Burmeister and Wain Copenhagen 1907	United Shipping Co. Copenhagen (Schoolship)	Gustav Erikson bought 1929	1933 – 108 days; 1934 – 137; 1935 – 97; 1936 – 116; 1937 – 103; 1938 – 116
Archibald Russell 4-m. steel barque	2354	291	Scott of Greenoch 1905	J. Hardie and Co. Glasgow	Gustav Erikson bought 1924	1933 – 119 days; 1934 – 130; 1935 – 111; 1936 – 104; 1937 – 98; 1938 – 130

Ship	Tonnage		Builder	Owner	Owner	Passage times
Winterhude ex *Mabel Rickmers* 3-m. steel barque	1980	285	Rickmers Bremerhaven 1898	Rickmers Bremerhaven	Gustav Erikson bought 1925	1933 – 144 days; 1934 – 126; 1935 – 105; 1936 – 117; 1937 – 126; 1938 – 165
Abraham Rydberg ex *Hawaiian Isles* 4-m. steel barque (Wireless Transmitter)	2345	261	Connell Glasgow 1892	Hawaiian owner	Abraham Rydberg Assn bought 1929	1933 – 125 days; 1934 – 107; 1935 – 147; 1936 – 134; 1937 – 112; 1938 – 120, via Cape of Good Hope
Kommodore Johnsen ex *Magdalene Vinnen* 4-m. steel barque (Auxiliary oil engines Wireless Transmitter)	3572	329	Krupps, Keil 1921	F. A. Vinnen Bremen	Norddeutscher Lloyd 1933 – 96 days; 1934 – 91; Bremen bought 1936	1935 – 99; 1936 – ; 1937 – ; 1938 –
Padua 4-m. steel barque (Wireless Transmitter)	3064	320	Tecklenborg Wesermunde 1926	Laiesz, Hamburg	Laiesz, Hamburg	1933 outward Elbe to Spencer's Gulf 66 days; 1934 – 109; 1935 – 100
Olivebank ex *Caledonia* 4-m. steel barque	2795	326	Mackie and Thomson Glasgow 1892	Andrew Weir Glasgow	Gustav Erikson bought 1924	1933 – 104 days; 1934 – 115; 1935 – 118; 1936 – 108; 1937 – 106; 1938 – 105
Moshulu ex *Kurt* 4-m. steel barque	3116	316	Wm Hamilton Port Glasgow 1904	G. H. J. Siemers and Co., Hamburg	Gustav Erikson bought 1935	1936 – 112 days; 1937 – 102; 1938 – 116
Killoran 3-m. steel barque	1817	261	Ailsa Shipbuilding Co. Troon 1900	Brown Glasgow	Gustav Erikson bought 1924	1933 – 110 days; 1934 – 125; 1935 – 131; 1936 – 120; 1937 – 116; 1938 – 130

MOSHULU – BELFAST TO PORT LINCOLN 1938–9

Date	Lat.	Long.	Distance	Locality	Days	General	Course
18.10.38				Belfast Lough			
19.10.38				Irish Sea	1	By Bardsey	
20.10.38				Irish Sea	2	By Bardsey	
21.10.38				Irish Sea	3		
22.10.38				North Channel	4		
23.10.38				North Channel	5	Flat calm all day then strong SW	
24.10.38	56°00'08"N	09°48'00"W	78	North Atlantic	6	Heavy swell	N66°W
25.10.38	53°56'07"N	13°31'04"W	183	North Atlantic	7	Wind moderate	S 2°W
26.10.38	50°01'00"N	14°46'09"W	240	North Atlantic	8	Wind W strong	S11°W
27.10.38	46°01'06"N	17°10'02"W	256	North Atlantic	9		S23°W
28.10.38	44°41'02"N	16°12'03"W	157	North Atlantic	10		S17°W
29.10.38	42°32'08"N	17° 04"W	130	North Atlantic	11		S19°W
30.10.38	40°14'02"N	16°58'02"W	156	North Atlantic	12		S 1°W
31.10.38	39°20'03"N	15°56'08"W	72	North Atlantic	13		S22°E
1.11.38	38°38'09"N	16°09'03"W	36	North Atlantic	14		S16°W
2.11.38	36°54'05"N	17°47'03"W	105	North Atlantic	15		S30°W
3.11.38	35°42'03"N	17°56'05"W	48	North Atlantic	16		S 9°W
4.11.38	34°29'08"N	18°28'03"W	62	North Atlantic	17		S12°W
5.11.38	32°14'04"N	19°14'03"W	142	North Atlantic	18		S16°W
6.11.38	31°27'00"N	20°19'04"W	87	North Atlantic	19		S50°W
7.11.38	30°44'01"N	22°13'05"W	127	North Atlantic	20	Moderate gale	S61°W
8.11.38	28°50'00"N	21°48'02"W	125	North Atlantic	21		S90°E

MOSHULU – BELFAST TO PORT LINCOLN 1938–9

Date	Lat.	Long.	Distance	Locality	Days	General	Course
9.11.38	27°15′09″N	20°24′07″W	119	North Atlantic	22		S24°E
10.11.38	25°40′03″N	19°28′00″W	112	North Atlantic	23		S27°E
11.11.38	23°10′00″N	19°13′04″W	151	North Atlantic	24	NE. Trades	S 2°W
12.11.38	20°05′01″N	20°22′09″W	193	North Atlantic	25		S13°W
13.11.38	17°00′00″N	21°03′06″W	190	North Atlantic	26		S 9°W
14.11.38	13°36′02″N	21°21′01″W	208	North Atlantic	27		S 4°W
15.11.38	09°48′01″N	21°12′08″W	86	North Atlantic	28	Entered Doldrums	S 1°E
16.11.38	No record	—	—	North Atlantic	29		
17.11.38	07°28′02″N	21°17′00″W	145	North Atlantic	30		S16°W
18.11.38	06°10′06″N	22°12′06″W	98	North Atlantic	31		S31°W
19.11.38	04°58′02″N	22°33′09″W	76	North Atlantic	32	SE. Trades	S29°W
20.11.38	03°14′01″N	24°48′07″W	212	North Atlantic	33		S50°W
21.11.38	00°40′03″N	25°17′02″W	245	North Atlantic	34	Crossed Equator about 4 p.m. in long. 29°W	S50°W
22.11.38	02°27′01″S	30°50′01″W	241	South Atlantic	35		S39°W
23.11.38	05°45′04″S	32°53′09″W	233	South Atlantic	36	Passed F. Norohna at night	S30°W
24.11.38	05°28′02″S	32°20′08″W	26	South Atlantic	37		N78°E
25.11.38	08°32′04″S	33°42′06″W	203	South Atlantic	38		S23°W
26.11.38	12°17′02″S	34°31′05″W	226	South Atlantic	39		S12°W
27.11.38	15°51′00″S	34°58′08″W	213	South Atlantic	40		S 2°W
28.11.38	18°26′09″S	34°13′00″W	163	South Atlantic	41		S15°W
29.11.38	20°50′09″S	33°25′02″W	139	South Atlantic	42	Trinidad Island invisible to Port. Lat. 20°30′S – Long. 29°22′W	S18°E
30.11.38	23°31′03″S	32°33′03″W	160	South Atlantic	43	*Karl Vinnen* 5-masted semi-schooner 5 miles to Port. Course ENE. Lost SE. Trades	

MOSHULU – BELFAST TO PORT LINCOLN 1938–9

Date	Lat.	Long.	Distance	Locality	Days	General	Course
1.12.38	26°01′15″S	31°36′05″W	163	South Atlantic	44		
2.12.38	29°46′05″S	30°02′04″W	230	South Atlantic	45		
3.12.38	32°51′15″S	26°43′06″W	244	South Atlantic	46		
4.12.38	35°12′05″S	20°36′01″W	315	South Atlantic	47	NW. Moderate Gale average 13½ knots 24 hours. 12–4 a.m. ran 55 miles	S69°E
5.12.38	36°39′03″S	14°15′01″W	316	South Atlantic	48	Inaccessible I. North 6–7 miles	S71°E
6.12.38	38°06′07″S	08°18′00″W	292	South Atlantic	49		S77°E
7.12.38	39°04′15″S	03°00′00″W	245	South Atlantic	50		S77°E
8.12.38	38°55′04″S	00°41′07″W	160	South Atlantic	51		S85°E
9.12.38	39°18′06″S	03°37′08″E	139	South Atlantic	52		S80°E
10.12.38	39°02′03″S	04°23′02″E	35	South Atlantic	53	No steerage way	S80°E
11.12.38	39°05′09″S	09°06′05″E	181	South Atlantic	54	West Wind	S80°E
12.12.38	39°05′09″S	16°17′02″E	292	South Atlantic	55		S71°E
13.12.38	40°33′08″S	20°40′10″E	253	Indian Ocean	56	Cross Long. Cape of Good Hope	S83°E
14.12.38	41°27′09″S	27°25′05″E	263	Indian Ocean	57		S83°E
15.12.38	42°08′03″S	32°40′06″E	246	Indian Ocean	58		S80°E
16.12.38	42°31′09″S	35°56′00″E	146	Indian Ocean	59		S89°E
17.12.38	42°42′09″S	40°22′02″E	192	Indian Ocean	60		S87°E
18.12.38	42°47′07″S	42°28′04″E	93	Indian Ocean	61		S86°E
19.12.38	42°56′01″S	45°13′03″E	121	Indian Ocean	62		S86°E
20.12.38	43°14′07″S	50°41′02″E	242	Indian Ocean	63		S86°E
21.12.38	43°06′09″S	57°02′00″E	277	Indian Ocean	64		E
22.12.38	41°15′00″S	63°05′06″E	227	Indian Ocean	65		N85°E

MOSHULU – BELFAST TO PORT LINCOLN 1938-9

Date	Lat.	Long.	Distance	Locality	Days	General	Course
23.12.38	41°37'09"S	65°33'09"E	106	Indian Ocean	66		S75°E
24.12.38	42°45'03"S	71°43'02"E	270	Indian Ocean	67		S74°E
25.12.38	43°34'03"S	75°56'07"E	208	Indian Ocean	68		S74°E
26.12.38	43°37'08"S	81°46'08"E	255	Indian Ocean	69	Starboard steering cable parted. After wheel manned	E
27.12.38	43°40'07"S	88°06'04"E	276	Indian Ocean	70		N88°E
28.12.38	43°46'03"S	92°48'04"E	210	Indian Ocean	71		E
29.12.38	43°37'08"S	81°46'08"E	255	Indian Ocean	72	59 m. by log between 4 and 8 a.m.	E
30.12.38	43°32'00"S	104°41'08"E	258	Indian Ocean	73		N87°E
31.12.38	43°33'03"S	110°41'03"E	251	Indian Ocean	74	Heavy NW. Gale. Continuous lightning	N81°E
1.1.39	43°03'02"S	117°03'04"E	276	Indian Ocean	75	Mizzen upper topgallant blew out	N71°E
2.1.39	42°03'06"S	123°45'03"E	288	Indian Ocean	76		N71°E
3.1.39	40°42'03"S	129°13'00"E	269	Gt Australian Bight	77		N57°E
4.1.39	38°33'03"S	132°21'05"E	198	Gt Australian Bight	78		N47°E
5.1.39	37°49'06"S	133°18'15"E	59	Gt Australian Bight	79		N40°E
6.1.39	36°24'09"S	134°01'00"E	82	Gt Australian Bight	80		N22°E
7.1.39	35°09'03"S	135°31'05"E	117	Gt Australian Bight	81	Sighted Cape Catastrophe 4 a.m.	N by W
8.1.39				Spencer's Gulf	82	Cape Catastrophe abeam 11 a.m. Anchored at 2.30 p.m. off Boston Island. Boston Point NW., Cape Donington SSE, Pt Lincoln about 8 m.	
9.1.39						In quarantine. *Lawhill* sighted noon. Anchored astern 85 days out	
10.1.39						Customs and doctor. Captain ashore – Letters	

MOSHULU – PORT VICTORIA TO QUEENSTOWN FOR ORDERS 1939

Days		Lat.	Long.	General Course	Miles Sailed	Locality
11.3		Sailed Port Victoria				
12.3	1	38°02'S	132°14'E	S 5°E	247	
13.3	2	40°38'S	139°21'E	S32°E	91	
14.3	3	40°59'S	139°34'E	S 5°E	76	Southern Ocean
15.3	4	43°35'S	140°40'E	S18°E	263	
16.3	5	45°30'S	146°00'E	S62°E	184	
17.3	6	46°49'S	149°56'E	S71°E	201	
18.3	7	47°44'S	153°55'E	S74°E	157	
19.3	8	48°24'S	158°14'E	S79°E	231	
20.3	9	49°24'S	164°10'E	S78°E	223	
21.3	10	49°46'S	169°15'E	S82°E	183	
22.3	11	49°56'S	171°37'E	S80°E	104	
23.3	12	no sight	176°59'E	S82°E	205	
24.3	13	51°09'S	176°37'W	E	282	Crossed 180th meridian
24.3	13	50°19'S	170°36'W	E	296	
25.3	14	50°07'S	164°21'W	N88°E	228	
26.3	15	51°12'S	158°34'W	N85°E	228	
27.3	16	51°34'S	152°31'W	N85°E	209	
28.3	17	51°17'S	146°21'W	N84°E	272	
29.3	18	50°59'S	138°06'W	N85°E	273	
30.3	19	no sight	130°44'W	N89°E	208	
31.3	20	81°27'S	125°10'W	E	245	
1.4	21	51°24'S	119°12'W	S85°E	186	
2.4	22	51°28'S	115°03'W	S88°E	148	
3.4	23	51°32'S	111°22'W	S87°E	118	
4.4	24	51°32'S	107°48'W	S89°E	192	
5.4	25	51°53'S	101°50'W	S74°E	227	
6.4	26	53°24'S	95°23'W	S74°E	252	
7.4	27	54°40'S	88°49'W	S70°E	248	
8.4	28	55°47'S	80°47'W	S76°E	283	
9.4	29	56°15'S	74°57'W	S78°E	200	Sighted *Passat*
10.4	30	56°57'S	68°36'W	S75°E	214	By Cape Horn
11.4	31	55°35'S	63°11'W	N64°E	194	
12.4	32	53°27'S	57°36'W	N54°E	211	By Falkland Is.
13.4	33	50°25'S	52°35'W	N51°E	256	South Atlantic
14.4	34	48°14'S	48°14'W	N53°E	210	
15.4	35	46°12'S	43°38'W	N57°E	227	
16.4	36	44°19'S	40°43'W	N47°E	157	
17.4	37	41°42'S	39°24'W	N29°E	175	
18.4	38	38°50'S	37°21'W	N29°E	177	
19.4	39	36°45'S	35°19'W	N38°E	155	
20.4	40	32°57'S DR	34°08'W	N15°E	236	
21.4	41	30°36'S	32°48'W	N31°E	155	
22.4	42	28°49'S	30°12'W	N48°E	158	SE. Trades
23.4	43	26°06'S	29°52'W	N14°E	158	
24.4	44	23°59'S	29°09'W	N13°E	130	South Atlantic
25.4	45	22°06'S	28°44'W	N16°E	110	
26.4	46	19°01'S	28°56'W	N 2°W	186	Passed Martin Vaz Is.

MOSHULU – PORT VICTORIA TO QUEENSTOWN FOR ORDERS 1939

Days		Lat.	Long.	General Course	Miles Sailed	Locality
27.4	47	16°12'S	29°11'W	N 2°W	171	
28.4	48	13°07'S	29°22'W	N 3°W	189	
29.4	49	10°26'S	29°23'W	N 7°W	161	
30.4	50	8°09'S	29°13'W	N 8°E	135	
1.5	51	5°32'S	29°12'W	N	138	
2.5	52	4°14'S	29°26'W	N10°W	79	Lost SE. Trades. Doldrums
3.5	53	4°00'S	29°55'W	W	20	
4.5	54	2°57'S	30°04'W	N16°W	51	
5.5	55	0°39'S	29°54'W	N 4°W	134	Crossed the Line
6.5	56	1°48'N	29°38'W	N	99	North Atlantic
7.5	57	2°56'N	30°27'W	N40°W	66	Doldrums
8.5	58	4°00'N	30°58'W	N26°W	58	
9.5	59	5°32'N	32°44'W	N46°W	130	
10.5	60	7°33'N	34°59'W	N49°W	167	
11.5	61	9°32'N	37°20'W	N53°W	177	
12.5	62	12°23'N	39°14'W	N38°W	198	
13.5	63	14°59'N	40°24'W	N27°W	168	
14.5	64	16°49'N	40°55'W	N14°W	105	
15.5	65	19°25'N	42°13'W	N26°W	167	
16.5	66	21°45'N	43°48'W	N31°W	145	
17.5	67	23°53'N	45°34'W	N39°W	152	
18.5	68	26°38'N	46°48'W	N24°W	180	
19.5	69	29°50'N	46°57'W	N 7°W	182	
20.5	70	31°45'N	47°18'W	N 6°W	100	Spoke a steamer
21.5	71	32°25'N	47°10'W	N 2°W	38	
22.5	72	33°43'N	46°19'W	N22°E	78	
23.5	73	34°44'N	45°38'W	N27°E	80	
24.5	74	35°50'N	44°56'W	N22°E	70	
25.5	75	36°54'N	43°03'W	N45°E	163	
26.5	76	38°57'N	41°00'W	N42°E	148	Spoke a Norwegian steamer. Reported at Lloyd's
27.5	77	40°52'N	37°33'W	N54°E	196	
28.5	78	41°19'N	34°10'W	N80°E	156	
29.5	79	42°10'N	33°11'W	N58°E	58	
30.5	80	44°28'N	30°40'W	N38°E	176	
31.5	81	47°08'N	26°07'W	N53°E	248	
1.6	82	48°52'N	21°43'W	N70°E	204	
2.6	83	49°32'N	19°33'W	N67°E	95	
3.6	84	49°56'N	18°40'W	N63°E	38	
4.6	85	50°17'N	18°16'W	N59°E	25	
5.6	86	50°32'N	17°47'W	N67°E	15	
6.6	87	50°37'N	16°09'W	N84°E	62	
7.6	88	50°20'N	12°31'W	N83°E	141	
8.6	89	51°00'N	10°32'W	N58°E	83	
9.6	90	noon				Fastnet bearing N by E dist. 5 miles
10.6	91	10.30 a.m. took pilot. 11 a.m. arrived outer roads Queenstown				

MOSHULU OF MARIEHAMN AFTER THE LAST GRAIN RACE

Sailed Glasgow 27 July 1939. Arrived Gothenburg 11 August.

Sailed Gothenburg 7 October 1939 for River Plate. Arrived Buenos Ayres 7 December 1939. Loaded grain.

Sailed Buenos Ayres 26 January 1940. Arrived Farsund 10 April 1940.

Seized by the Germans on putting into Farsund.

Sent to Christiansand to unload cargo.

Stripped of Masts and Yards which were stored and destroyed by bombing.

18 September 1947 broke her moorings and went ashore.

Sold to Gidsken Jakobsen and J. P. Skotnes, Andenes.

Refloated May 1948 by salvage vessels *Uller* and *Traust* – taken to Narvik.

Arrived Bergen 13 June in tow in order to contact eventual buyers more easily.

Bought by Trygve Sommerfelt, Oslo – towed to Stockholm to be used as grain store.

Arrived Stockholm 4 November 1948.

Grain store at Stockholm until 1952.

Bought by Heinz-Schliewen, Hamburg, for conversion to cargo carrying and sail training ship.

Arrived Hamburg in tow about 30 August 1952.

1953 Sold to Svenska-Lautmanners Riksforbund as grain store.

Arrived Stockholm in tow 16 November 1953.

Information from Lloyd's Shipping Index.

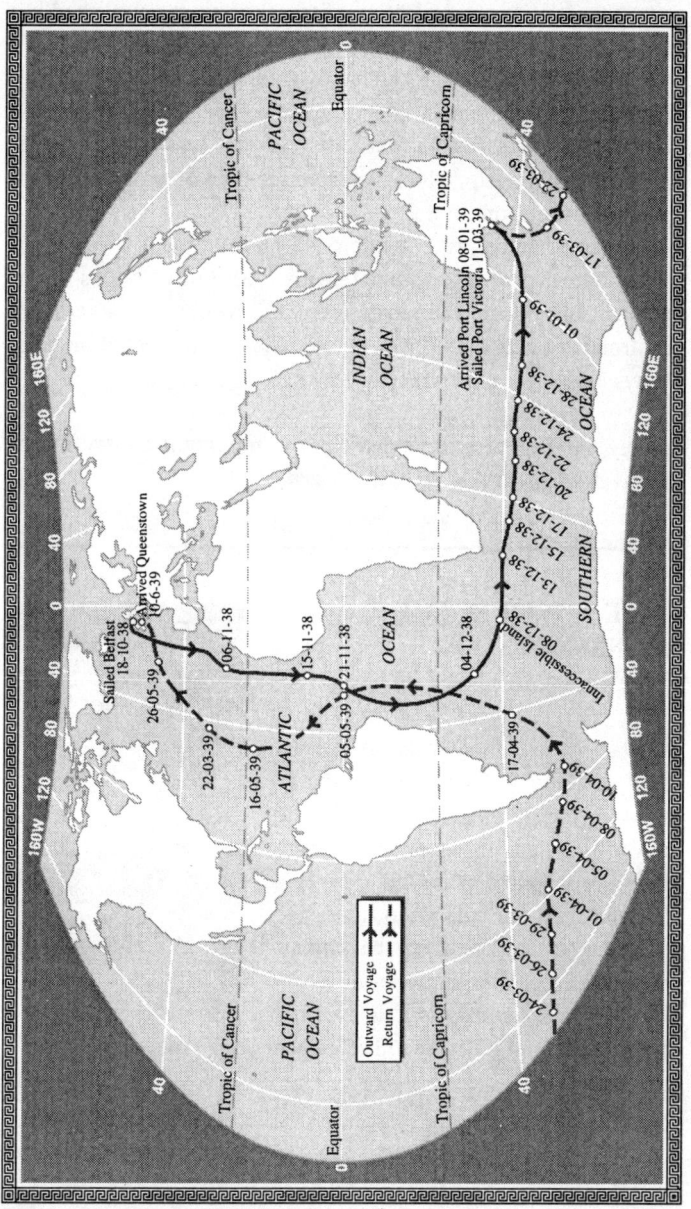

LONELY PLANET JOURNEYS

JOURNEYS is a unique collection of travel writing – published by the company that understands travel better than anyone else.

It is a series for anyone who has ever experienced – or dreamed of – the magical moment when they encountered a strange culture or saw a place for the first time. They are tales to read while you're planning a trip, while you're on the road or while you're in an armchair, in front of a fire.

These outstanding titles explore our planet through the eyes of a diverse group of international writers. JOURNEYS books catch the spirit of a place, illuminate a culture, recount an adventure, or introduce a fascinating way of life. They always entertain, and always enrich the experience of travel.

'Lively, intelligent and varied . . . an important contribution to travel literature' – *Age (Melbourne)*

LOVE & WAR IN THE APENNINES
Eric Newby

In 1943 Eric Newby was an escaped POW in Italy. With the Nazis advancing from the north and no certain way back to England, his situation was grim. Hiding in shepherd's huts and a cave, he survived with the help of local farmers and villagers - among them the woman who would become his wife. *Love and War in the Apennines* is Eric Newby's gripping account of the months he spent on the run.

Not available in Australia, Canada, Europe or the UK

ALSO BY ERIC NEWBY

A SMALL PLACE IN ITALY

In 1967 Eric and Wanda Newby bought a run-down farm-house in northern Tuscany, which they gradually restored. With his characteristic wry humour and sharp eye for the quirks of human nature, Eric Newby paints an unforgettable picture of rural Italy and its people, lovingly evoking the rhythms and rituals of country life.

A SHORT WALK IN THE HINDU KUSH

Feeling restless in the world of London's high-fashion industry, Eric Newby asked an old friend to accompany him on a mountain-climbing expedition in the wild and remote Hindu Kush, in north-eastern Afghanistan. His frank and funny account of their expedition is one of the classics of travel writing.

ON THE SHORES OF THE MEDITERRANEAN

Whether explaining the workings of a Turkish harem or the Mafia, pondering King David's choice of Jerusalem as the site for a capital city or enjoying a dinner produced by one of France's finest chefs, Eric Newby's erudite and entertaining tale takes us not just around the Mediterranean's shores but through the civilisations born there.

ROUND IRELAND IN LOW GEAR

Having decided to explore Ireland by bicycle, Eric and Wanda Newby set out one December. From Dublin to the Aran Islands, their rain-soaked journey is beset by minor disasters, and aided by stops for Guinness, tea and soda bread. Along the way, Eric Newby deftly summons up a world of hermits and horse-fairs, peat-cutting and poetry.

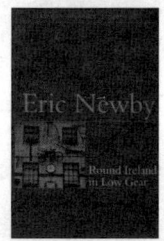

SLOWLY DOWN THE GANGES

Travelling in a variety of boats, as well as by bus and bullock cart, Eric Newby becomes intimately acquainted with the river: its shifting moods, its colourful history, the people who live on its banks. He brilliantly captures the sights and sounds, frustrations and rewards, the sheer enchantment of travel in India.

Note: Eric Newby titles are not available in Australia, Canada, Europe or the UK.

THE LONELY PLANET STORY

Where it all began…

A beat-up old car, a few dollars in the pocket, and a sense of adventure.

That's all Tony and Maureen Wheeler needed for the trip of a lifetime. They met on a park bench in Regent's Park and married a year later. For their honeymoon, they decided to attempt what few people thought possible – crossing Europe and Asia overland, all the way to Australia. It took them several months and all the money they could earn, beg or borrow, but they made it. And at the end of it all, they were flat broke… and couldn't have been happier.

It was too amazing an experience to keep to themselves. Urged on by their friends, they stayed up nights at their kitchen table writing, typing and stapling together their very first travel guide, Across Asia on the Cheap.

Within a week they'd sold 1500 copies and Lonely Planet was born. Two years later, their second journey led to South-East Asia on a shoestring, which led to books on Nepal, Australia, Africa, and India, which led to… you get the picture.

Fast-forward over 30 years.

As Lonely Planet became a globally loved brand, Tony and Maureen received several offers for the company. But it wasn't until 2007 that they found a partner whom they trusted to remain true to Lonely Planet's principles. In October of that year, BBC Worldwide acquired a 75% share in Lonely Planet, pledging to uphold Lonely Planet's commitment to independent travel, trustworthy advice and editorial independence.

BBC Worldwide is the main commercial arm, and a wholly owned subsidiary of, the British Broadcasting Corporation (BBC).

Today, Lonely Planet has offices in Melbourne, London and Oakland, with over 500 staff members and 300 authors. Tony and Maureen are still actively involved with Lonely Planet. They're travelling more often than ever, and they're devoting their spare time to charitable projects. And the company is still driven by the philosophy in Across Asia on the Cheap: 'All you've got to do is decide to go and the hardest part is over. So go!'